Politics as F̣ ̣ ̣ ̣ ̣ ̣in Lars von Trier

Politics as Form in Lars von Trier

A Post-Brechtian Reading

Angelos Koutsourakis

Bloomsbury Academic
An imprint of Bloomsbury Publishing Inc

B L O O M S B U R Y
NEW YORK • LONDON • NEW DELHI • SYDNEY

Bloomsbury Academic
An imprint of Bloomsbury Publishing Inc

1385 Broadway	50 Bedford Square
New York	London
NY 10018	WC1B 3DP
USA	UK

www.bloomsbury.com

BLOOMSBURY and the Diana logo are trademarks of Bloomsbury Publishing Plc

First published 2013
First published in paperback 2015

Library of Congress Cataloging-in-Publication Data
Koutsourakis, Angelos.
Politics as form in Lars Von Trier : a post-Brechtian reading / Angelos Koutsourakis.
pages cm
Includes bibliographical references and index.
Includes filmography.
ISBN 978-1-62356-345-5 (hardback : alk. paper)
1. Trier, Lars von, 1956 – Criticism and interpretation.
2. Brecht, Bertolt, 1898-1956 – Influence. I. Title.
PN1998.3.T747K68 2013
791.4302'33092 – dc23
2013027924

ISBN: HB: 978-1-6235-6345-5
PB: 978-1-5013-0769-0
ePub: 978-1-6235-6133-8
ePDF: 978-1-6235-6027-0

Typeset by Integra Software Services Pvt. Ltd.

For David J. Barnett
Friend and Teacher

Contents

Preface and acknowledgments

This book was born out of an interest in exploring the politics of form in the films of Lars von Trier. So far, the formal and the political aspects of his films are not sufficiently theorized, partly because of the prominence of his life and his idiosyncratic persona in the interpretation of his work. I was an undergraduate when Lars von Trier established himself as one of the most important contemporary filmmakers during the mid-to late 1990s. I still recollect my confusion when I first watched *The Idiots* (1998) and my inability to mark the boundaries between inside and outside largely due to von Trier's tendency to challenge the safe borders between film and reality, by constantly returning the gaze and the questions to the auditorium. His films provoked endless debates and strong responses (positive or negative) in the cinema foyers and during film seminars. But most importantly, I cannot forget the ways these debates generated a romantic feeling, as if we had suddenly returned to the 1960s and 1970s, when there was a certain belief in the power of cinema to challenge the politics of perception and turn into a radical medium, instead of a consumerist one. One thing was indubitable: One could not just watch a film by von Trier without spending the rest of the evening trying to fill the narrative and the hermeneutical gaps. At times, spirits were agitated and the arguments in the cafes, in the amphitheaters, and in the bars were interminable. Reminiscing on these days, I am more convinced of the validity of my understanding of von Trier as a political filmmaker, who offers the audience unfinished material and asks them to sort it out themselves. But in a way, von Trier's revitalization of the medium by means of his productive rather than reproductive (a central point of this book) engagement with the technological possibilities of cinema, his employment of fragmentary structures that show analytically the very process of showing instead of relying on mimetic narrative tropes, and his combination of formal experimentation with provocative subject matters that promote a revolutionary metacritique of conformist tendencies in cinema is a return to the cinematic debates of the past. Nevertheless, I see this return to the past as far more complex and not simply as a postmodern gesture tout court. That said, to historicize von Trier, one needs to identify the ways that he returns to the past not in a nostalgic way, but as a way of politicizing the present.

Politics as Form in Lars von Trier: A Post-Brechtian Reading aspires to unlock the formal complexity of von Trier's films and reveal the political implications of form. The central figure that will facilitate the task of identifying the interrelationship between form and politics in the Danish filmmaker's work is none other than one of the fathers of political art, namely Bertolt Brecht. I employ a materialist approach to von Trier's films and suggest that our knowledge of his formal experiments can be deepened and enlivened by discussing them in conjunction with Brecht's theory. Brecht's understanding of political art was predicated on the urge to challenge the politics of perception, so as to involve the audience in more productive ways and even to divide it so as to activate conflict, which is the essence of politics. The book intends to historicize both von Trier and Brecht, and thus, I do not treat the latter as a sacred cow, who can provide definite hermeneutical answers to von Trier's films. Antithetically, I focus on the post-Brechtian aspect of von Trier's work, deeming him as a filmmaker who pushes forward certain aspects of Brecht's theory and practice. Anglo-Saxon film criticism has been keen to pick up certain stylistic devices associated with "Brechtianism," ignoring at the same time Brecht's political philosophy and his dialectical method, which aims to make the audience think in oppositions and question values and ideas that are taken for granted. In other words, form cannot be dissociated from the dialectical method, and when form is divorced of dialectics, it does not subscribe to Brecht's formal politicization of representation. Thus, the book's role is twofold: It aspires (1) to analyze the dialectics of form in von Trier's films showing that Brecht is more important to his work than most critics seem to acknowledge and (2) to rethink the widely used and at times abused epithet Brechtian and establish a post-Brechtian methodological framework. This methodology can show that Brecht and film studies are to invoke Habermas, an "unfinished project."

Von Trier has a sizeable body of work. He has directed ten early films (including eight assignments as part of his student years), a graduate one, and twelve feature ones, while his latest film *Nymphomaniac* (2013) is upcoming shortly. He has also been involved in the unfinished film project *Dimension*, in one television film, and in four television projects as a director. He has contributed to scripts for other TV and radio shows, and to a conceptual work that merges cinema, installation, and performance art. To this, we should add his short film, produced as part of an anthology commissioned by the Cannes film festival. He has also acted as a scriptwriter for two films made by Thomas Vinterberg and Jacob Thueson, respectively. Finally, he has also directed a number of video clips. In view of this impressing body of work, this book privileges selected objects, in an effort to identify recurring formal elements and politics. I mainly privilege examples from earlier films, perhaps because I feel that we need a historical distance in order to abandon a biographical interpretation of a filmmaker's work and adopt more intricate hermeneutical strategies. For example, owing to such a historical distance we can now see how scholarship has started historicizing a filmmaker like Fassbinder, whose critical reception relied heavily for many years on the director's eccentric persona and his background. This study, therefore, is not intended to be a "career" book. Hopefully, von Trier will continue making films which challenge film language and audience expectations in the years to come. Thus, I do not see the point of such an endeavor in the present historical context. Hopefully, my formal/political analysis of the objects under consideration will help the reader reexamine von Trier's latest films within the context of formal and political debates, and make her or him see how von Trier adopts a working model which returns to the same themes and formal experiments so as to rework and renew them.

Drawing on Hayden White's idea that "the Manifesto has no interest in the past except as part of the problem to be solved" (2007, 220), I include in the appendix von Trier's Manifestoes to facilitate the reader's understanding of how his work bridges productively the past with the present. Some of them have been included in previous studies and others are relatively unknown. A closer examination of these texts shows that they do not simply act as mere provocations but they showcase a filmmaker who has a theoretical understanding of cinema. The Appendix also includes an interview with Lars von Trier and one with his mentor, Jørgen Leth. Leth's body of work had its effect on certain formal aspects of von Trier's oeuvre. Indicative of this perspective are the nonharmonious relationship between images and sounds, the "naïve attitude to reality," and the performative employment of the camera; these formal experiments are congruent with a post-Brechtian aesthetic that concerns me in this book. But this interview is also a homage to this great filmmaker, whose work has influenced not only von Trier but also the Dogme movement and numerous contemporary Danish filmmakers.

This book would not have been possible without the support of a great deal of people. I am most grateful to the Danish Agency for International Education for giving me the chance to spend ten months in Denmark as a guest researcher at the University of Copenhagen. Many thanks also to the Department of Media Cognition and Communication at the University of Copenhagen for hosting me there. I am indebted to John David Rhodes and David Barnett, who read an early version of the manuscript and offered me incisive comments. My deep gratitude goes to Lars von Trier, who allowed me to interview him, and his secretaries Katrine Sahlstroem and Emilie Spliid. I would also like to thank von Trier and Zentropa Productions for allowing me to incorporate the former's Manifestoes along with stills from the films I discuss. I am grateful to Jørgen Leth and Alexander Kluge, who also gave me an interview. During my stay in Copenhagen, I was privileged to discuss von Trier's films with Peter Schepelern, and I am grateful to him for all his help as well as for setting up my interview with von Trier. The help and support of a great deal of people at the University of Copenhagen was invaluable. Tine Weidick and Nete Nørgaard Kristensen were always there to help me with any practicalities. Jespe Kappel from the University's audiovisual archive provided me with materials that have enriched my knowledge of von Trier's cinema. I am also grateful to Camilla Dindler, Eva Novrup Redvall and Yiannis Stamatelos, who shared my concerns about the project. I am thankful to the staff at Bloomsbury and, especially, to Katie Gallof, who believed in this book from the beginning. I am also grateful to Caroline Wake, Darrow Schecter, Julian Murphet, Sean Pryor, and George Kouvaros. Thanks to Jens Peder Søndberg, who helped me translate Danish texts. A final note of gratitude goes to my family, my brother Vangelis (who introduced me to the films of Lars von Trier), and my partner Eszter Katona for sharing a passion for European Art Cinema.

A part of Chapter 2 appeared in *Journal of Contemporary European Studies* 20:4 (2012).

A part of Chapter 3 appeared in *The Brecht Yearbook* (37) (2012).

A part of Chapter 4 appeared in *New Review of Film and Television Studies* 11:3 (2013). A smaller part of the same chapter appeared in *Cinema: Journal of Philosophy and the Moving Image* 3(2012).

Notes to the text

Spelling in all quotations is left untouched. To facilitate the reader, I use English translations of Brechtian texts with the exception of untranslated resources or quotations that lose their clarity in the English versions. I provide in brackets the year of release only for the first mention of each film. Similarly, for each character mentioned I provide in brackets the name of the actor portraying the character only the first time the character is named in the text.

Brechtian terms

Verfremdungseffekt (+*e* in plural): the process of making the familiar strange. I use the term "defamiliarization" rather than the problematic one "alienation."
Gestus: a gesture that reveals the ideological and social component in an individual behavior.
Haltung (plural *Haltungen*): the German word for postural attitude. For Brecht, the postural attitude reveals social connections too.

Abbreviations

Schriften: refers to Brecht's *Schriften zum Theater* volumes 1–5, Frankfurt: Suhrkamp Verlag, 1963; and volumes 6–7, Frankfurt: Suhrkamp Verlag, 1964.

Introduction: Looking back

When I was young the medium was enough ... Now one should be able to use the film for something ... to raise some questions, but not to answer them

Lars von Trier

You the viewers should be amused and humiliated at the same time ... Please watch this film in the same way you play, work, fight, hate and love

Nagisa Oshima

In the course of a shaky camera movement, a series of abstract visuals are arranged, followed by a number of antirepresentational colorful images. Suddenly, a set of intertitles appears on screen posing the following questions: "Why run away from that which you know you cannot escape? Why try to escape from the image that penetrated into your retina?" This is the opening of *Hvorfor Flygte Fra Det Du Ved Du Ikke Kan Flygte Fra?Fordi Du Er En Kujon* (1970), an early film shot by von Trier in the age of 15. The specific problem posed by this question, which is also part of the film's title, is whether it addresses the character within the film or the audience, or both; or maybe it challenges the boundaries between inside and outside, the diegetic and the metalevel. Seventeen years later, von Trier was a well-known filmmaker, and in a scene from his second feature film, *Epidemic* (1987), we see him acting as a character in the film. In the film, he pauses and says to his collaborator, Niels Vørsel, "a film should be like a stone in your shoe." Again, this line is part of the narrative but also extends outside of it, as if the filmmaker merges the story line with a thesis about filmmaking itself, refusing to adhere to standardized distinctions between art and life. But this blurring of the boundaries between in and out is not just a skillful formalist exercise; it has rather deeper politicized implications, and a thorough formal consideration of the whole corpus of his filmography reveals that this is one of the fundamental characteristics of his work.

This book is directed by a specific theoretical intent, which is to identify the ways form is the key to comprehending the politics of von Trier's films. There is a growing tendency among film scholars to read von Trier's films as objects that have biographical points of reference and/or to understand his formal experimentation with the medium and his characters as reflections of the director's eccentric persona. To an extent, von Trier is moderately responsible for the prevalence of discussions about his life and his own phobias over broader formal and political analyses. As Peter Schepelern intimates, "continuously, Trier has worked on the making of Trier, the Auteur" (2005c, 120). On the face of this argument, I am convinced that one needs to take von Trier's words with a grain of salt. I take quite seriously his views on the film medium, his justifications of certain formal choices, and his polemical critique of conventional cinematic tropes. However, I do not let his biography and his own interpretations overdetermine the complexity of his work. In this fashion, this study follows a different line of argument and is concerned with marrying formal analysis to a discussion of the films' politics.

One important thing that eludes critics' attention is that von Trier's first filmmaking ventures called for a return to form, since he reacted against a very popular genre of Danish cinema of the 1970s and 1980s, namely social or humanistic realism. Filmmakers of the time, like Erik Clausen and Kaspar Rostrup, adopted conventional sentimentalized narrative tropes which privileged content over form. Particularly, Clausen's films dealt with overtly political issues, but without questioning the frame of representation. The effect was a moralizing sentimentalism that did not omit standardized cathartic dramaturgical effects that failed to implicate the audience's social role in the depicted social relationships. Contrariwise, von Trier's practice is concerned with politicizing perception and assigning a more productive participation to the audience, instead of trying to propagate clear-cut theses by means of canonical, emotional, and moralist narrative tropes. His film aesthetics was formulated by his interest in Danish filmmakers, such as Jørgen Leth, who advocated experimental narrative structures. Leth was very much influenced by the theory and practice of Bertolt Brecht and Jean-Luc Godard. His films inaugurated a type of cinema which employed formalist experiments so as "to adopt an analytic stance towards what is most natural, obvious and mundane" (Leth cited in Hjort and Bondebjerg 2000, 61).

Challenging the established film language as a means of allowing the audience to think beyond the limits of the obvious is crucial to understand the dialectics of politics and representation. To a large extent, all films are political because, consciously or unconsciously, they propagate certain values, beliefs, and evaluations of certain aspects of social reality. But, political cinema, which is committed to questioning and not just reproducing the reality outside the narrative, experiments with film language so as to negate a static and permanent understanding of social relationships and reveal their changeability. Seen through the prism of this definition, political cinema aims at "denaturalizing" our perception of the world and revealing its constructedness, instead of treating it as "natural" and fixed. The prerequisite for this politicization of representation is a film practice that interrogates the familiar—both the socially familiar and the representational one—with the view to questioning the medium of its own articulation and pressing on the ways certain aesthetic practices shape our understanding of "the real."

The connection between formal complication and political effects has been acknowledged by von Trier in an interview given after the completion of his graduate film *Images of Relief* (*Befrielsesbilleder*, 1982). When asked whether Erik Clausen's films are more politically dangerous than his own, von Trier stated that a film that has an "oppressed people is always right" thematic content can be easily co-opted by the industry.

> I mean that if you make a film that is reactionary in its form, then the contents are insignificant. This is the way it is: you can't have rebellious or reformist content without adapting the form at the same time. You can't separate the one from the other. (cited in Scwander 2003, 23)

Form is key to politicizing representation, so as to utilize strategies that make the audience productive and give them the chance to step out of the story and reflect on the material on screen. In simple terms, the prerequisite for denaturalizing one's understanding of social reality is to take the audience seriously and not to deploy conventional moralist tropes that force them to accept uncritically the filmmaker's arguments. Taking the audience seriously means also to point to their own social responsibility. The Austrian filmmaker Michael Haneke has described this eloquently in an interview with Alexander Kluge, where he states that showing respect for the audience stands also for articulating "uncomfortable truths" and not using narrative manipulative strategies albeit in the service of progressive ideas.

> Costas Gavras' Z (1969), a brilliantly made film. I remember when I first saw it, I loved it and I was raging about the fascists. Raging without reflection. In its historical context the film was important. It was a film of agitation. Nonetheless, one must not forget that its means are exactly those used in the political manipulation films. In other words, this film makes people more stupid maybe for a good cause in this example. But the question remains. Is that permissible?

Is it permissible to make an anti-fascist film with fascist means? That is one dilemma if one wants to make a political film. (cited in *News and Stories*, 2008)

Haneke's point rests on the assumption that by preventing the audience from critically reflecting on the narrative, one follows the dominant frame of representation which is grounded in the separation between producers and consumers. But the propagation of this separation not merely disrespects the audience and makes it accept the director's viewpoints without reflection but also lays the groundwork for the commodification and the institutionalization of the most radical ideas. This practice reduces both cinema and politics to plot/drama, without analyzing the language that connects the reality inside the narrative with the one outside of it.

Both von Trier's and Haneke's above-mentioned comments are consonant with the theory and practice of Bertolt Brecht. The cornerstone of Brecht's political aesthetic is that one needs to change the medium's function and render the familiar strange, so as to present the audience with a series of dialectical oppositions. Brecht argued that changes in social and historical reality demand new representational modes that create a distance between reality and representation, which could make the audience step out of the story, analyze the represented material, and identify its connection with the extra-diegetic reality. In this context, Brecht's advocation of formal abstraction derived from a dissatisfaction with the established dramatic tropes, which reduced social processes to dramas of self-determined individuals failing to grasp phenomena that take place on a mass level. Character is equally important in Brechtian dramaturgy, under the proviso that the individual is shown as the product of social relationships and not as self-determined. Part of the aims of the *Verfremdungseffekt* was to offer deictic analytical representational strategies that connected the character's attitudes with the broader social environment.

Brecht's formal radicalism was devoted to showing the world dialectically, and in this context, one had to question the medium's language so as to produce contradictions instead of offering straightforward "messages." Brecht defines dialectics "as a method of thinking, or rather, an interconnected sequence of intellectual methods, which permit one to dissolve certain fixed ideas and reassert praxis against ruling ideologies" (2003, 124). It is imperative to understand that the term "Brechtian" marries formal experimentation with dialectics, something that dismisses moot points by contemporary film scholars, who tend to argue that Brechtian and modernist experiments have been absorbed by the Hollywood industry. Thus, the deployment of formal elements that interrupted the narrative and reflected on the process of its own making was not an end in itself, but intended to make the audience adopt new ways of thinking. Brecht's political modernism was a form of negation, and it is this gesture of negation that is missing from Hollywood products which manipulate certain formal elements, but ignore the dialectical method. While certain formal traits associated with Brecht and political modernism, for example, self-reflexivity and montage, are used by Hollywood so as to enhance narrative pleasure, it is a mistake to think in tautological terms and suggest that certain stylistic elements are in themselves equal to Brechtianism. For example, blockbusters and advertisements employ modernist and Brechtian elements, but they do it to "reproduce" a set of relationships as natural and not to challenge habitual understandings of intricate issues. It is this dichotomy between production versus reproduction which may help us understand film radicalism beyond the limits of tautology. This sort of tautological mistake was conducted by the 1970s film theory, which, as Sylvia Harvey points out, understood Brecht's writings as a set of formal devices that divorced a dialectical understanding of art and social life (1982, 51). Aware of the risk of a simply aestheticized *Verfremdungseffekt*, Brecht suggested, "Man wird daraufhin untersuchen müssen, wie denn nun der V-Effekt einzusetzen ist, was, für welche Zwecke da verfremdet werden soll" (one shall investigate how the V-effect is employed and what and why should be defamiliarized) (*Schriften* 7 1964, 292).

In this book, Brecht provides the methodological framework that will bring to the fore the politics of form in von Trier's cinema. In this context, the book stages an attempt to explore the filmic applications of Brecht's theory in a historical reality where his certainties are not applicable. En route to stimulate new perspectives on von Trier's formal politics, I situate von Trier under the rubric of the "post-Brechtian," a term to which I shall return below. Let us first discuss von Trier's connection with Brecht, even though it is far from the book's intentions to discuss the latter's "influence" on von Trier. Primarily, von Trier's dialogue with Brecht dates back to the past and is not something to be restricted to films like *Dogville* (2003) and *Manderlay* (2005). Peter Schepelern acknowledges this while discussing films like *Epidemic* (1987) and *Europa* (1991) (2000a, 100, 132). Similarly, von Trier himself admits this in various interviews. In an interview after the completion of *Dogville*, which along with *Manderlay* is one of the few films that has been critically received as "Brechtian," he stated:

> Brecht was something of a domestic God when I was growing up, whereas my generation has tended to view him as a rather old-fashioned genius. Fashions

and tastes are constantly changing, of course.... I experienced Brecht's dramas at a fairly young age and have never returned to him or his work. They exist in my memory mostly as feelings and atmospheres. (cited in Björkman 2003, 243–244)

Similarly, after the completion of *Manderlay*, von Trier discussed the film's formal austerity in relation to Brecht's practice.

I thought of Brecht's work, which is not exactly the same as this, but requires stylized settings. My mother was crazy for Brecht and dragged me to the theater to see his plays. I'm always looking for ideas that I believe are good for film. (cited in Merin 2011)

In an interview he gave me during the editing of *Melancholia* (2011), von Trier explained that while being familiar with the central tenet of Brecht's theory, namely the *Verfremdungseffekt*, "truth" is something more complex and has to do with "all aspects of cinema" and not just with the acting style (Interview, Appendix). Von Trier's comments merit elaboration, because they point albeit indirectly to the whole idea of the *Verfremdungseffekt*, which is not, as it is routinely assumed, simply a matter of acting, but it embraces all the aspects of representation, something which I shall discuss in Chapter 1. Furthermore, von Trier's problematization of the whole notion of "truth" in the aforementioned quotation indicates a different perception of the author's/director's role in the sense that the artist is not the person who holds epistemological mastery and communicates an unequivocal piece of knowledge to the audience. This position helps to expose the shift from an aesthetic that intends to align dialectical contradictions so as to communicate knowledge effects to one that brings together points of tension that remain unresolved.

The above-mentioned comments provide a useful background for clarifying the very term "post-Brechtian." Years ago, Roland Barthes discussed the fragmentary aesthetics of Brechtian dramaturgy, explaining that each fragment/tableau has a sense of autonomy and is infused with meaning. The accumulation of fragments intends to bring together antithetical materials that the audience has to assemble. While this aesthetic aspires to produce knowledge effects, Barthes envisages the possibility of a post-Brechtian one:

marked by the dispersion of the tableau, the pulling to pieces of the "composition" the setting in movement of the "partial organs" of the human figure, in short the holding in check of the metaphysical meaning of the work—but then also of its political meaning; or, at least, the carrying over of this meaning towards another politics. (1977, 72)

In light of Barthes' comments, the politics of von Trier's films does not reside in the dramatization of political subject matters. It is rather his employment of deictic representational strategies which "show the act of showing," rather than reproducing cohesive plot, and challenge the politics of perception. This practice diminishes the concreteness of iconic information, complicates the narrative structure, and draws attention to the processes that intervene in the transformation of the given raw reality into filmed object. The deictic representational elements downplay dramaturgical cohesion and shift the emphasis from the script to the image, something that he understood to be countercinematic from the beginning of his career: "We have to make some 'counter-films', that give you the opportunity to experience something broader than this plot-bound thing, which is so hackneyed and only exciting from a craftsmanship point of view, like when a carpenter makes a table" (cited in Schwander 2003, 15). Furthermore, in many films von Trier engages in a dialogue with various media and employs a Brechtian separation of elements, which produce a "literalization" of the medium, a term that I qualify in Chapters 2 and 4. In these terms, von Trier's cinema is also an "anti-cinema"; formal experimentation acts as a negation of the conventional film language without striving to stabilize a master-voice, which makes the audience uncritically accept the directors' viewpoints.

The question that arises then is this: In what ways does the Brechtian differ from the post-Brechtian and how can we understand von Trier as a post-Brechtian filmmaker? This is the subject of Chapter 1. The chapter proceeds to clarify some misunderstanding apropos Brecht's writings on cinema and then moves to position von Trier within a post-Brechtian context, referencing examples from his early student films to the more recent ones. Particularly, I focus on specific formal elements from his early films that are reworked in the latest ones too.

A skeptic could then ask whether von Trier shares Brecht's historical view and his Marxist interpretation of history, according to which the dialectic can be led to a close. This is the subject of Chapter 2, which discusses the *Europa* trilogy. These three films, *The Element of Crime* (1984), *Epidemic*, and *Europa*, revisit historical traumas of the European past. Focusing on the films' visual dramaturgy, I explain how the ruptures in dramatic linearity defamiliarize our sense of temporality, question teleological stories, and valorize processes over concrete dramatic narratives. I suggest that von Trier follows Brecht's mistrust of a historical representation based on pictorial verisimilitude, without, however, sharing his view of history as Marxist science. Retrospectively, the

Europa trilogy's interest in the historical traumas of the past acquires a renewed historical significance in light of the financial crisis that has cast doubt on the concept of the integrated Europe.

Throughout his career, von Trier has insisted that filmmakers should develop new techniques for the new contradictions that society levels at us, a gesture which clearly invokes Brecht. In this context, Chapter 3 concentrates on Dogme 95. The chapter analyzes the reasons why the Dogme Manifesto employs a political modernist rhetoric, so as to understand the historicity of this gesture. Unlike other critics, I do not see Dogme as postmodern parody or solely as a marketing trick. What I find worthwhile analyzing is that Dogme reconciles a political modernist language that alludes to Brecht with a realist aesthetics, something that was out of the question during the late 1960s and early 1970s when Brecht's theory was received keenly by scholars in *Cahiers du Cinéma* and the British journal *Screen*. Secondly, the chapter focuses on *The Idiots*, while also bringing examples from the unfinished project *Dimension,* which can reveal the broader politics of Dogme. The chapter concludes with reference to other objects, *D-Day* (*D-Dag:* 2000), *The Five Obstructions* (2003), and *The Boss of It All* (*Direktøren for det hele*, 2006), which push forward the fundamental idea of the Dogme project.

The last chapter focuses on *Dogville* and *Manderlay*, perhaps the only films that have been unanimously received as political by the critics or have been discussed through a Brechtian critical angle. I suggest that the critical reception of the films under the rubric of "anti-Americanism" has obscured their politics and innovations. A crucial point to comprehend both films' politics is that despite their employment of Brechtian tropes, they go beyond the Brechtian *Fabel,* and their dialectical openness can make us understand their pessimistic tenor politically. Furthermore, the chapter unveils the ways von Trier politicizes emotions and feelings. Among the misunderstandings of Brecht's theory is the oft-repeated truism that he wanted to abolish emotions. The chapter shows how von Trier analyzes the characters' corporeal attitudes to show emotions as contingent on broader social processes and not as subjective ones. The book's epilogue brings this post-Brechtian angle up-to-date with reference to the latest developments in von Trier's oeuvre.

One could object that by going back to Brecht to understand von Trier might be a conservative approach. I would refer the skeptics to Jacques Derrida's argument that in moments of crisis radical thought needs to return to the past and proceed to criticize it and borrow from it at the same time. Derrida intimates that Marxism is still alive when it is ready to undertake its "self-critique" (1994, 111) and I suggest that the same applies to Brechtian theory, which can still enliven film theory and practice. For Derrida, the radical "specters of the past" can play the same role as the ghost in *Hamlet*, namely they can enhance our visibility of the present. Taking a cue from his point and, given that the end of history proved to be a naïve illusion, Brecht can help us historicize film criticism. Changing historical circumstances alter the ways we use certain theoretical apparatuses, and, as Thomas Elsaesser and Malte Hagener explain, film theory does not necessarily extend into the future but to the past as well, so as to rethink certain arguments from a different perspective (2010, 6). On this basis, the book's goal is to "defamiliarize" von Trier, by focusing on the formal complexity of his films, rethinking the questions he poses, and omitting any biographical discussions. The point of the book is not to deliberate that my reading gets von Trier "right" but to create more productive ways of understanding the formal and thematic complexity of his films and the reasons why his work divides the audiences worldwide.

From Brechtian to Post-Brechtian Cinema: Lars von Trier and the Post-Brechtian

Brecht on the film medium

Exam Question:	What in your opinion has Brecht to offer to a person who wants to make a movie?
Fassbinder:	The *Verfremdungseffekt*, which in movies can be applied in a variety of ways.

In an interview with Peter Schepelern for the Danish magazine *EKKO*, von Trier outlined his understanding of political cinema arguing that an object can be understood as political given that one analyzes its subject from multiple viewpoints. As he said, "Hvis det er politisk, så er det jo for mig analyserende. Både psykologisk analyserende, men også politisk analyserende. Det er at stille spørgsmål til både den ene og den anden holdning og meget gerne forsvare de holdninger, jeg ikke selv har" (If a film is political, then it is analytical. Analytical both on the psychological and on the political level. It is a matter of questioning a position and its conflicting one and I am very happy to defend a position that goes against my own one) (cited in Schepelern 2005a). In the same interview, von Trier explained that part of the politics of his films is that he shows things in an extreme way and lets the audience deal with them. "Dér kan man godt tale om Verfremdung, fordi jeg hiver historien så langt ud, at alle kan se, hvad den er bygget af" (This is my *Verfremdungseffekt*, because I pull the story so far that everyone can see what is made of) (Schepelern 2005a). These comments are heuristic to understanding von Trier's post-Brechtian aesthetic. Yet, in accounting for the question "what is post-Brechtian cinema" and how can we position von Trier in the post-Brechtian, one needs to go back to Brecht's own film essays, to shed some light on the very term "Brechtian," which is at times used inadvertently by film scholars.

One of the reasons lies in the fact that Brecht's reception on the part of the 1970s film theory did not focus considerably on his film fragments, but mainly on his theater theory. Brecht's film writings are concerned with finding ways of politicizing the medium by means of formal experimentation, as well as by criticizing cinema as an institution. Certain aspects of his cinematic writings, such as the representation of the individual, the aesthetics of interruptibility, the loose dramaturgy, and his dissatisfaction with the commodification of cinema, are crucial to our understanding of a post-Brechtian cinema, which employs formal experimentation and proceeds to criticize the institution of cinema. The politicization of form aims at liberating thinking out of a motionless understanding of social reality and presenting crises and contradictions, but unlike Brechtian orthodoxy it does not offer clear-cut suggestions on how to overcome the impasse. Put simply, questions are valorized over answers so as to provide an excess of negativity, which intends to make the audience productive.

Brecht as a modernist was fascinated by the film medium and its potential to offer representations of reality that could encourage critical reflection on the part of the audience. One of the aspects of the medium that he considered to be revolutionary was its ability to do away with character psychology and show the individual as representative of his or her social role. Influenced by Marx's theoretical antihumanism, Brecht saw the individual as the product of the historical and social circumstances as opposed to the bourgeois concept of "human essence." According to Marx, a theory of subjectivity cannot allow for a scientific investigation of human relationships and lapses into an abstract humanism. But such an abstract humanism fails to see the individual as a historical emergent and as a producer of history (Marx and Engels 1970, 47).

One of the aims of Brecht's *Verfremdungseffekt* is to demonstrate the individual's dependence on processes that defy his or her self-determination. For Brecht, cinema could show the individual as historically defined in a more effective way than the theatrical and literary dramaturgy. As he explains, in contrast to bourgeois drama's and novel's psychologically driven characters, cinema presents socially motivated type characters. Consequently, the audience cannot dissociate the portrayed characters from their historical and social positions:

> For the theatre for instance, the cinema's treatment of the person performing the action is interesting. To give life to the persons, who are introduced purely according to their functions, the cinema uses available types who encounter

specific situations and assume in them particular attitudes. All motivation from within the character is excluded; the person's inner life never provides the principal cause of action and seldom its principal result; the person is seen from the outside. (2001, 164)

From these comments, one can see that Brecht draws his conclusions from early cinema's experiments, which treated characters as types motivated by their social functions and not by psychology. Equally important is to acknowledge Brecht's interest in the Russian avant-garde and in particular in Eisenstein's cinema. Martin Walsh suggests that Brecht's meeting with the Russian director in Berlin in 1929 was crucial for the formulation of his film and theater theory too (1981, 16). Indeed, Eisenstein's paradigm partially fits into Brecht's perception of the cinema as a medium that does away with psychological motivation. Eisenstein's concept of the dialectical conflict created by the juxtaposition between seemingly unrelated materials and his prioritization of actions and historical events that surpass the characters might be the type of cinema that Brecht had in mind.

Early cinema's portrayal of type characters was also influential in Brecht's valorization of a gestic acting as opposed to a dramatic one. For Brecht, the social *Gestus* can offer simplification, through an exposition of attitudes that minimize psychological traits. *Gestus* assists in the depiction of the individual as the product of forces and laws that cannot be discerned in the phenomenology of human relations. According to Brecht, a gestic acting is concerned with showing an action ("Gestus des Zeigens"), that is, quoting it rather than imitating it. This acting activates the audience's critical faculties and allows them to reflect on the characters' attitudes. Of paramount importance in Brecht's favoring of a gestic acting was Charlie Chaplin's depiction of characters in his films. As Wolfgang Gersch explains, Brecht saw in Chaplin a tendency to isolate generalized rather than individual patterns of behavior. "Auf diese Weise war es Brecht möglich, Simplizität zu konstatieren, die er als Prinzip der Filmdramaturgie verallgemeinerte" (It was thus possible for Brecht to establish simplicity, which he describes as a generalized principle of film dramaturgy) (1975, 42).

Brecht considered Chaplin as an actor who did away with past dramatic traditions based upon the imitation of feelings. His acting placed emphasis on the very process of creating a character. By shifting the emphasis from the act of imitation to that of showing the act of showing, Chaplin presented characters who were motivated by their social roles and conditions. In effect, Chaplin's acting corresponded with Brecht's Marxist conviction that the individual is changeable and not fixed. In the same manner that Chaplin's acting demonstrated the process of creating a character and his or her actions, Brecht thought of film as a medium that had the potential to represent dramatic actions and include the very process of copying them. Thus, film could turn into a nonempathetic medium given that the focus would be on actions over characters' psychology. "In fact the film demands external action and not introspective psychology…. For the cinema the principles of non-Aristotelian drama (a type of drama not depending on empathy, mimesis) are immediately acceptable" (2001, 171).

This quotation reveals Brecht's utopian view of the medium and his belief that certain formal principles can lead to the production of radical effects. By valorizing actions—and it is important to note that Brecht implies social actions rather than dramatic plot as an end in itself—over psychological interpretations of characters, cinema could become a means of teaching historical awareness. The prerequisite for this effect is that the medium adopt an external point of view that de-individuates the narrative and focuses on the social processes and their changeability. By implication, Brecht aspired to make the act of representation more complex so as to encourage responses on the part of the audience. In encouraging the audience to reflect on the filmic material, Brecht thought that the viewers would be able to see the historicity of human relationships and the very falsity of their "naturalization" on the part of the bourgeois society.

Brecht's understanding of cinema as a medium that could analyze social relations aimed at stimulating the audience's capacity for action in the social sphere. One important document that offers some practical examples of his predilection for external actions at the expense of conventional character-based dramaturgy is the film *Kuhle Wampe, or Who Owns the World?* [*Kuhle Wampe, Oder: Wem Gehört Die Welt?* (Bertolt Brecht, Slatan Dudow, Ernst Ottwald:1932)]. *Kuhle Wampe* tells the story of a German working-class family in Berlin and raises questions regarding the rise of unemployment in Germany during the 1930s. The film consists of four independent parts that are interrupted by musical compositions accompanied by images of factories and council houses. It is an object immensely influenced by Eisenstein's intellectual montage and, as Marc Silberman observes, the montage sequences in the film interrupt the narrative with material that does not serve diegetic purposes. Story development is minimized in favor of a loose sequence of episodes that deconstruct dramatic actions. This deconstruction aims at linking dramatic actions with the social conditions of their construction (2009, 321).

As a result, characters are shown as representatives of their social roles and not as individuals with unchanged psychological traits. Emblematic of Brecht's interest in identifying the social drive in the characters' behavior is a scene portraying Franz's suicide, the youngest member of the Bönike family. What precedes this incident is a family argument regarding the son's inability to find work. Tired of the lack of prospects, the boy decides to end his life. The camera remains immobile focusing on the character, while the lack of extra-diegetic music heightens the grotesque atmosphere. A different frame follows and shows a banner hung in the kitchen wall saying, "Don't blame the morning that brings hardship and work. It is wonderful to care for those one loves." This banner juxtaposes a capitalist ethic into a working-class environment, with the purpose of demonstrating the *oppressed's complicity in their* oppression. Later on, the boy approaches the window in a very "clinical" manner—as if it is part of an everyday routine—and takes off his watch. While preparing to jump from the window he is careful enough not to damage the family's flowers.

The mechanical approach toward the portrayal of the suicide fails to establish empathy for the victim. The filmic treatment of the material draws upon Brecht's concept of *Gestus,* which aimed at connecting an inner attitude with the outside social reality. In this scene the camera becomes "gestic" and as Silberman points out, "The camera here becomes the ideal instrument for looking from the outside" (1995, 43). To "look from the outside" stands for connecting the personal with the political via a method that does not portray suicide as a personal tragedy, but as a phenomenon that can be understood historically. This passage of the film summarizes some of the fundamental Brechtian tenets, such as the valorization of social forces over characters and the detached portrayal of dramatic actions, which intend to identify the social laws that regulate one's actions.

As maintained by Brecht, certain formal choices make the cinematic medium more effective with regard to the minimization of character-based dramaturgy and produce a fragmented form that de-individuates actions and reveals their social/historical significance. Thus cinema's political effectiveness lies in its ability to create a fragmentary diegetic pattern. This preference for an incomplete and episodic narrative served the purpose of preventing the audience from being carried away by the plot. This episodic form could freeze the actions and give the viewer time to ponder on the represented social relationships and the contradictions introduced by the narrative. His argument is reminiscent of his point in the "Notes to Mahagonny," in which he explains that the episodic form of the epic theater expects the audience to stand outside and question the portrayed events instead of adopting an empathetic attitude. The following quotation clarifies Brecht's perception of the cinema as a medium that benefits from an episodic/paratactic style.

> Film obeys the same laws as static art. It is essentially static and must be treated as a series of tableaux. Its effect must arise from the clear interruptions, which would otherwise just be common errors. The tableaux must be so composed that they can be taken in at a single glance like a sheet of paper, but yet they must withstand separation into details so that every detail corresponds in the larger scheme with the centre. (2001, 7)

Underlying Brecht's preference for arranging a film as a series of tableaux is his conviction that this visual style leads to a formal abstraction that renders the represented reality enigmatic. In this way, the audience's critical faculties are aroused and the viewer is confronted with material that she or he has to either conform or dispute.

Brecht's emphasis on an aesthetics of interruptibility by means of a succession of fragments/tableaux aims at confronting the viewers with images of reality, in which they are asked to recognize themselves and see, at the same time, reality as a construct (Silberman 2009, 321). The collection of different fragments brings together contradictions that are offered to the audience to be resolved. This attitude of detachment could make the audience doubt the images' veracity and negate the stereotypical perception of representation as reproduction of a seemingly unified reality. Evidently, this argument draws upon the Marxist rejection of empiricism, according to which the outward appearance of social phenomena does not offer an understanding of their historical/social significance. Thus, Brecht distinguished between the reproductive and the productive use of the medium. The former paradigm is keen on reproducing the empirical reality, whereas the latter is more interested in showing that what appears as "real" is subject to transformation, because reality is socially constructed. As such, a productive use of the medium presupposed the presentation of a familiar reality in a way that it would appear strange and changeable.

The productive method is predicated upon a process of selecting fragments of reality and of showing, at the same time, this very process of assembling. In this way, the relationship between the profilmic material and its reproduction is made evident and the final cut does not appear as an uncritical portrayal of the empirical reality. The key principle of the constructive method is "montage," a term Brecht employs in his theater writings too. Montage stresses representational discontinuity and serves the role of isolating moments that can reveal aspects of reality which are not necessarily visible. As Brecht says:

> The film image is limited by its frame, everything which is inside of this frame takes on dimensions and a significance which is relative to this frame and does

not exist outside of it. In other words, the frame limits and delimits a field which determines a number of geometric, architectonic and plastic relations which do not exist in reality. At least, by limiting certain relations which in reality are lost among an infinity of others since reality is not limited by a frame, it underlines them. (cited in Mueller 1987, 483)

In Brecht's view, montage is a formal element that reinforces the productive over the reproductive use of the medium, a point which was very influential in the post-1968 film theory.

In many respects, this preference for the fragment indicates an interest in the process over the product. Montage operates as a means of interrupting the diegetic flow, in order to enact questions that go beyond the film's dramaturgy. Of particular interest in Brecht's theory is the connection between montage and his concept of the gestic acting, which has been acknowledged by Roswitha Mueller (1987, 477). Neither of the practices is content with the reduplication of reality; both are interested in the very process of interruption, with the view to preventing the audience from being absorbed by the story development. With this in mind, it is important to understand that for Brecht, what matters most is the productive interruption of the dramatic narrative and not montage in itself, as it was mistakenly understood by the 1970s film theory. I shall return to this in Chapter 3, where I discuss the ways von Trier employs a film practice that pushes forward Brecht's concept of *Gestus*. The distancing effects are achieved by a film style that does not employ montage sequences, but long-takes that focus on the actors' performances. The produced gestures create clashes between the diegetic and the metalevel and reveal unforeseen connections between the bodies.

Brecht's writings on film are infused with enthusiasm over the new medium and its potential to create complex representations of reality. Yet Brecht is busy identifying "intrinsic properties" in film, without taking into account the fact that the medium is also subject to historical transformations. As a modernist, he was fascinated by the possibilities offered by technological development. However, his initial enthusiasm over the film as medium fades away, and the main reason for that can be attributed to the fact that he became suspicious of cinema's ability to make the audience participate productively, because

In the theatre the public regulates the representation. The cinema in this respect has enormous weaknesses which seem theoretically insurmountable...the rigid fixation of the perspective: we see nothing except what the single camera eye has registered.... Due to the fact of mechanical reproduction, everything tends to present itself as a finished result, constraining, unchangeable. We return to the fundamental reproach: the public has no opportunity to modify the actor's performance, he does not find himself confronting a production, but the result of that production, which was produced in his absence. (cited in Walsh 1981, 60)

This quotation taken from a discussion between Brecht and Theodor Adorno is directly reminiscent of the latter's suspicion of the political efficacy of the film medium. Brecht maintained that theater's division between text and performance allowed for a more productive spectatorship, in which the actor is influenced by the auditorium. Brecht concluded that cinema was prone to producing dramatic material that is consumed without critical reflection on the part of the audience. An important factor that made him doubt the medium's ability to make the familiar strange was the fact that the audience's viewpoint in the cinema is always fixed. As he says: "we only see what one eye, the camera, saw. This means that the actors have to act for this eye alone" (cited in Brewster 1977, 45).

Certain directors, such as Alexander Kluge, Jean-Marie Straub/Danièle Huillet, and Jean-Luc Godard, who have consciously adopted Brechtian strategies in their films have tried to solve the unalterability of film's performance through a representational strategy that makes the relationship between text, performance, and camera viewpoint problematic. Similarly, von Trier's preference for uneven camera movements that destabilize the represented material pays equal attention to the process and the product so as to create a perceptual instability. For example, in *The Idiots*, *Dancer in the Dark* (2000), and *Dogville* and *Manderlay*, the camera's role is not that of the panoptic master that determines and controls every movement on the part of the actors. The camera is rather dedicated to a process of movement and readjustment and generates conflicts and contradictions that defy the understanding of the object as a "finished result."

Undeniably, Brecht's evaluation of the film medium is, to a large extent, restricted by his historical experiences. For instance, his initial optimism regarding cinema's ability to break with the dramatic realism that characterized other art forms, such as literature and theater, has been invalidated. The merit of his cinematic writings lies in his dissatisfaction with the mere duplication of the empirical reality and his valorization of representational strategies that aim at activating the audience's responses. It is his distinction between productive representation and reproduction that has much to contribute to film theory and practice.

Brecht's critique of the institution of cinema

Brecht, aware of the film industry's understanding of film as a commodity, argued in favor of a radical film practice that would be combined with a criticism of the institution of cinema. "As long as cinema's social function is not criticized, film criticism remains a critique of the symptoms and has itself only symptomatic character" (2001, 169). The argument rests on the assumption that film's means of production are capitalist and without questioning its commodity status the filmmaker unconsciously reproduces the capitalist ideology. Hence, the redefinition of the relationship between the filmed object and the audience is a necessary step for overcoming the commodity aspect of the medium. Brecht explains that mainstream film production does not question the reduction of the audience to the status of a consumer and the dominant view of the film object as a saleable product. In effect, the institution of cinema ends up reproducing a division of labor, in which the film director and the crew are perceived as the producers of work, while the audience is relegated to the status of the consumers.

As a result, the public's influence on the produced works is analogous to the customer's influence upon the product. The root of the problem is social, since the relegation of the audience to a position of "non-production" serves the interests of the capitalist mode of production. Brecht's point is clearly based on the assumption that the film industry's *modus operandi* reproduces a normalized image of the social structure, which cannot be influenced by the collective body, namely the auditorium. As he says:

> But mainly the sharp description between work and recreation characteristic of the capitalist mode of production divides all intellectual activities into those serving labour and those serving recreation and makes of the latter a system for the reproduction of labour power. Recreation is dedicated to non-production in the interest of production…. Those who buy tickets transform themselves in front of the screen into idlers and exploiters. Since the object of exploitation is put inside them, they are, so to speak, victims of "imploitation." (Brecht 2001, 170)

By participating in this exchange-value process, the audience unintentionally becomes an accomplice in the legitimation of its status as "non-producer," something that has consequences on the viewers' understanding of themselves as social subjects. While cognitivist film theory discounts these arguments on the grounds that a film is cueing the audience "to execute a definable variety of operations" (Bordwell 1985, 29), Brecht acknowledges that film-viewing is an active process, but he points to the ways this process is institutionalized or "routinized" according to J.D. Rhodes' discussion of Adorno's critique of cinema (Rhodes 2012, 63).

Thus, Brecht's critique of the institution of cinema is dedicated to rethinking the role of the audience, with the intention of reevaluating its role and transforming it from a passive observer to a producer. To achieve its productive potential, cinema should go beyond the industry's adherence to "public taste." For Brecht, "public taste" is a synonym for the reproduction of the familiar. Here the familiar stands for the production of objects that show a harmonized image of social reality and perpetuate the division between producers and consumers. A productive use of the medium, on the other hand, is concerned with the exposition of the familiar as commodity, so as to demonstrate the interrelation between aesthetics and politics. Thus, producing for a medium without changing its function is not enough. To politicize the medium, one needs to draw attention to the relationship between the institution and political conformity, so as to highlight what Gersch names "das Verhältnis von Destruktion und neuer Funktionalität" (the relationship between destruction and new functionality) (Gersch 1975, 84).

The latter point constitutes one of the most crucial aspects of Brecht's theory. To change the medium's function, it is not enough to introduce revolutionary topics within the established language. A mere portrayal of a political subject matter leads to comfortable contemplation and consumption of the material. On the contrary, a political utilization of the medium is predicated upon the preference for the unfinished, for the object that raises questions and makes the audience respond actively. Consequently, a radical rethinking of the institution of cinema is concerned with altering the established relationship between screen and audience, so as to activate the latter's productive faculties.

To achieve this transformation, Brecht proposes a practice that pays equal attention to the process and the product. In demystifying the productive process, Brecht aims at denying bourgeois society's distinctions between the artist and the public and the very idea of the artist as a gifted individual. In this context, technological development is seen as a positive evolution that can reveal art's reliance on apparatuses that are social *tout court*. These apparatuses defy the bourgeois concept of art as something deriving from an individual experience. The nub of Brecht's analysis is that the director's dependence on these apparatuses renders the understanding of cinema as a reflectionist medium obsolete. The social aspect of the apparatuses denies the idea that cinema can offer a candid/

neutral depiction of reality. Without perceiving the role that the apparatus plays in the finished product, the director reproduces the traditional forms of expression, which are determined by the capitalist reality.

Brecht's argument rests on the assumption that film does not rely much on the "creative individual" but on the technological apparatus. As Steve Giles points out, for Brecht, this concept is not something restricted to film. Human activity involves apparatuses that traditional art theories fail to acknowledge, partly due to their essentialist approaches toward the "artistic" and the "human" (1997, 149). From this perspective, Brecht understands the technological aspect of film production to be a form of transcending the bourgeois perception of art. The intervention of the technological apparatus brings to the surface art's dependence on technological developments and, as an extension, on the economic and productive forces. The camera is engaged in a process that records reality and produces a copy of it at the same time. This dual function collapses the distinction between the original and the copy. In this way, cinema's dependence on mechanical reproduction could strengthen the audience's understanding of the "visible"—and here the term refers to the filmic visible and the social one— as something that can be constructed and not as unchangeable.

Brecht's critique of the institution of cinema aspires to address film's reliance on the capitalist means of production. On this account, a demonstration of film's dependence on social factors can be beneficial for film practice too. The core of his argument is that cinema cannot be politically effective unless it is liberated from capitalist exploitation. Presently, film criticism can keep from Brecht's critique of the cinematic institution his call for objects that denounce the relegation of film to a medium that reproduces the commodity. Additionally, his idea that spectatorial passivity conditions people to be socially passive is historically pertinent, something that I shall return to below and in Chapter 2, in my analysis of von Trier's critique of cinematic voyeurism. Brecht thought that passive spectatorship relegates the audience to the status of the consumer, whose power relies on its purchasing and not on its productive capacity.

What is post-Brechtian cinema?

A core aspect of Brecht's theory is that forms are changeable and changing historical circumstances pose different questions. The terms "familiar" and "defamiliarization" are thus dynamic and subject to historical changeability. This was not comprehended by the 1970s film theory, which adopted a tautological understanding of Brecht's formal experiments, arguing that certain formal elements in themselves, for example, montage, can produce radical effects (see Heath 1974, 125). The same methodological mistake is conducted by scholars in Hollywood cinema, who tend to argue that Hollywood has become modernist, simply understanding modernism as the production of specific formal elements, and not as a gesture of negativity which aims at liberating human thought and perception from the shackles of banality and conformity.

In the current postmodern reality, where simulations of reality and real historical conditions merge, film radicalism lies in reevaluating the modernist negation of the institutionalized, in order to restore a more "responsible" spectatorship in the literal sense, that is, one that activates responses. Such a "responsible" spectatorship is not predicated upon the audience's confirmation of some preexisting theoretical ideas that run the risk of institutionalization. The restoration of responses can be rather achieved by a process that calls attention to form as a means of aligning contradictions that make the audience more productive.

Let us now offer a definition of the post-Brechtian. Very schematically, the term "post-Brechtian" describes a postmodern rethinking of Brecht which shares his preference for a fragmented representation and formal abstraction, but not his political certainties. In the introduction, I mentioned Barthes' argument that a post-Brechtian aesthetic intends to disturb secure hermeneutical exegeses including the ones that are shaped by the Marxist methodology. The question that arises is how such an aesthetics produces political effects. A valid starting point would be that a film interested in questioning current political reality should follow Brecht's *modus operandi*, according to which challenging the audience's perceptual abilities by means of formal abstraction can make one question aspects of reality that one takes for granted. In valorizing points of tension and contradictions, a post-Brechtian aesthetics is not interested in the reproduction of a political content to be consumed. Brecht's conviction that the medium needs to enter into self-criticism is still valid; what the post-Brechtian questions is his certainty that the complication of representation can result in precise enlightening effects and in social change based upon the socialist doctrine.

Along these lines, a post-Brechtian aesthetics follows Brecht and places the audience at the center of the action; it is a paradigm of radical postmodern practice consistent with the modernist ambition to renew perception. Martin Brady suggests that a post-Brechtian film can be broadly defined as the deployment of "Brechtian devices in films which no longer adhere to the principles of ideology or leftist political modernism" (2008, 297). Brady's brief definition is accompanied by two examples: von Trier's *Dogville* and Michael Verhoeven's *The Nasty Girl* [*Das Schreckliche Mädchen*: 1988]. While this definition has some validity, it does not address dialectics as a constitutive element of post-Brechtian cinema. Dialectics, namely the production of formal abstractions that produce oppositions that liberate understanding from the limits of the "innate" and the "natural," is still the principal method. Yet this method does not aim at subordinating the contradictions to a totalized metanarrative, but reflects its very motion and the very inadequacy of the medium of its own articulation.

Illuminating from this perspective is David Barnett's discussion of the very term "post-Brechtian," even though his discussion focuses on the medium of theater. Barnett explains that post-Brechtian theater practice builds upon Brecht's willingness to present relationships motivated by social impulses. The difference is that post-Brechtian performance is not restricted by the Marxist metanarrative. "Dialectics are preserved as a method of investigating the social; yet, under the condition of epistemological uncertainty, points of reference taken for granted in Brechtian theatre are not available and have to be created onstage" (2011b, 337). Thus, the post-Brechtian complication of form produces dialectical contradictions that cannot be understood in binary terms, as it was the case in orthodox Brechtian practice. Brecht's interpretive system is altered and the episodes presented on stage are concerned with offering unfinished material to the audience without interpreting it. Barnett proposes five "founding theses" that clearly illuminate the fundamental principles of a theater practice that finds Orthodox Brechtian practices insufficient:

(1) Epistemological uncertainty.
(2) Dialectics are preserved, and thus Brechtian stage-craft is modified and not rejected.
(3) The Brechtian emphasis on showing is retained.
(4) Criticism of Brecht is limited to a criticism of his interpretive system.
(5) The stage is no longer concerned with interpretation but association (Barnett 2011b, 337).

Barnett provides the basis which can help us understand the politics of a post-Brechtian aesthetic. The first principle, that is, "epistemological uncertainty," is the most important one, as post-Brechtian aesthetics presents a collision of theses that defy synthesis.

This link between the crisis of epistemology and Brechtian practices has been clarified by Alexander Kluge, who is renowned for his employment of Brechtian elements in his films. Kluge gave me an interview, and when I asked him to comment on the shift from the Brechtian to the post-Brechtian he explained that the difference lies in the fact that the author/director does not offer the audience hints on how to interpret the material. "The author analyses, or counter-analyses, or repeats, or makes comments" (Koutsourakis 2011, 223). This point suggests that the dialectics between the medium and interpretation is not a matter of an agitational call for change. Conversely, the role of dialectics is to turn the medium inside out so as to pose the problem of interpretation itself. The produced interpretations play against themselves and aim at undoing a stable relationship between ideas and representations. Jørgen Leth, a filmmaker, whose films employ a plethora of Brechtian elements, describes this process as a way of posing the most awkward questions, not in order to corroborate a previous conclusion, but to learn things while experimenting with the medium (Interview, Appendix).

In many respects, this demonstrates a preference for the process, and here process stands for aligning points of tension without resolving them. The French philosopher Jacques Rancière has also illuminated that contemporary art achieves its political function not by way of moral polarizations and messages, but through a process of disturbance that seeks to shock and disorientate the audience.

> The dream of a suitable political work of art is in fact the dream of disrupting the relationship between the visible, the sayable and the thinkable without having to use the terms of a message as a vehicle. It is the dream of an art that would transmit meanings in the form of a rupture with the very logic of meaningful situations. As a matter of fact, political art cannot work in the form of a meaningful spectacle that would lead to an "awareness" of the state of the world. Suitable political art would ensure, at one and the same time, the production of a double effect: the readability of a political signification, and a sensible or perceptual shock caused by the uncanny, by that which resists signification. (2004, 63)

Rancière's argument helps us bracket the very idea of the post-Brechtian and illuminate some of the previous points. In the current historical circumstances, art does not become political by harmonizing contradictions via definite solutions. The production of defamiliarizing effects does not aspire to lead to a cognitive revelation that simply leads the audience to a privileged position of knowledge. Formal complication aspires to create hermeneutical obstacles that make the audience more productive, so as to reflect on its own social role, since the crisis of meaning is also the outcome of the existing social/historical relationships.

Locating von Trier in the post-Brechtian

The question is how does this relate to the cinema of Lars von Trier? On the face of the previous comments, it is useful to explain that von Trier's films prioritize experimental formal practices that intend to challenge subject matter, habitual film-viewing, and the very cinematic institution. Von Trier employs representational strategies, which are not simply concerned with reproducing dramatic actions, but with pointing out contradictions that cannot be resolved within the limits of the films' dramaturgy. Things are viewed from a distance with the view to changing the subject and object relationships. It is noteworthy that this distance, or, to use a Brechtian term, *Von-Aussen-Sehen*, manifests itself in different ways in each film. For instance, films such as *Images of Relief*, *The Element of Crime*, *Europa*, *Antichrist* (2009), and *Melancholia* manipulate the spectacular aspects of the industry; objects such as *Epidemic*, *The Idiots*, *Dogville*, and *Manderlay* show a preference for cinematic austerity, whereas other films, for example, his student ones, *Orchidégartneren* (1977) and *Menthe—la Bienheureuse* (1979), and the later ones, *Breaking the Waves* (1996) and *Dancer in the Dark,* combine austerity with spectacular fragments that foreground an excess of artifice in the *mise-en-scène*.

Yet both the austere as well as the excessive visuals become analytical, in the sense that they create a gap between reality and representation which produces a sense of critical distance and detachment. Hence this distance transmits a feeling of authorial uncertainty which is communicated by means of a filmmaking process that privileges a visual rather than a text-bound dramaturgy. This is something that characterizes the whole corpus of his filmography. In his first filmmaking attempts, he strived for absolute control and precision in the filmmaking production. However, this absolute control did not favor the making of images that simply reproduced a script, while the relationship between sound and image was not necessarily harmonious. For example, in the *Europa* trilogy, which I discuss in detail in the next chapter, the voice-over is used in a radical way that creates a disjunction between the speaking subject and language. This disjunction complicates chronotopic reality and the boundaries between historical past and present.

In this first trilogy of films, as well as in his student films, for example, *Orchidégartneren* (1977), *Menthe—la Bienheureuse*, and *Images of Relief*, von Trier follows the practice of his mentor, Jørgen Leth, and sets forth the narrative by way of visual tableaux that have a sense of autonomy. The dramaturgy is always loose and the tableaux do not subordinate image, sound, and meaning into a unitary whole. Consequently, the final outcome is far from being, as Brecht would say, a *Schmelzprozeß* (melting process), and forces the audience to make interconnections which are not necessarily predetermined. These interconnections defy authorial sovereignty. In an interview he gave after the completion of his graduate film, von Trier referred to the need to make films which go beyond the authority of the text and do not follow the classic psychological formula in which the actions justify the characters and the other way around. In his words, "the storyline is the pretext of the film, but the other elements don't have to point in the same direction" (cited in Schawander 2003, 14).

A significant example of this preference for visual tableaux not restricted by a logocentric connection is his early film *Orchidégartneren*. The film's story is minimal and it is about a young artist Victor Marse (von Trier) who meets two nurses and falls in love with one of them—Eliza (Inger Hvidtfeldt)—while being interned in a sanatorium. The arrangement of the tableaux has no sense of clear-cut narrative orientation, while throughout the film there are minimum sequences of dialogue. As Peter Schepelern explains, "Filmens historie er kryptisk. Scenerne står hovedsagelig som enkeltstående situationer En ledsagende voice-over-stemme (Jakob Hoffmeyer) giver en distanceret og affekteret speak til Victors historie, men alligevel er det umiddelbart ikke muligt at bestemme, præcis hvad der fortælles." (The film's story is puzzling. The scenes are mainly individual situations. An accompanying voice-over—Jakob Hoffmeyer—narrates in a distant and affectionate manner Victor's story, yet it is not possible to determine exactly what is told) (2000a, 27–28). The voice-over does not serve the role of the conventional offscreen narration which is joined with the image tracks. Instead of being homogenized, it is used as material that encourages the audience to make associations between sounds and images.

At one moment in the film, we see an unknown woman masturbating, while an offscreen sound of a baby crying is persistent. The voice-over comments: "Victor Marse knew that the worst thing they could do to him was not to smile. And he had learned that women always—always—despise that which is weak. And he truly dreamt of strengthening himself." The following image shows the male protagonist dressing himself in a Nazi uniform, while the uniform and the visual paraphernalia that come with it express a change in the character's *Haltung*. The character's *Haltung* is for Brecht an expansion of his term *Gestus*, which aspires to connect the body with the social environment. Marc Silberman explains that "*Haltung* can be translated both as 'attitude' in the intellectual sense of a cognitive category and as a stance in the pragmatic sense of physical component" (Silberman 2006, 38). For Brecht, the *Haltung* is always variable, since corporeal dynamics are demarcated by the variable social relationships and environments.

Brecht thought that the film medium has the exceptional potential of presenting a series of *Haltungen*, something that was manifested in Chaplin's emphasis on physical/gestural movement. A character has a variety of *Haltungen* which vary according to the different situations. A film committed to the exploration of *Haltungen* does not need to overdramatize and can liberate the object from absolute authorial intentionality. This is certainly clear in *Orchidégartneren*, in which the arrangement of antithetical *Haltungen* acts as experimental exercises in kinesics aiming to examine the politics of sexuality. Initially, Victor's *Haltung* signifies passivity, but after rehearsing the Nazi clothes his posture and attitude change. The individual is not only shown as changeable, but as role-playing too.

The film's arrangement of a plethora of visual and acoustic materials places the actions in a social context. Thus, sexuality is not treated in an existential or psychological way, but as the repetitive play of domination and submission. The camera registers the performing body in an analytical way so as to capture the variability of the power dynamics in the portrayed relationships. Neither the camera nor the actors conceal the fact that they quote and von Trier uses the performing body and the sound and image counterpoints to investigate the social and political aspect of sexual relationships. In a noteworthy scene, we see Victor observing Eliza powdering herself in front of a mirror. Eliza is humming the German song *Lili Marleen*, which is renowned for its historical links with the traumas of fascism. While the character is framed in a close-up, we can see that the humming's origin is offscreen rather than on-screen, a stylistic choice which once again divides the individual. Hence, the song's connotations placed in a context of sexual antagonism make one rethink the micropolitics of everyday life, which is a recurring theme in von Trier's oeuvre.

One can certainly observe parallels with the work of another post-Brechtian director, that is, Reiner Werner Fassbinder, whose work is also busy identifying social connections in the characters' bodies. The political implications of Fassbinder's cinema develop from his preference for a segmented narrative style which prioritizes the examination of social relations instead of stories of self-determined characters. Von Trier's combination of stylized visuals and the employment of the voice-over as linguistic material follows Fassbinder's *modus operandi* and shifts the interest from the reproduction of dramatic action motivated by psychology to the production of gestures that suspend the cause-and-effect connection of the episodes. Toward the end of the film, the camera frames Victor threatening Eliza with a gun. She, on her part, asks him to give her a second chance and while addressing him she talks directly to the camera. There is a systematic omission of the reverse shot and this prevents us from looking at the character—Victor—whom she addresses. Instead, images of Victor's revolver interject and the camera constantly returns to Eliza linking the audience's gaze with the gun, a choice that lays bare von Trier's hyperawareness of the apparatus of cinema (figure 1.1).

The tableaux here produce a metaeffect which is evidenced by Eliza's exit from the frame, which remains temporarily empty. She then repeatedly returns and exits again, as if she is consciously entering a theater space and addressing an audience. Ultimately, Marse throws his revolver and in the next frame a zoom-out reveals that Eliza holds a whip behind her back. Directly after Marse has disarmed himself, we notice that she is preparing to flagellate him (figure 1.2). Again, this passage captures a variety of *Haltungen* that reveal the changeability of power relationships and depict the individual as a possibility rather than an entity, showing that the victims can turn to perpetrators and the other way around.

In one of the film's final sequences, Marse is driving his car and a diegetic radio sound reproduces an advertisement in English: "I was in his warm embrace. Our eyes met and he pressed his lips firmly against mine. Phew! What a let-down! His breath reeked of stale tobacco and his mouth tasted like an old fag end." This

Figures 1.1 and 1.2: *Orchidégartneren* (1977).

is immediately followed by a male voice advising the listeners that sometimes cigarettes can damage more things than your health. This small scene is indicative of von Trier's tendency to accumulate visual and acoustic materials which do not necessary form a unified narrative, but produce contradictions which make the viewer more productive. But most importantly, this passage makes a clear connection between the sexual and the social, openly acknowledging gender identity as performative. The practice of contrasting visuals and acoustic materials loosely connected with each other downplays the conventional narrative structure, in which all the aspects of the *mise-en-scène* are subordinated to clear storytelling. On the contrary, von Trier's practice draws attention to all the formal elements, such as image, sound, lightning, and camera movements, so as to expose the object as a system of narration and to make connections between the filmic and the extra-filmic reality. Instead of a causal linking of the episodes which present a crisis, its development, and the climax, the film's visual dramaturgy produces visual and acoustic shocks which suspend the cause-and-effect narrative order.

In place of a development of a central crisis, the material confronts us with a series of crises forcing us to make connections. *Menthe—la bienheureuse* is another important document which exemplifies this point. Similarly to *Orchidégartneren* the film's dramaturgy is unfixed and is busy investigating performative connections between images and sounds as well as corporeal connections which refute any sense of dramatic linearity. An unnamed female character addresses her female lover Menthe (Annette Linnet), trying to make her recollect a series of memories from the past. For the most part, the voice-over does not connect with its originating source, namely Menthe's lover (Inger Hvidtfeldt), and the effect is a collection of materials which have no straightforward connection with each other. Throughout the film, Menthe does not speak at all and her thoughts and memories are doubled by her lover. Sounds and images are not united harmoniously, and this experimental structure eschews the production of concrete spatiotemporal relations. The focus shifts from the individual speaker, and visual and verbal language becomes the protagonist, as if language speaks the character and not the other way around, something which is a central characteristic of postdramatic theatrical representation (Lehmann 2006, 88).

Exemplary in this regard is a scene in the film that focuses on Menthe's lover. While we hear her voice in the background, the character looks directly into the camera without speaking, making plain that the voice-over is extra-diegetic.

Figure 1.3: *Menthe—la bienheureuse* (1979).

Language here divides the speaking character and the voice-over reads: "they offered you these blessed chains that took you away from yourself." The image that follows shows a woman's genitalia chained, followed by a large figurine of Jesus on the cross. A cut to Menthe's lover follows, who gazes at the camera and (at this point her voice is diegetic) says: "You have difficulty in interpreting what one tells you. Always" (figure 1.3). The camera does not reverse to Menthe and this absence of a reverse shot implies that the character addresses the audience; here the film produces a metacommentary on its own deliberate banishment of certainty.

There is a plurality of material in these vignettes which do not promote dramatic plot but depersonalize the narrative and foster a plethora of interconnections between desire, power, and domination. By analyzing verbal communication, visual arrangements, and body language, the film turns upon itself and blurs the distinctions between life and performance and self and world. Language becomes unstable and characters are reduced to linguistic and visual constructs. One is asked to think beyond autonomous identities and to focus on the character's dependence on verbal and visual systems which are unfixed and present the relationships as an ensemble of complex and ever-changing processes. The crisis of identity applies also to issues of authorial expression, since the film ceaselessly quotes Alain Resnais and Marguerite Duras and the renowned novel *Histoire D'O*. As Peter Schepelern observes, von Trier quotes Resnais' *Last Year at Marienbad* [*L'Année dernière à Marienbad*: 1961] and like the French auteur he refrains from showing dramatic actions, but experiments with sounds and images. "De er ingen dialog, kun kvinde stemmernes stadige ordstrømme som ledsagelse" (They [the characters] have no dialogue, only steady female voices, and word-flows are their companions) (2000a, 37).

Consequently, the narrative is polyphonic and this aspect of the film complicates the diegesis, given that each visual and verbal utterance is not necessarily connected with the ones that follow. This also results in spatial and temporal defamiliarization, whose task is not to fuse all the materials in service of the story. This practice is also evidenced in the first part of the Europa trilogy, *The Element of Crime*, which I discuss in detail in the next chapter. The role of this polyphonic narrative is to offer a variation of perspectives, which resist the dramatic convention of the unified individual character and the view of the narrative as the vehicle for the director's ideological positions. The narrative is structured in terms of oppositions which do not reach a climax. As Mikhail Bakhtin—the major theorizer of polyphony—explains, conventional dramatic form aspires to resolve contradictions by uniting the author's point of view, the characters' function within the narrative, and the audience in an integrated world. Antithetically, polyphony produces a variety of voices and incompatible materials that cannot be reduced to a single ideological entity. Like Brecht, Bakhtin suggests that the connection between language and the speaking subject is partial, because language cannot be understood outside a social context. Language is "interindividual" and the role of polyphony is to establish a dialogic relation between the narrator and the audience (Bakhtin 1984, 6–7).

Von Trier's employment of polyphony favors the role of indeterminacy, and this is key to our understanding of the post-Brechtian. This indeterminacy does not invite the audience to respond within a demarcated realm of signification. Story development and characterization are downplayed and replaced by a performative excess that favors the production of ruptures in the film's narrative. In the case of *Menthe*, these ruptures depersonalize a narrative, which appears ostensibly subjective, placing sexuality and desire in a social framework. Characteristic of this, for example, is a scene in which Menthe's lover asks her to "remember the blacks." Immediately a still image of four emaciated African kids follows (figure 1.4) and another one shows two men dressed in traditional African turbans. Meanwhile, a series of landscape images succeed one another, communicating an "exotic" and peaceful atmosphere. These oppositions are significant because they force us to perceive two extreme contradictions simultaneously that could be summed up as follows: "to desire is to dominate and to control" and "one person's fantasy is another's misery and submission."

Figure 1.4: *Menthe—la bienheureuse* (1979).

The deindividuation of the narrative reaches a zenith toward the end of the film, when we get to realize that the woman, who is addressed as Menthe by her female lover, is not Menthe. The camera registers a letter written by her, in which she reveals the identity confoundment, and once again language is separated from the individual speaker. The film's stylized antinaturalism eschews the harmonious relation between characters and language with the view to exploring contradictions that are flattened in classical narratives. Representational consistency is replaced by a performative arrangement of images and sounds which prioritize the fragmented exploration of relations and *Haltungen*.

A skeptic could interject that contemporary Hollywood high-concept films and blockbusters have also disturbed the classical hierarchies between images and sounds and are also concerned with loosening dramaturgy and storytelling. Once again, one needs to think of the different effects that some outwardly similar formal elements produce. Contemporary Hollywood minimizes dramaturgy and changes the hierarchy between images and sounds, so as to create a visual excess that aims at maximizing pleasurable consumption. Spectacle replaces traditional storytelling and the story is not the blockbusters' primary attraction; but this choice does not aim at politicizing the object, that is, at making the audience more productive. By contrast, the reduction of the narrative to an excess of visuality aims at oversimplifying the object and creating visual marks that can be further exploited in ancillary markets, for example, computer games, advertisements, DVDs that can produce more profits than the films themselves (King 2000, 2). At times, as Thomas Schatz rightly observes, "it is hard to distinguish a film's aesthetic or narrative quality from its commercial imperatives" (1993, 10). Thus, blockbusters go beyond classical Hollywood storytelling so as to encourage responses, but these responses are placed in a consumerist framework; they do not aim at making the audience rethink the social relations outside the narrative world. On the contrary, they expect the audience to reconfirm these relations by enhancing spectacular pleasure so as to facilitate the purchase of products circulated by sister companies.

While the Hollywood *modus operandi* strives to stabilize unproblematic narrative consumption as well as the audience's consuming habits in the extra-filmic reality, von Trier aims at destabilizing the narrative so as to maximize ambiguity. Exemplary in this regard is his graduate film *Images of Relief*. The film is a prime example of a polyphonic narrative that separates the voice from the speaking subject, casting doubt on the idea of the speaker being the originator of the spoken material. *Images of Relief* is the progenitor of the *Europa* trilogy and tells the story of Leo (Edward Fleming), a Nazi soldier betrayed by his Danish girlfriend Esther (Kirsten Olesen) the first day after the liberation of Copenhagen. Documented images of humiliation and violence toward suspected Nazi collaborators are followed by dream-like images accompanied by Leo's voice-over. The effect is that the object appears as a quotation of antithetical materials that point to the limitations of representation. Consequently, the variety of stimuli has its effects on the portrayal of history, which is not shown as a photographic reproduction of events, but as fragments that need to be assembled by the audience.

Despite the centrality of the two main characters, the film's complex form subverts principles of classical narration and portrays history in an undramatic way, which challenges the view of history as an additive series of events that mark out precise boundaries between the past (here the Nazi occupation) and the postwar reality. The narrative is communicated through a series of static tableaux, while characters are again reduced to visual constellations and linguistic quotations. For the most part, von Trier refrains from placing the central characters in the same frame, even in scenes loaded with conflict. For instance, during the first encounter between Leo and Esther, there is nothing to indicate a spatiotemporal change from the previous tableaux.

In a rather lengthy tableau we see Esther kissing with a black soldier; the camera suddenly cuts to Leo and then captures images of no dramatic importance. When Esther realizes that Leo is present, the camera observes her in an analytical way, but once her monologue starts, it cuts to Leo, again followed by prolonged unconnected visuals. In the next tableau, Esther moves in a slow stylized way while talking to Leo and the camera moves from left to right in a choreographic movement. Interpersonal communication is rendered problematic, given that the characters look like voicing inner thoughts instead of engaging in a dramatic dialogue. This stylization adds an oneiric element to the narrative and the characters within the tableaux appear as role-players in the broader theater of history.

Accordingly, this dissolution of the dramatis personae is used as a means of placing the relationships into history, rather than using history as a setting for the production of drama. The narrative draws attention to the historical changeability and the shift in the power relationships, asking the audience to conduct a dialectical experiment and consider how the process of denazification ends up reproducing the same practices that it negates. It is a concrete contradiction which aspires to make the spectator comprehend history beyond the limits of historical determinism. Corresponding to Brecht's view of dialectical experimentation as a process that aspires to reveal contradictions instead of solving them, von Trier shows the victims adopting the attitudes of the perpetrators. Brecht did something similar in his failed collaboration with Fritz Lang for the film *Hangmen Also Die* (1943). In a scene which was omitted from the final cut, Brecht had some detainees in a concentration camp singing an anti-Semitic song minutes prior to their execution by the Nazis. As Gerd Gemünden explains, "this scene was to convey the startling and contradictory impact of totalitarianism on the population" (1999, 71). In a similar dialectical way, *Images of Relief* shows how historical changeability does not always eliminate the previous state of affairs. History justifies the winners, who can easily replicate repressive practices after their victory. Von Trier explained that: "Jeg har ikke taget parti for den tyske officer, fordi han er nazist, men fordi han er tabe ren" (I have not taken the side of the Nazi soldier because he is a Nazi, but because he is the loser) (Schepelern 2000a, 59).

The film represents the historical shift in a very distant manner, asking the audience to consider history beyond the ideological certainties of the established historical narrative, a point to which von Trier returns to in the *Europa* trilogy. The unexpected interruption of the story line with newsreels of the time puts forward this conjecture in a very forceful way. After Leo's and Esther's meeting, a lengthy newsreel shows images of violence against Nazi collaborators and German soldiers (figure 1.5). As opposed to the static quality of the main narrative, these newsreels are characterized by an excess of physical movement on the part of the Danish people, who are brutally attacking the defeated side. This antithesis between mobility and stillness, documentary images and fiction calls attention to the film's quotation of antithetical materials. Apart from the

Figure 1.5: *Befrielsesbilleder* (*Images of Relief* 1982).

lengthy quotation of newsreels, the fictional tableaux's stylization intentionally foregrounds a feeling of artificiality, which reduces the characters to mere deliverers of a text.

The quotation of antithetical materials is a method that can also be identified in the Europa trilogy, aiming at provoking questions with respect to the opposition between the official history and aspects of it that have been overlooked. In *The Element of Crime,* von Trier self-consciously quotes the film noir genre to produce a failed mystery story that defies any sense of linear development. The narrative consists of decomposed fragments that bring together historical references torn out of context with quotations from prominent films and literature verses. These references function as historical indices with which the audience is expected to interact. In *Epidemic,* von Trier incorporates the filmmaking process in the film's fabula. The film appears as a quotation of its own making and this has its corollary on the portrayal of history, which appears as non-chronologically ordered material. Hence, *Europa,* which deals explicitly with history and in particular with the postwar West Germany, adopts formal strategies such as overt back projections and superimpositions that express a dramaturgical skepticism regarding the medium's ability to portray history.

This predilection for non-plot-bound/fragmented narratives is also evidenced in von Trier's subsequent works. The major difference is that after the publication of the Dogme 95 Manifesto, extreme attention to visuals is replaced by a more performative use of the camera, aiming to abandon absolute control. A careful examination of his camera work since *Breaking the Waves* can illustrate this point more clearly. The meticulous and calculated composition of images is replaced by an interest in using the camera as an investigative tool. Again, the objective is the making of performative connections between images and sounds, but as he says, the camera's role is to search for things and not to frame material (Interview, Appendix). One should also consider von Trier's preference for avoiding detailed rehearsals and allowing the actors to improvise while performing a character. Commenting on his experience as an actor in *Manderlay*, William Dafoe said that von Trier had a preference for the moments when the struggle between the actor and the scene was made clear (cited in *The Road to Manderlay*: 2005). This *modus operandi* focuses on gestural details and contradictions at the expense of concrete characterization. This evokes Brecht's idea that the camera becomes productive when it does not seek to capture material solely in the service of the drama. In one of his film scripts, Brecht says that "der Apparat sucht sich sozusagen Motive, er ist ein Soziologe" (the camera searches for motives, it is a sociologist) (1983, 333). In assuming an investigative rather than a reproductive role, the camera prioritizes the capturing of a range of materials which resist the closed dramatic form of mainstream cinema.

Likewise, von Trier's employment of the camera is concerned with discovering things rather than creating a coherent dramatic cosmos. He employs the camera in a performative way so as to explore the irreconcilable words, gestures, and actions which do not lead to a monocausal thesis, but explore the political dimension of everyday relationships. While I discuss this in depth in Chapter 3, it is instructive to offer here a brief explanation of the very terms "performative" and "performativity." My understanding of performativity is informed by Derrida's reading of John Langshaw Austin's writings on the speech act. Derrida interprets the term "performative speech act" as a practice that is not solely referential and does not simply communicate the intentionality of the speaking subject. It is rather a transformative process, not concerned with the communication of "a semantic content" (Derrida 1977, 13).

Within this framework offered by Derrida, one can define performativity in the cinema as the camera's interaction with the actors' performances in ways that the communication of storytelling material is not prioritized. The camera interacts with the performing body in an analytical way, whose function is not strictly diegetic. In many respects, performativity refers to a process in which the act of showing/analyzing an action is privileged over the action itself. That is, representation shifts from the reproduction of actions to an aesthetics of showing the process of making a scene; performativity destabilizes the narrative so as to render the very act of interpretation problematic.

Particularly telling with reference to von Trier's performative use of the camera is one of the final sequences in *Dancer in the Dark* (2000). Selma's (Björk) execution is approaching and we get to see the character being distressed while walking toward the gallows. At one point, Selma faints and Brenda, the female police guard (Siobhan Fallon), whom she has befriended, helps her stand up and regain her consciousness. Meanwhile, Brenda performs her institutional role and assists the guards in lifting Selma up using a board (figure 1.6). There is a wealth of material in this scene which piles contradictions upon contradictions without offering any sense of hermeneutical relief to the audience. On the one hand, we see Brenda offering her sincere sympathy to Selma. She strokes and consoles her, while at the same time she aids the guards in placing the rope over Selma's neck. This passage reveals the clash between the individual's persona and her social function. Von Trier emphasizes this conflict by using the camera in a way that captures dramatic and aleatory material. This practice denaturalizes the performing body combining the presentation of dramatic material and a reflection on it. The major contradiction is that Brenda, who is sympathetic toward Selma, is part of the institutional establishment that kills her. Her expression of sympathy is a gesture that facilitates Selma's smooth execution. This passage is symptomatic of von Trier's indifference in treating the story as an end in itself, as well as of his preference for a loose story line, which accumulates points of tension that increase uncertainty.

Figure 1.6: *Dancer in the Dark* (2000).

Challenging the cinematic institution

As mentioned earlier, the core of Brecht's writings on cinema is that one cannot produce for a medium without transforming its social function. Brecht intended to emphasize cinema's reliance on social and economic factors, with the purpose of showing that cinema's technological means of production, as well as narrative forms, are primarily social. Brecht celebrated the very forces that produced commodification, on the basis that the exposition of the film as commodity could become a means of debunking bourgeois values that appear as natural. His objective was to expose the apparatuses that are involved in our perception of social life and affect all forms of culture and narration; in his view, these apparatuses are suppressed by canonical forms of narration which do not question the medium of their own articulation.

The exposition of cinema as an institution, and the demonstration of the social aspect of certain narrative forms, as well as of the processes of commodification and consumption serve the purpose of changing the institution from an apparatus of consumption to a productive one. This argument is a complex one and refers to the ways the institution of cinema plays a dual function; that is, it produces commodities and at the same time it relegates the audience to the status of the consumer. Brecht's inference resonates with Marx's argument in the 23rd chapter of the *Capital*, in which he explains that capitalism reproduces itself not simply by means of the productive processes but also through an incessant reproduction of the very conditions which facilitate the reproduction of the worker not as a productive being, but as a reproductive one. As Marx says:

> The capitalist process of production, therefore, seen as a total, connected processes, i.e. a process of reproduction, produces not only commodities, not only surplus-value, but it also produces and reproduces the capital relation itself; on the one hand the capitalist, on the other the wage-labourer. (1990, 716)

Marx's argument hinges upon the consideration that the sole production of commodities is not sufficient for the continuation of capitalism. Equally important is the smooth reproduction of the existing conditions and social relations that can maintain the existing processes of production.

Marx's line of reasoning provides the framework that can make us rethink other forms of reproduction. In particular, one can reexamine how canonical forms of cinematic narration do not simply ensure the reproduction of commodities, but they simultaneously reproduce the institutionalized subject and object relations. Von Trier's films confront the cinematic institution and challenge the institutionalized relations by frustrating the audience's expectations and by treating them as coproducers of the narrative as opposed to consumers. He achieves this by means of metacinematic strategies; in this context, the films are not solely committed to the narrating of stories, but they are also reflections on cinema itself. Roland Barthes suggested something similar about Brecht's work, arguing that Brecht abolished the "mythic distinction between creation and reflection." His literary works are not just literary objects, but metaliterature as well (2000, 262).

Comparably, von Trier's films are always semitreatises on cinema itself, expressing skepticism toward image and sound-making production. At the same time, certain films rework cinematic genres so as to analyze them and expose their institutionalization as well as their ideological banality. As he says: "De film, jeg har lavet, har altid handlet meget om at lave film" (the movies I have made are always about filmmaking itself) (cited in Schepelern 2000a, 100). On this account, metacinematic tropes figure importantly in his films and this is not simply a matter of postmodern intertextuality, but a way of revealing social processes by focusing on the medium itself. It is rather a utopian belief in the power of cinema to denaturalize the material on screen and it is reminiscent of Brecht's film writings in which he compares the process of making social realities visible to the process of producing a picture from a photographic negative (cited in Giles 2008, 123).

Interestingly, this practice permeates the whole corpus of his filmography, from the very first student films to the latest ones. A scene from *Orchidégartneren* shows this eloquently. In a sequence, taking place in a cinema theater (and serving no diegetic purpose whatsoever), we see Victor, Eliza, and her girlfriend watching a movie. The camera cuts abruptly from the characters to the film they are watching. The characters in the film within the film have their eyes covered with black streaks, refusing to be looked at (figure 1.7). Through the use of shot reverse shot, von Trier cuts from the film within the film to the diegetic cosmos, showing the characters acting as spectators. But their spectatorship is frustrated, since the metafilm opposes canonical cultural habits of viewing depending on the assumption that the individuals seen cannot return the gaze.

By cross-cutting from the metafilm to the main narrative, von Trier draws our attention to issues of cinematic voyeurism and the ways habitual forms of spectatorship are linked with a particular social and political framework. This point is clearly confirmed in the next sequence, when Eliza and her girlfriend

Figure 1.7: *Orchidégartneren* (1977).

are kissing and fondling each other. In the meantime, Eliza's girlfriend returns the gaze to the camera and says "look at him," acknowledging the presence of a voyeur. Eliza moves toward the camera and slaps a person, whom we cannot see. The camera trembles and immediately after that, Eliza shuts the door. The fact that we cannot see the person addressed by the two women makes one assume that they are breaking the fourth wall to disrupt our orthodox structures of looking.

Apart from bringing to light the dominant gendered structures of the habitual forms of film-viewing, the aforementioned scene breaks the secure patterns of spectatorship which assume that spectatorial pleasure derives from the comfort that the act of viewing remains secret. Quite the reverse, von Trier's films always return the gaze to the audience and this is not just a formalist exercise, but a gesture that epitomizes his willingness to get the audience involved, to provoke them to rethink their roles, not only as viewers but also as social and historical beings. In a characteristic scene in *Images of Relief*, Esther accuses Leo of having poked out the eyes of a partisan boy along with a group of Nazis. When Leo's offscreen voice counteracts that the SS are responsible for this, Esther gazes at the camera and asks, "Don't you see that you have a responsibility too?" (figure 1.8). The camera remains focused on her without cutting to her addressee; the character's words address the audience, making a parallel between passive spectatorship and social inertia. The inference is that standardized forms of spectatorship are equivalent with standardized forms of social existence, which lead to the docile acceptance of social and historical reality.

In subsequent films, the critique of institutionalized subject and object relationships manifests itself by means of the manipulation of familiar genres. Von Trier reworks certain established genres, such as melodrama in *Breaking*

Figure 1.8: *Befrielsesbilleder* (*Images of Relief* 1982).

the Waves, musical in *Dancer in the Dark*, the horror film in *Antichrist*, and defamiliarizes them. The produced objects have a dual function: On the one hand, they rework certain narrative patterns in much more radical ways, and on the other, they turn into metacommentaries on the genres themselves. *Breaking the Waves* is a good example in this regard. Von Trier's manipulation of generic melodramatic tropes in this film is remarkable, because he has removed some of melodrama's constituent elements, such as the overwhelming of the narrative with *melos* and the genre's overemphasis on the domestic sphere.

Throughout the film, music is solely used in the beginning of each chapter and it is accompanied by some static tableaux. Each chapter has a title which summarizes the action that follows and the songs act more as commentaries. Music here acquires, what Brecht calls, "an independent function" (2001, 14), and liberates the material from the conventions of the genre. The absence of extra-diegetic music in the main narrative complicates matters more, since there is no sound that duplicates the people's emotional states. The story is stripped to its essentials, forcing us to focus on the contradictory relationships instead of using an excessive mise-en-scène that mirrors the characters' psychology. Moreover, the film's pseudo-documentary realism comes in opposition to the melodramatic tropes of excessive lightning, music and décor, while for the most part action takes place outside domestic spaces, clearly linking Bess' (Emily Watson) story to the social rather than the private/domestic sphere.

Yet the material becomes more complex, due to von Trier's questioning of melodrama's oversimplistic understanding of social relations through the reductive binary of good versus evil. In employing these reductive binaries, *Breaking the Waves* does not necessarily validate them, but reveals their banality so as to urge the audience to block any generic produced meaning. It is worthwhile quoting some parts of the director's statement that can reveal some irreconcilable paradoxes. Von Trier says that the film is "about good" and describes both Jan (Stellan Skarsgård) and Bess as good characters. Bess is good in a "spiritual sense," and she cannot perceive things outside the dichotomy of good and evil. Jan is mainly good, because he marries "simple-minded" Bess despite society's misgivings. After his accident, Jan does not want to deprive Bess of the gift of physical love. "When Jan asks Bess to find another lover, he is being completely sincere and genuine. He wants to do 'good'... Bess is fooled; she is doing 'good' for him. He is doing 'good' for her. Nobody is forcing anybody. They both act from the will to do 'good' " (1996, 21).

Von Trier's commentary indicates the film's intention to criticize the genre from within by seemingly accepting its moralizing language. The reduction of the story to a naïve, oversimplified minimum acts as a form of experimentation which questions the genre's moral polarizations. This naïve attitude is one that produces the major questions and contradictions that aim at intensifying the social aspect of the produced paradoxes, instead of accepting melodrama's presentation of the crises under the rubric of tragic destiny. The constitutive intersection between naiveté and defamiliarization evokes the work of Carl Theodor Dreyer and Brecht. Dreyer thought that the film medium becomes productive and innovative when employing formal abstraction that gives rise to a naïve exploration of reality, which is the exact opposite of a naturalistic portrayal of characters and story. Coming from a different direction, Brecht introduced a term—*die asthetische Kategorie des Naiven* (the aesthetic category of naiveté)—which is committed to a naïve exploration of the most obvious and self-evident aspects of reality, with the intention of creating misunderstandings that can encourage the audience to comprehend the social complexity of human relationships. As Johannes Goldhahn explains, "Solcherart Naivität meint differenziertes Beobachten des Verhaltens Von Menschen" (This naiveté is meant to offer a different observation of peoples' behavior) (cited in Schoeps 1989, 196).

The film employs naiveté to observe and analyze a commonplace subject matter, namely love. Referencing Fassbinder, the argument set forth by *Breaking the Waves* is that love and "goodness" can be the route to social oppression and domination. Each character wants to help somebody else but their actions produce antithetical outcomes. Furthermore, the film develops the interconnections between love and the will to control, and this is evidenced in Dodo's (Katrin Cartlidge), Jan's, and Dr. Richardson's (Adrian Rawlins) behavior.

Symptomatically, Jan's good intentions transform him into an authoritative persona, which exercises absolute control over Bess. Antje Flemming observes that "Jan nutzt Bess' Abhängigkeit aus und schwingt sich trotz seiner körperlichen Machtlosigkeit zum Inhaber der geistigen Macht auf. Es gehört zur Ambivalenz der Trier's schen Filme, dass kaum zu entscheiden ist, ob die Motivation der Figuren 'evil' oder 'good' ist" (Jan has been using Bess' dependency and despite his physical impotence he is the holder of the intellectual power. It is part of the ambivalence of Trier's films, which make it difficult to decide whether the motivation of the characters is 'evil or good') (2010, 65).

Von Trier's problematization of melodrama's clearly defined moral universe exhibits the very fallacy of the binary good versus evil and insists on a more complicated understanding of human relationships. In the end, the reconstitution of the family, which is typical of melodrama, is denied and the film's irony forces us to think beyond the ideological obviousness of Christian love and suffering. If the foundation of Jan's rescuing is Bess' death, then the latter's good intentions lead to the former's misery, moving further in a vicious circle. On this basis, the pseudoreligious ending turns into ironic cynicism. Years ago, Thomas Elsaesser demonstrated the link between irony and formal complexity, explaining that there is such a thing as a "cinema of irony." As he explains, the term does not refer solely to films that propagate sarcastic assertions, but to all the formal elements that negate the singularity of meaning. As he says:

> It names all the strategies of displacement, reversal, detachment, suspension— verbal, visual, structural—whereby a statement, a message, a communication, image or action may be qualified, put in question, inverted, parodied or indeed wholly negated while still preserving as visible that to which it refers itself ironically. As such, irony is dialectical in intent and invariably points out a potentially significant gap or break between the signifier and the signified. (1973, 1–2)

In light of Elsaesser's comments, irony in *Breaking the Waves* draws on metacinematic strategies which lead to a hermeneutical break, urging us to think beyond the story, to reflect on the very strategies of representation and on the ways the object manipulates familiar cinematic tropes, resisting at the same time established narrative-generic meaning.

The employment of metacinematic tropes as a means of criticizing the cinematic institution is more straightforward in *Dancer in the Dark*. Both the film's form and content thematize the very relationship between reality and cinema, denouncing the conventional escapist role of the medium. Set in Washington in the 1960s, the film tells the story of Selma, a young immigrant from Czechoslovakia working in a factory. Selma's hereditary handicap is gradually making her blind, but she is indefatigably working to save money to pay for an operation that will prevent her son—who suffers from the same disease—from becoming blind. An avid fan of musicals, Selma has created an idealist image of the United States, which is eventually negated by her own experience in the country. The film manipulates all the familiar tropes of the genre, such as the backstage musical, since Selma takes part in an amateurish production of *The Sound of Music*. References to maternal melodramas abound, as Selma eventually sacrifices herself for the sake of her son.

Yet the most important aspect of the film is its own metacommentary on film as medium and its critique of cinematic illusionism, and here I refer to illusionism strictly in the Brechtian meaning. It is crucial to understand that Brecht equated "illusionism" with "nonreflexive film/theater practices," but his understanding of both terms is not just formal, as many critics wrongly assume. Illusionism is rather a philosophical and political concept referring to works of art that do not reflect on the reality that they represent, but depict sets of social relationships, as if they are "natural" and thus unchangeable. On this basis, formal anti-illusionism does not refer to practices that expose the virtuoso of the filmmakers, but to the ways that films question the social and cultural dominant. This distinction discredits debatable points in contemporary film theory that Hollywood has become "anti-illusionist." Put simply, anti-illusionist formal reflexivity is a means of setting up dialectical clashes that are smoothed by representations structured upon the premise of mimesis. Von Trier points toward Hollywood illusionism when suggesting that Selma's initial utopian and idealized understanding of the United States derives from her passion for American musicals, that is, for films which are inclined to alleviate and not to reveal social contradictions.

The genre is particularly renowned for its thematic interest in the very myth of entertainment. Hollywood musicals are reflexive, but their reflexivity does not call into question the cinematic institution; they rather portray an idealized image of the entertainment industry and of the world. As Rick Altman explains, musicals merge "the real with the ideal" (1987, 62), and their overemphasis on visual extravaganza, colorful spectacle, and the positive aspects of life comes in stark contrast with the harsh social reality outside the world of the narrative. In this context, a central thematic concern of *Dancer in the Dark* is the very critique of the wish-fulfilling function of the medium. This is communicated by way of a stark antithesis between the main narrative and the musical sequences. A Dogme-style handheld camera captures the action throughout the main narrative, giving a feeling of grim realism, while the musical sequences are shot with 100 digital cameras and they are excessively colorful.

Prior to the film's premiere, von Trier published a Manifesto in which he justifies this stylistic choice. The antithesis between the musical numbers and the main narrative serves the purpose of underscoring the antithesis between art and life. The first paragraph of the Manifesto explains that the character resorts to popular culture to escape from her difficult circumstances.

> She loves musicals. Her life is hard, but she can survive because she has a secret. When things get too much to bear she can pretend she's in a musical...just for a minute or two. All the joy that life can't give her is there. Joy isn't living...joy is there to make it bearable for us to live. (Selma Manifesto, Appendix)

Later on, the Manifesto addresses the film's form.

> In order to tell Selma's story the film must be able to give concrete form to her world. All the scenes that don't contain her musical fantasies must be as realistic as possible as far as acting, décor and so on are concerned, because the scenes from Selma's daily life are the model for what she adds to her musical numbers...and these have to be true to life. What she sees at the cinema is flawless...painless..., in other words entirely at odds with real life...where it's the flaws and the pains that make it shine. The intimation of humanity...of nature...of life. (Selma Manifesto, Appendix)

The Manifesto echoes Brecht's "Notes on Mahagonny" particularly in the way that it describes the contrast between the main narrative and the dance sequences.[1] In "Notes on Mahagonny," Brecht explains that he wanted to make an opera which would take advantage of the very operatic traits that produce pleasure, so as to expose opera as "merchandise." Brecht's conviction was that "real innovations attack the roots" (1964, 41).

Analogously, *Dancer in the Dark* is a musical that narrates a story and at the same time criticizes the very generic elements that it manipulates. Selma draws our attention to this when she says that she likes musicals because "in a musical nothing dreadful ever happens." The film strips the genre from all the elements that produce pleasure: the oversimplification of complex and unpleasant social relationships, such as class differences; the perfect duet in the backstage musical which concludes with a heterosexual happy ending; and, most importantly, the valorization of "pure entertainment" as an alternative utopia to the burdensome everyday reality. There are six musical interludes that interrupt the narrative and they only appear when Selma faces a crisis. The first interlude takes place when Selma's impaired vision prevents her from working.

Figure 1.9: *Dancer in the Dark* (2000).

Immediately after the colorful and optimistic interlude, she returns to the humdrum reality and injures herself. The second interlude follows her dismissal from the factory and after its completion Selma confronts Bill (David Morse), who has stolen her savings. The third interlude occurs after having murdered Bill and the fourth one precedes her arrest by the police. The fifth interlude interrupts the narrative during her trial and prefigures her death sentence, and the final one is prior to her execution (figure 1.9). While the musical sequences ostensibly serve the purpose of liberating a set of desires that can compensate the character for her real-life drabness, there is no crisis that is not followed by another crisis straight after the interludes. Consequently, formally and thematically the film polemicizes against the conventional entertainment apparatus aiming to rethink the medium's social function and foster new connections between cinema and social life. As Flemming points out, "Denn auf einer semantischen und narrativen Ebene ist *Dancer in the Dark* ein Hybrid, ein Anti-Musical, ein entgrenztes Werk das gegen seine eigene Genrekonvention anrennt" (On the semantic and narrative level *Dancer in the Dark* is a hybrid, an antimusical, an open work that protests against its own genre conventions) (2010, 75).

The film's form and content thematize cinema as a commodity, only to bring this principle under discussion and to question the social reality that produces escapist forms of entertainment. Perhaps, this is why Selma insists that her son has his eyesight healed. He shall be able to "see" and not be fooled like her, whose passion for musicals made her imagine the United States like a depoliticized utopia. The Selma Manifesto labels the film as "punk" object: "as I see it punk is a collision between tradition and nature. It isn't destructive ... it isn't solemn, because it's trying to get back to basics ... by confronting the system with a more honest view of life ... and forcing life into something that has become stale and enclosed"... (Selma Manifesto, Appendix).

The same practice of confronting "stale" narrative systems and practices can be seen in more recent films by von Trier, such as *The Boss of It All, Antichrist*, and *Melancholia*. In the vein of his earlier films, these objects act as theses on film as medium, aiming to go beyond established tropes of cinematic pleasure. For instance, in *The Boss of It All* von Trier experiments with comedy, but the film's farcical form produces conflicts that energize an ironic critique of the institutionalization of art and its dissociation from social life. In *Antichrist*, the manipulation of horror film tropes brings to the fore some of the most reactionary aspects of the genre. However, the horror is not the outcome of an outsider's intrusion into the lives of the main characters, as it is the case in the genre. The narrative repeatedly cultivates generic expectations, only to frustrate them and deny generic pleasure. Lastly, in *Melancholia* von Trier references the Armageddon films, but the final object is more complicated, since the form combines art cinematic visual abstraction with a loose dramaturgy that once again negates standardized generic meanings. In many respects, one senses that the characters are constantly playing roles, rather than following the dramatic principle of the unified character and the films quote established cultural and generic norms, so as to question them. Effectively, the objects are self-reflexive, but in the broader sense, that is, they comment on the institutional tropes of narration so as to reestablish the medium's productive instead of its reproductive function. As von Trier says, "for mig er det ved ethvert kunstværk vigtigt, at man kan se dets tilblivelseshistorie. De film, som jeg holder af at se, handler altid også om, hvordan man laver en film, hvordan man gør det gennemskueligt" (For me at any work of art it is important that you can see its genesis. The movie, which I like to see, is always also about how to make a movie, how to make it transparent) (cited in Schepelern 2000a, 100). Concomitantly, film as medium assumes an important place in the narratives and this medium-reflexivity performs a radical critique of the "familiar"/conformist subject and object relationships produced by the cinematic institution.

Artaudian cruelty as *Verfremdungseffekt*

In 1999, von Trier and Christian Braad Thomsen reimported in Denmark Pier Paolo Pasolini's film *Salo, or the 120 Days of Sodom* [*Salò o le 120 Giornate di*

Sodoma: 1975]. From their point of view, this film is an important document that had to be reexamined and reevaluated by contemporary audiences. For anyone familiar with von Trier's work, it is not surprising to hear the latter's high regard of Pasolini's particular film. Furthermore, Pasolini along with Rainer Werner Fassbinder—whose films have been influential in von Trier's oeuvre—are two filmmakers who have successfully combined Brechtian *Verfremdungseffekte* with Artaudian cruelty. Fassbinder's and Pasolini's combination of these two traditions served political purposes; they both aimed at liberating film form from the shackles of psychological realism as well as protesting against the institutionalized forms of representation that avoided confronting the audience with unpleasant and painful truths. In tune with these directors' practice, numerous films by von Trier bring together Brechtian with Artaudian practices.

Before moving to von Trier, it is crucial to elucidate the similarities between the two theorists. For many years, in theater and performance studies there was a distinction between Brecht's politicized aesthetic and Artaud's theater of cruelty. Nonetheless, the theater of Heiner Müller, as well as other post-Brechtian practitioners, such as The Living Theatre, and Robert Wilson have confirmed that there are many signs of convergence between these two aesthetic traditions. In cinema, apart from the films of Pasolini and Fassbinder mentioned above, contemporary directors such as Michael Haneke and Yorgos Lanthimos have made films that fuse Brechtian and Artaudian elements, so as to politicize form and protest against mainstream cinema's reduction of the audience to consumers of images.

Brecht and Artaud denied the Western theatrical tradition of the verbalized drama and aimed at reanimating theater by utilizing physical and gestural representational strategies, which could show the individual as the product of social and power relations. Both argued in favor of iconoclastic representations that would question institutionalized theatrical forms. Judith Malina from The Living Theatre rightly observes that both traditions serve the same political purposes. The Brechtian tradition deals primarily with "a movement of perception and reflection and change of attitudes," while the Artaudian one prioritizes "a visceral experience" that the audience shall experience physically. Yet both of them denied the "tyranny of the text" to challenge the politics of perception and the separation between art and social life (cited in *Signals Through the Flames*: 1989).

Additionally, Artaud's writings on cinema correspond with Brecht's, since he valorized iconoclastic/episodic narratives that would take advantage of the medium-specific elements with the purpose of opposing the reduction of cinematic narrative to "visual interpretations of a text." He repeatedly argued in favor of a "visual cinema where psychology itself is devoured by the action" and showed preference for fragmented narrative structures concerned with "the problem of expression in every domain and to its full extent" (1989, 58, 60). Significantly, Artaud considered visual abstraction as the route to an aesthetics of cruelty interested in "irritating the audience" by breaking with the cultural and ideological norms. Michael Haneke, whose films are well known for joining Brechtian with Artaudian elements, has described cruelty as an essential way of negating ideological banality: "In my definition, anything that could be termed obscene departs from the bourgeois norm. Whether concerned with sexuality or violence, or another taboo issue, anything that breaks with the norm is obscene" (cited in Coulthard 2011, 182). Haneke here refers to an Artaudian tradition which is concerned with producing unpleasure and irritating the audience.

By the same token, Lars von Trier's cinema combines formal elements, which experiment with film language and force the audience to question the "obvious," with Artaudian elements that are set to encourage physical responses too. Charles Martig has acknowledged this aspect of von Trier's oeuvre and argues that similar to Haneke, David Lynch, Abel Ferrara, David Cronenberg, and Kim Ki-duk, von Trier's films are part of an iconoclastic representational tradition committed to a cinema of unpleasure and irritation. Martig's reading completely ignores Artaud and understands this cinematic unpleasure in terms of theology. As he says, "Die Beschäftigung mit dem Kino der Irritation ist eine Chance für eine moderne Theologie nach dem 'Tode Gotte' " (The study of the cinema of irritation is an opportunity for a modern theology after the death of God) (2008, 13). The weakness of Martig's account lies in the fact that it utterly disregards the political implications of cinematic "irritation," that is the ways that cruelty produces "shocks" dedicated to fostering political opposition to the cultural dominant.

It is of cardinal importance to illuminate that Artaudian cruelty cannot be simply restricted to images of horror and gore violence. Artaud himself noted that "it is wrong to make cruelty mean merciless bloodshed, pointless and gratuitous pursuit of physical pain" (1989, 119). In essence, as Artaud refused the separation between mind and body, one cannot separate cruelty taking place at the level of the intellect from the physical one. With this in mind, one can identify aspects of cruelty in von Trier's propensity to attack the audience by means of representational methods, which drive representation at its limits and expose the mediations which make the dominant forms of cinematic narration harmless and inoffensive.

Symptomatic of this practice is the absence of political correctness in von Trier's films. In *Images of Relief*, the images of brutal violence against the defeated Nazis intend to shatter the illusions of standardized liberal thinking which understands fascism as an isolated historical phenomenon, that is, as an unproblematic opposition between "good versus evil." There is a very distinctive passage from *Images of Relief*, in which Esther is given a knife by the Danish partisans and stabs Leo's eyes. We do not see the act depicted, but we hear the sound of the knife hitting his flesh repeatedly, something which strengthens the shocking quality of the scene. In a rather Artaudian fashion of physical aggression against the audience, the sound of the stabbing creates a corporeal connection between the audience and the scene. It activates a feeling of actual danger, which seeks to point toward the terror of history. Similarly, in the *Europa* trilogy von Trier confuses the boundaries between oppressors and the oppressed and proposes a more complex understanding of history outside political correctness. When I asked von Trier about his avoidance of political correctness, he responded that a filmmaker who is politically correct has no respect for his audience (Interview, Appendix). One senses a link between aggression, cruelty, and political incorrectness and this is rooted in the understanding of the object not as a static and finished work, but as a work in process. In line with Artaud's opposition against the understanding of cinema as a photographic reproduction of a straightforward narrative with an unambiguous "message," political incorrectness turns into an aggressive confrontation of the audience.

Typical in this regard is *Dancer in the Dark*, where there is a mixture of cruelty and ironic distance that shifts the emphasis from the individual story to broader social issues. One need only recall the film's clinical portrayal of the death penalty. The protracted length of the final scene draws attention to the ordinary banality with which the state officials approach their duty (figure 1.10). Meanwhile, the detailed depiction of Selma's suffering does not follow the logic of Hollywood melodrama's justification of the maternal sacrifice. The camera's frantic movement combines distanced coldness with emotional excess, showing the character as a social being in interaction with a set of social and political circumstances that can account for her death by the state. Simply put, Selma's death is not tragic; that is, it cannot be understood as "inevitable." This concluding passage from the film is meant to provoke anger rather than pity and fear, forcing the audience to think beyond the limits of tragic unavoidability, implying that different social conditions could have prevented this violent finale.

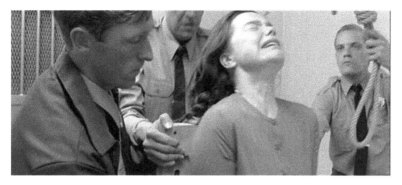

Figure 1.10: *Dancer in the Dark* (2000).

While in *Dancer in the Dark* the politics of cruelty is much more blatant, in subsequent films cruelty is employed as a means of stimulating conflicts and divisions that oppose the ethical/moralist conception of intricate issues. For instance, in *Antichrist* the battle of the sexes implicates the audience in ways that negate the liberal ethics of harmony, aiming to provoke controversy that goes beyond conservative ethical clichés. Playing with the horror film genre's pleasurable flirtation with fear, the film disregards the cliché of the "monstrous other," contending that the horror is to be identified in the micropolitics of everyday relationships. Unlike horror films, violence is kept to a minimum, but it is the very analytical portrayal of horror (e.g., the scene of self-mutilation) that de-eroticizes it and attacks the hedonistic pleasure in shocking images. Lothar Mikos maintains that the major principle of the horror film genre is that "audiences accept that emotions, such as anxiety, fear, shock, disgust, horror, and so on will be played on. They know that the viewing contract will not be violated and that the conventions of the genre will be adhered to" (1996, 42).

At odds with the genre's conventions, von Trier in *Antichrist* violates the viewing contract and this violation aims at the transformation of institutionalized ways of thinking, both about politics (here the battle of the sexes), as well as about cinema itself. What one can clearly see here is the Artaudian relationship between "knowledge" and violence reconciled with the Brechtian understanding of political art as *kämpferisch* (polemical). But then, knowledge here is not founded upon epistemological certainties; it is rather the product of experimentation with the very cinematic conventions that produce pleasure, with the intention of disrupting the assurance that the horror on the screen cannot affect the audience's "safety." This violation of the viewing contract, as well as the critique of ethical banality, is set to initiate controversies that divide the audience and the cultural apparatuses. A glaring example of a comic contradiction generated from this practice is the UK conservative tabloids' response to *Antichrist* as "a misogynist film," a quite paradoxical response given that *The Daily Mail* is not renowned for being a "feminist" paper or a champion of civil liberties (Hart 2009; Tookey 2009). Thus, this visceral attack on the audience turns into a political attack on the cultural dominant. Politics is the very product of divisions which oppose the indisputable acceptance of "universal ethical categories," and, as Alain Badiou maintains, the essence of politics is the disruption of a homogeneous public sphere and of the "ethics of consensus." Politics is predicated on a violent antithesis to the norm, and, as he says, "For what every emancipatory project does, what every emergence of hitherto unknown possibilities does, is to put an end to consensus" (2001, 36). In this context, politics starts when the opposition to the ideological orthodoxy asserts itself in an aggressive way, not with the aim of integrating the alternative thinking to an existing institution, but with the intention of transforming it.

In view of that, von Trier's dalliance with Artaudian cruelty operates as a means of turning genres, "viewing contracts," and the medium's institutionalized function upside down, so as to arouse divisive tensions that can reinforce the medium's transformative potential. Susan Sontag says that Artaudian cruelty is "a commando action against the established culture" (2004, 91), a verdict which aptly describes von Trier's *modus operandi*. Illustrative on this account is *Occupations* (2007), the short humoristic film that von Trier directed as part of the anniversary for the 60 years of the Cannes film festival. In this film, we see von Trier in the auditorium of a cinema theater watching his own film *Manderlay*. An obviously uninterested man (Jacques Frantz) next to him keeps on interrupting the film, discussing business matters and boasting about his riches. Visibly irritated, von Trier ignores him and when the man asks him about the nature of his occupation, he responds "I kill!" In a scene that plays with the horror films tropes, he starts beating him to death with a hammer, only to resume his seats and continue watching *Manderlay*. This short black-humored narrative synopsizes the employment of cruelty as a form of cultural and political resistance, which is also the case in *Epidemic*'s finale, to which I shall return in the next chapter.

A similar gesture of resistance is evidenced in *Melancholia*, in which Justine's (Kirsten Dunst) depression becomes a force of negation of the prevailing bourgeois normativity, making her welcome the end of the world. In the first chapter of the film, Justine's melancholy is amplified by the bourgeois triteness of her wedding dinner ritual. Suddenly, the contrived and dramaturgically unjustified impending collision of earth with planet Melancholia prefigures the imminent end of the world. Justine is no more a melancholic postmodern Ophelia—the film includes many visual references to Jørgen Leth's *Ophelia's Flowers* [*Ofelias Blomster*: 1968]—but now she turns into a vengeful Electra, celebrating the doomsday.[2] Following a proactive pessimism, *Melancholia* suggests in a controversial way that the world can be changed, provided that we belligerently do away with the present conformism and banality. It is a negative affirmation with positive undertones. This constructive negativity is also expounded by the film's "beauty," which in its own way welcomes this apocalyptic ending of the world. Formally and thematically, *Melancholia* returns to previous motifs explored by von Trier. During the production of his first feature film, *The Element of Crime*, von Trier argued, "Jeg synes, det er at udnytte Ragnarok eller muligheden for Ragnarok til noget positivt, til at lave billeder af Ragnarok som har en stor skønhedsværdi" (I think it has a great beauty value to use Ragnarok [term from the Nordic mythology which stands for the end of the world], or the possibility of Ragnarok into something positive, and to make pictures of it.) (cited in Schepelern 2000a, 86). Such an excess of negativity is symptomatic of the crisis of epistemology, which frustrates any fixed positive historical insights into the future. This reconciliation of politics with historical pessimism also permeates von Trier's first trilogy of films, which is the subject of the next chapter.

Notes

1 In an interview with Stig Björkman, von Trier showed his awareness of the connection between opera and musicals (Björkman 2003, 234). Furthermore, Schepelern notes von Trier's admiration of Kurt Weil's (Brecht's collaborator) operas (2000a, 256).

2 A similar transformation takes place in Heiner Müller's *Hamletmachine*.

Historical Fragments in the *Europa* Trilogy

Europe is painful

"If you want me to help you get rid of these headaches we must go back," reads the voice-over in the beginning of the first part of the *Europa* trilogy—*The Element of Crime*—and continues, "all I know is that Europe has become an obsession to you." In *Epidemic*'s finale, a woman is hypnotized and asked to enter the fictional universe of a film in process, dealing with the European past. The woman complains that she visualizes painful images of people who "are scared of each other. They are scared of infection and death." In *Europa*, Max von Sydow's hypnotic voice-over asks the audience and the main character to "go deeper into Europa," only to realize that we have ended up in a nightmarish period of history, back in Germany 1945. Europe in von Trier's first trilogy is a place which produces "headaches," and while the therapist (Ahmed El Shenawi) in *The Element of Crime* suggests that returning back will alleviate the pain, this proves to be an *ignis fatuus*, since the trilogy's journey into the past exposes the troublesome historical present.

Though different in many ways, the common characteristic of these films is their deployment of loose dramaturgy, segmented plot, and metafilmic effects, which are features that can be identified in the rest of von Trier's filmography. The films' formal complexity, such as the weak causal nexus of the portrayed events, the ambiguous temporality, and their preference for a fragmented representation complicate historical depiction. Teleological stories and linear patterns are abandoned in favor of non-chronologically ordered fragments and constellations that do not follow the strict narrative laws of dramatic cinema. This *modus operandi* corresponds to a post-Brechtian aesthetic which retains Brecht's favoring of exposing the transitory character of history, without sharing the forward-looking politics of the *Fabel*—a term to which I shall return below. The trilogy's refusal to portray history as a positive teleological progress can also help us trace its meaning from the viewpoint of the current European crisis.

The first movie, *The Element of Crime,* borrows stylistic elements from German Expressionism and the film noir genre. *Epidemic,* a black-and-white film shot on location in Denmark and in Germany, plays a lot with the tension between documented and fictional material. *Europa*—like the first film of the trilogy— draws upon the cinematic tradition of film noir and German Expressionism. In *The Element of Crime*, a police officer, Fisher (Michael Elphick), is hypnotized by a psychiatrist to go back to Europe to reconstruct the facts of a case he was in charge of, in which an unidentified person named Harry Grey committed murders of girls selling lotto tickets. The location is unspecified, but the names of the cities, some of the characters' surnames, and certain words, such as *polizei* instead of police, are in German. Furthermore, some allusions are made to German history, for example the appearance of a group of skinheads conducting a collective ritual and sporadic references to Auschwitz.

References to German history and culture appear also in *Epidemic,* in which von Trier and his collaborator Niels Vørsel impersonate themselves in the process of making a film inspired by the plague that took place in Europe during the fourteenth century. Along with all the information that they collect from archives and museums, the characters decide to visit Cologne, in order to get material from contemporary history related to the bombing of Germany on the part of the allies. Throughout the film, images of their work in process appear on the screen without prior notice. The film within the film tells the story of Dr. Mesmer, an idealist (played by von Trier again), who wants to cure Europe from the plague and turns out to realize that he is the carrier of the disease. Finally, *Europa* deals explicitly with German history and in particular with the postwar period. Max von Sydow's extra-diegetic voice-over addresses Leopold Kessler (Jean-Marc Barr) to go back to *Europa*, that is, Germany in 1945. Leo goes to postwar Germany and gets a job in Zentropa, a railway company owned by Max Hartmann (Jørgen Reenberg), a former Nazi collaborator. After falling in love with Katarina Hartmann (Barbara Sukowa), Leo is embroiled in a Nazi terrorist conspiracy and faces Germany's inability to erase its past.

Niels Vørsel, who acted as a cowriter of the scripts, contributed decidedly to the trilogy, both formally and thematically. The films' thematic interest in the traumas of the European past derived from Vørsel's fascination for German history and art, which pervades his own writings, such as his radio play *Transistor* (1977), in which one of the characters says, "Jeg er ved at være forpulet træt af

Europa" (I am getting fucking tired of Europe) (cited in Schepelern 2000a, 126). The fundamental idea of the trilogy is that Europe is in a state of crisis. As von Trier says, "De tre film er for mig et forsøg på at skitsere et stort maleri af Europa, der fortæller meget om dette kontinent" (The three films are like a sketch painting of Europe that tells us much about the continent) (Schepelern 2000a, 126). The first film places emphasis on images of the "European" (the exact location is unknown) landscape and has a plethora of references to Germany that can be identified in the expressionist aesthetics and the unmotivated allusions to the fascist past. In *Epidemic*, the narrative starts in Copenhagen but the characters have to return to the German space. With *Europa*, von Trier concludes the trilogy and locates the narrative in Germany year zero.

As Peter Schepelern points out, for von Trier the word *Europa* stands for Germany. Germany is a repository of cultural elements and historical memories that have influenced contemporary Europe. As he says, "Men trilogiens centrale fællestema er først og fremmest Europa-tolkningen, der igen peger på Tysklands—(og nazi) temaet" (The central theme of the trilogy is first and foremost Europe that points to Germany and Nazi culture) (2000a, 126). Von Trier has also explained that both he and Vørsel see Germany as Europe: "For mig og min medforfatter, Niels Vørsel, er Tyskland meget vigtig, fordi vi ser Tyskland som Europa… og taler om tysk kultur som en hel masse smukt og en hel masse farligt" (For me and my coauthor, Niels Vørsel, Germany is very important because we see Germany as Europe... and speaking of German culture as a whole, we think that it combines beauty with danger cited in Schepelern 2000a, 127). Von Trier's equation of Europe with Germany is a very bold decision that has to do with the view of Germany as a country whose history and culture has produced visuals that are as powerful as a "drug." In a way, Germany appears as the "crime scene" where one is repeatedly asked to return, in order to understand the European past and present. Intertextuality plays an important role as well, since the films reference many films dealing with German history and Nazi culture. Another quotation by Schepelern can illuminate things further.

> The *Europa* trilogy is one of the great feats of European cinema in the so-called postmodern phase. These films are full of quotations from other films, from history and other ideas. It's a fantastic cinematographic, historical and ideological puzzle, full of references. (cited in *Europa* DVD extras)

The films also share some key thematic elements. In all of them, an idealist embarks on a trip to "save" Europe and ends up causing a catastrophe.

Despite the trilogy's postmodern position, I am inclined to maintain that its formal complexity cannot be understood under the rubric of postmodern helplessness. Previous readings have focused on the films' intertextuality and their deployment of postmodern strategies, but they have ignored the political implications of their form as well as the ways we can understand their pessimism politically (Badley 2010, 40–43; Bainbridge 2007, 45–59). Discussions of content give a lower profile to form, and when issues of form are raised they are reduced to the status of postmodern trickery (Simons 2007, 102). A more nuanced formal analysis of the objects uncovers the relationship between aesthetics and politics, in view of the fact that these three films negate classical cinema's representation of history as a linear sequence of events. History saturates their narratives, but all of them prioritize the fragment and raise a set of questions regarding the medium's relation to history. The matter that deserves more scrutiny is that these three films stockpile material from different historical temporalities so as to challenge the continuum of history. Characterization is problematized and the individual is presented as a product of forces that cannot be understood by psychology. At the heart of this strategy is an aspiration to challenge "official" history by intensifying the historicity of the present. This gesture counters what Fredric Jameson describes as the postmodern "erasure of temporality and loss of historicity" (1991, 25), which makes the collective perceive contemporary time as an ahistorical perpetual present dissociated from the past. Therefore, the trilogy's references to the past intend to historicize the present.

Beyond the *Fabel*

In other words, the complex narrative structure seeks to indicate that the mistakes of the past are the product of social processes that can be identified in the present. This gesture is Brechtian tout court, given that Brecht singled out the affinity between canonical narrative forms and official history. The latter tends to treat history as an evolutionary development and understands the historical present as a process unhindered by the past. However, Brecht argues that portraying things historically stands for showing the interconnectedness between the past and present, so as to oppose the predominant historical hermeneutics. This is exemplified in the work of a number of filmmakers, such as Straub/Huillet, Fassbinder, and Angelopoulos, who adopted a Brechtian aesthetics in films such as *Not Reconciled* (*Nicht Versöhnt Oder Es Hilft Nur Gewalt Wo Gewalt*

Herrscht: 1965), *The Marriage of Maria Braun* (*Die Ehe der Maria Braun:* 1979), and *The Travelling Players* (*O Θίασος:* 1974) so as to rewrite history through the film medium. This understanding of representation as productivity, that is, as a destabilization of tradition, is a pivotal aspect of Brechtian theory and practice. Brecht proposes estrangement as a means of overcoming the "naturalization" of social phenomena, and eliciting their historical function. The affinity between estrangement and showing things historically is manifested in the following quotation: "Er [Verfremdungseffekt] bezweckte hauptsächlich die Historisierung der darzustellenden Vorgänge" (Making the familiar strange aimed primarily at historicizing the processes that are about to be represented) (Schriften 5 1963, 178).

The nexus between estrangement and representing things historically acknowledges two very important factors. The first one lies in the Marxist belief that the appearance of the historical phenomena does not provide us with an understanding of the workings of history. It is only by means of a theoretical reconstruction and re-viewing of the facts that historical effects can be appreciated and understood. The second one is based upon the notion of the historical past and present being nothing but an established narrative. Thus, viewed from an atypical angle, it can offer a different assessment and understanding of the workings of history. Hence, the representation of history becomes a matter of *praxis*, of transformation of the solidified narrative and, in the utopian dimension of Brecht's theory, a transformation of the audience's historical consciousness.

Brecht's refusal to reduce historical phenomena to "mere presence," that is, to offer an additive reconstruction of historical events, is indicative of his view of history as an active process and not as an authentic background. As he says:

> The field has to be defined in historically relative terms. In other words we must drop our habit of taking the different social structures of past periods, then stripping them of everything that makes them different; so that they all look more or less like our own, which then acquires from this process a certain air of having been there all along, in other words of permanence pure and simple. Instead we must leave them their distinguishing marks and keep their impermanence always before our eyes, so that our own period can be seen to be impermanent too. (1964, 190)

The impermanence of history is put forward through the representation of historical conditions, which, as Brecht suggests, are not mysterious forces in the background, but are manifested in the relations between individuals. In other words, history and the social state of affairs can be brought to the surface via a constant questioning of the individual and his or her place in it. Instead of showing characters operating in an authentic historical background, one needs to place emphasis on questions that reveal the very historicity of human relationships. This feature does not treat history as a reflection of reality, but as a host of possibilities and an instigator for action. In other words, there is a sense of uncertainty/unrepresentability in Brecht's work that aims at undermining the older certainties and showing historical reality as transitory.

This unrepresentability is the point most meriting analysis with respect to the *Europa* trilogy, since the transition from modernism to postmodernism has complicated Brecht's certainties and our ability to represent history. One important consequence of this crisis of representation is the complication of the distinction between historical facts and fiction. As Jean-Francois Lyotard explains, the spreading out of the media has reformulated the understanding of historical memory. The vast amount of information transmitted shapes the collective perception of the historical past and present. Yet the paradox is that in the last analysis, collective memory is nobody's memory. "But 'nobody' here means that the body supporting that memory is not an earth-bound body" (1991, 64). Postmodernism, therefore, takes uncertainty as a given element of contemporary reality, and the individual's relation to history is complicated, since the latter seemingly appears to be an impersonal structure.

The dialectic between the individual and history constitutes one of the major tenets of Brecht's Marxist view of history and his critique of historical transcendence. Historical reality and the individual are not shown as given but as subject to constant change. This stress on changeability serves the purpose of revealing the possibility of transforming the established political reality. The fundamental condition is that human beings have to perceive themselves as products and producers of history. For Brecht, the Marxist dialectic operates as a means of investigating human relationships and revealing their dependence on structures and forces that are not visible. His view of history as Marxist science is founded upon the principle that capitalism produces the historical conditions for its own defeat.

In other words, Brecht's epistemology is grounded in the belief that by understanding the world dialectically, one can comprehend history and change social reality. Historical progress is grounded on the condition that "people derive dialectics from reality" (Brecht 1993, 47). This is the point of rupture between von Trier's depiction of history and Brecht's. On the one hand, von Trier follows Brecht's refusal to offer an "additive method" in the portrayal of history and prioritizes historical/social forces over the view of subjects as the sole historical agents. On the other hand, the *Europa* trilogy aspires to think history in terms of Benjaminian constellations that do not share Brecht's understanding of history as the route to human emancipation and progress. These constellations offer a materialist view of history that negates the conformist understanding of the past historical catastrophes as aberrations. The concept of history as a heterogeneous temporality which resists teleological progress has been theorized by Walter Benjamin. As he says:

> The concept of the historical progress of the mankind cannot be sundered from the concept of its progression through a homogeneous empty time. A critique of the concept of such a progression must be the basis of any criticism of the concept of progress itself. (1999, 252)

Benjamin's argument is in line with a dialectical view of history that is not restricted by Marxist teleology, something that characterizes the work of certain post-Brechtian practitioners in film and theater.

The works of Straub/Huillet, Hans-Jürgen Syberberg, Alexander Kluge, and Heiner Müller are some important pieces of evidence of such a representation of history, which does not propose any unambiguous solution for human emancipation. These directors follow Brecht's favoring of discontinuity and fragmentation but they deny the logic of the Brechtian *Fabel*, which strives to produce a unified meaning out of the collision of different fragments. The *Fabel* is a complicated term normally translated as narrative in English. David Barnett has illuminated the complexity of the term arguing that the *Fabel* stands for "the plot interpreted through a dialectical notion of history" (2011a, 337). The *Fabel* has a pedagogical value, for it deploys contradictions to reveal the laws of history, their effect upon a specific society, and the ways history shapes the characters' attitudes.

For Brecht, this dialectical view of history was predicated on the idea of progress, while the post-Brechtian view questions the likelihood of dialectical closure. From this perspective, the *Fabel* is not the central driving element in the *Europa* trilogy; productivity emanates from the production of shock-effects that intend to reveal how the historical present is saturated with practices and conventions from the past. The three films employ a Brechtian "presentational" mode of narration and correspond to Brecht's preference for quoting cinematic materials, gestures, and genres. Then again, the trilogy's complication of historical reference discloses the epistemological break between representation and history and goes beyond the understanding of history as a positive movement.

Audiovisual plenitude: The individual in crisis

One of the most intricate qualities of the first film of the trilogy is the way it fuses a variety of voices and images that do not necessarily have a precise storytelling function. The film's dialogue with various films and genres, which allude to the European legacy of fascism, downplays dramaturgy and favors visuals at the expense of plot. On a narrative level, stories interlock within stories and render narrative agency problematic. Thus, the audience is confronted with a multiplicity of perspectives that prevent the viewer from being anchored to a character's point of view. *The Element of Crime* accumulates visual and acoustic materials that dispute the linear and self-sufficient cinematic representation of history. This aesthetics produces a variety of voices and incompatible materials. The valorization of disintegration over unity questions not only the unity of the fictive world but of the extra-filmic reality too.

Let us first see how many filmic materials resonate polyphonically within the film's narrative. In *The Element*, action takes place somewhere in Europe which appears as a locus of traumatic memories. The film offers glimpses of history that do not solidify into a coherent narrative. There is no precise temporal and geographical specificity, while the narration consists of intertextual references and images that allude to the European legacy of fascism. During the shooting of the film, von Trier discussed the film's Brechtian presentational mode of narration. He stated that the film is like a "picture book film," which places emphasis on the act of "showing," as if telling the audience, "here you see a house" (cited in *Ennenstadt Europa* 1984). This emphasis on a type of narration which privileges "showing" over "telling" minimizes psychological motivation, since, as Seymour Chatman explains, what interests the narrator is the presentation of conflicts and of the narrating devices instead of narrative causality (1980, 192). As von Trier says:

> We are trying to get the most out of the pictures we are showing. We are trying to incorporate as much history into them as possible. We've employed a futuristic set which is very patinated. And everything in the film has a history which is also patinated. A chair tells you how it's used through its patina. If you transfer the idea to the landscape you can tell how the landscape has been used through its patina. The same goes for the people. Their patina will tell you how they've lived their lives. (cited in *Ennenstadt Europa*, 1984)

History, therefore, does not emerge solely out of the script but through certain metaphors and allegories created by means of visual effects and intertextual references. The construction of a hallucinatory landscape and soundscape points to Resnais's *Last Year at Marienband* (1961). Hence, the combination of film noir and dystopian aesthetics is a direct reference to Godard's *Alphaville* (1965) and Tarkowsky's *Stalker* (1979). These references are used as a set of historical materials and are not simply part of a postmodern pastiche aesthetics.[1] In other words, von Trier treats these intertextual references as materials which merit historical reassessment and reevaluation, and not as recycled "dead styles" and objects. Far from the postmodern view that the historical referents have vanished altogether, the employment of these references as historical materials suggests that by going back to the historical/cinematic past we can get a better understanding of the contemporary present.

Von Trier admits that in many respects *The Element* "is a film about film" (cited in Larsen 2003, 43), and, as Schepelern points out, an important driving facet in the film's narrative is the productive utilization of metafiction, which places materials from the past in a contemporary context (2000a, 89). The manipulation of German Expressionism and film noir results in a sort of apocalyptic decay that at a first viewing can lead someone to see the film as an aestheticization of desolation, as it has been pointed out by many reviewers (Larsen 2003, 41). This aesthetics is concerned with producing temporal and geographical defamiliarization, opening old wounds from the past, and reflecting on the contemporary, seemingly ahistorical reality.

The manipulated genres are well known for their association with the traumas of fascism. Siegfried Kracauer's famous treatise suggested that German Expressionism's interest in the madness that permeates authority was symptomatic of the collective German soul in the years that preceded fascism (1990, 244). Film noir, on the other hand, draws on the postwar traumas of fascism, showing a predilection for fatalistic narratives that frustrate the characters' best intentions. Moreover, film noir's critique of the capitalist social imaginary proposes a radical negation of the commodity culture and of the postwar narrative of historical progress (Naremore 1995, 24).

Von Trier's handling of these genres draws upon common clichés and stereotypes of authority, such as the police officer Kramer (Jerold Wells), who stands for a pro-Nazi image, suggestive of an authoritarian figure. Moreover, the story of Fisher, who goes back to Europe with the best intentions and turns out to become part of the reality he negates, is evocative of film noir's fatalistic narrative patterns. The crisis of individual freedom comes to the fore and the collision of different narrative levels goes against the very notion of the monadic subject. Downplaying issues of individual psychology, the narrative favors fragments that point to historical processes and memories. Such a fragmented representational strategy follows Brecht's *dialektische Geschichtsauffassung* (dialectical conception of history), according to which historical actions and events surpass the monadic dramatic hero. Linda Badley suggests that the film's stylization is not interested in historical representation, but in the depiction of the central character's "subjective vision" (Badley 2011, 23). This seems doubtful, however, since the film's narrative and visual tropes contradict the very idea of the autonomous individual.

Critical vis-à-vis the crisis of the individual is the emphasis on the European landscape at the expense of dramatization. The landscape acquires a voice of its own and fuses contradictory voices and images. As von Trier admits, people appear as part of the scenography and not as characters (cited in Björkman 2003, 76). Thus, the European landscape turns into a canvas, in which the director combines cultural stereotypes with inconclusive images that allude to European history. In this fashion, the landscape becomes a dehumanized place, which interlocks visual fragments from nature, history, and culture. This visual preeminence of the landscape leaves little room for a unified subjectivity and puts forward the primacy of historical forces. On this basis, the emphasis on debris and natural disaster points to a post-Enlightenment era, in which the mythologies that accompanied the age of reason have been invalidated in the course of history.

The employment of "landscape images" as a means of putting forward the primacy of historical forces has been utilized by post-Brechtian directors in film and theater too. For instance, Syberberg in his film *Hitler: A Film for Germany* (*Hitler—Ein Film Aus Deutschland*, 1977) uses the landscape as a theater of history, in which images and figures from the past and the present are amalgamated. Anton Kaes understands this formal element as part of a "post-histoire" culture (1989, 48). Counter to this ahistorical reading, the use of the landscape as a canvas that accumulates antithetical materials does not imply that history "has disappeared." It is rather a different understanding of historical representation which denies the use of history as a backdrop for dramatic purposes. The purpose of such a method is not the establishment of "historical truth," but the proliferation of visual and aural constellations that reveal the discontinuity between past and present. This discontinuity exposes history as an active process but not as epistemology.

The same applies to the theater of Heiner Müller, in which the landscape does not function as a concrete historical background but as the locus, in which "'the nightmare of history' emerges" (cited in Malkin 1999, 31). Unattributed voices meet with figures from European historiography and mythology, offering an ever-shifting perspective. This emphasis on the landscape as a living agent draws upon the Marxist approach, according to which historical events can be seen in the light of conflicting forces and broader collective institutions, and not as actions instigated by autonomous subjects. By implication, the landscape brings to the surface questions regarding the relationship between self and world, going beyond an anthropocentric view of history. Characters lose their preeminence and dissolve into linguistic and visual fragments. One is asked to consider whether the subject is thrown into history rather than being an active agent.

The landscape in *The Element* has a similar function. It appears as a nonplace of cultural and historical fusion somewhere in Europe, in which characters speak English in accented language. An atmosphere of solipsistic withdrawal overrides dramatic forms of story development (figure 2.1). The result regarding the portrayal of characters is complicated given that the seemingly ahistorical depiction of Europe gives the impression that subjects are abolished altogether. In conjunction with the self-conscious incorporation of genre figures and the intertextual references, the actors look as if they quote cultural stereotypes instead of embodying dramatic figures. This practice reinforces the questioning of individuality in relation to history, and the historical reality outside the world of images.

The most conspicuous example can be drawn from a scene in which Fisher meets Kramer. Here the landscape predominates over story development. As Fisher informs us, "Europe lies dormant and everything seems very peaceful." In the midst of a lengthy camera movement, the camera focuses on the natural environment, which is dilapidated—an effect that is heightened by the semisepia color. Later on, a scene of police violence is followed by an image of a horse sinking inside the water. As Fisher and Kramer are walking to the scene of the crime, we see images of wretched people placed in beds, hammocks, and rooms that are surrounded by water. Another image of a dead horse sunk into the water emerges (figure 2.2) and the camera ends up in a sand hill that looks completely dissociated from the previous images (figure 2.3).

Yet the voice-over constantly informs us that the place is Europe and the portrayed European landscape cannot be dissociated from the crime scenes. Europe appears as a permanent locus of crime and inertia. Following Fisher's and Kramer's visit into the crime scene, the ensuing frame heightens the sense of temporal and spatial uncertainty (figure 2.4). People are shown running in

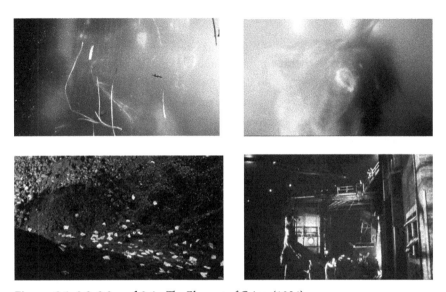

Figures 2.1, 2.2, 2.3, and 2.4: *The Element of Crime* (1984).

various directions and more images of dead horses are interlocked, while the extra-diegetic music intensifies the dream-style narration. Multiple fragments are attached and the audience's eye cannot absorb them at once. What is particularly suggestive for the viewer is that the uncertainty communicated by the landscape intimates the film's lack of interest in dramatic realism, showing preference for constellations infused with history instead of a historically accurate *mise-en-scène*. At odds with postmodern nostalgia films—for example, *Cinema Paradiso* (Tornatore: 1988) and *Life Is Beautiful* (*La Vita è Bella*, Benigni: 1988)—which employ landscape images to suggest historical specificity, evoke a past historical period, and trigger audience emotivity, in *The Element of Crime* the landscape plays a different function, since its appearance is not simply narratively motivated and it does not provoke questions of national identity and specificity. Unlike the aforementioned period films that employ landscape images to erase any contradictions between nature, culture, and history, von Trier creates a "landscape effect" which conveys a feeling of historical and cultural failure.

Subsequently, the European landscape is not just a dramatic setting, but it carries a meaning that exceeds character interiority and action. Despite Fisher's attempts to solidify his memories into a concrete narrative, his view of Europe as a locus of traumatic memories predominates and infuriates his therapist, who repeatedly asks him to stay focused on the story. In this landscape, von Trier fuses cinematic and historical references, so as to voice a historical anxiety regarding the medium's relationship to an ever-changing historical environment. Thus, one can understand this predilection for visuals at the expense of plot as a means of addressing the crisis of referentiality. This can be brought to the surface via an examination of the accumulation of different narrative levels, which result in a collision of materials that fail to integrate into a concrete narrative structure. Questions of story development are minimized in favor of questions of narrative agency. In other words, the film's unfolding leaves unanswered questions with respect to who is narrating to whom. Subjective memory, textual/filmic references, and collective historical memories overlap, problematizing the main character's capacity to map the world around him.

On the surface, *The Element* appears as a narrative that addresses individual memories. The film starts in Egypt and Fisher is hypnotized by an Egyptian psychiatrist to go back into the past and assemble the pieces of a traumatic experience. In the frame story, Fisher is always absent and the therapist gazes at the camera addressing him and the audience simultaneously. As the therapist implies, what follows is the recounting of a subjective experience on the part of the main character. Fisher's voice-over interjects the reality of the story-time with its recounting. The time of the story and the time of its narrating are intertwined. In effect, the relationship between individual and story becomes problematic. Fisher is a character in the story and an observer at the same time, something that is equivalent to Brecht's objective to split the character and reveal her or him as a construction. Von Trier pushes things further to the extent that there are moments when one senses a radical separation between voice and body. As a result, voices are privileged over a unified identity.

Fisher the narrator is the person who is asked to go back to Europe by means of hypnosis so as to clarify the traumatic past events and refamiliarize himself with the memories that cause him pain. In the film within the film, which is the revisualization of these memories, Fisher is the character whose pursuit of the serial killer Harry Grey becomes the film's plot. Within the story another story intervenes, which is the theory of *The Element of Crime*, a book written by Fisher's mentor, Osborne (Esmond Knight). According to the book, crimes can occur in a certain element and environment. Thus, the prerequisite for a successful discovery of a criminal is the pursuer's identification with her or him. In the end, a puzzling switching of identities takes place, since Fisher kills a girl he uses as a decoy to lay the killer in ambush. He turns out to assume the identity of the murderer and later on the identity of his mentor, who commits suicide having taken the responsibility for the killings.

The switching of identities and the clash between different narrative levels create a disjuncture between individual experience and pictorial representation, something that defies the films' ostentatious narrative as the recounting of a subjective story. While Fisher is hypnotized in the frame story, a dream-style narration typifies the film's narrative, in which von Trier presents many narrative layers. In his explanation, the reason for this is that "it's all about trying to convey the fact that the world is so much more than a trite little story that's inside the head of the film's protagonist" (cited in Larsen 2003, 38).

The different story layers emanate from an aesthetics that polarizes action and narrative voice. A prime example can be seen in the beginning of Fisher's recollection, in which there is a disjunction between the image-track and the sound track. Fisher says that he visits Europe again; but instead of a clearly identifiable and recognizable location, we see images of dead horses (figure 2.5). What is clear beyond doubt is that these durational images are not establishing shots. Uncertainty is heightened by the voiceover, which does not aim at clarifying the visuals. Both the voice-over narration and the images play with the dialectic between "showing an action" and telling, something that does not render the storyteller reliable. In this, von Trier follows Jørgen Leth's deployment of the voice-over as a way of doubling the image on the screen, or even obfuscating it. The disjunction between image and sound creates an audiovisual collage devoid of a storytelling function. The figures of the dead horses are accompanied by a quotation from *The Rime of the Ancient Mariner* on the part of the main character: "water, water everywhere and not a drop to drink." Fisher's quotation is interrupted by the therapist's reprimand to stay focused on the story.

Obviously, there is dissociation between the speaking utterances and the body of the narrator. In this regard, the role of hypnosis that provides a dream-style narration is crucial to our understanding of the disconnection between

Figure 2.5: *The Element of Crime* (1984).

subject and language. The recounting of Fisher's traumatic experience in Europe by means of hypnosis accords the narrative an element of artificiality, since the aesthetics of the dream is not based upon the experience of a concrete story. Conversely, the dream is always a quoted narrative, which cannot be attributed to a unified subject. As Michael Lambek explains:

> The experience of dreaming is not based upon a concrete, bounded narrative or image that we can then repeat verbatim; instead the telling replaces the dream. In other words, it is impossible to know where the images perceived or originating in sleep break off and those in waking life, elicited in what is ostensibly a reproduction but becomes its own creative process, begin. Once formulated in words, it is this version we remember, the representation, not the original experience. What we call the dream is actually the highly mediated retelling. (1996, 242)

In light of these comments, one can perceive the film's complex narrative as a representation revolving around quotation. The act of recollection replaces the authoritative narrative and refutes the notion of a unified identity. Another element that heightens ambiguity regarding the identity of the narrator is that, despite the fact that the film purports to be a subjective-flashback, the origin in the frame story is not Fisher, who is absent, but the therapist.

Thus, the world that is narrated collides with the narrating process itself. At times, Fisher's suspended critical abilities, which are the outcome of hypnosis, are transferred to the main story and the very act of "witnessing" is problematized. Fisher's function as a narrative agent is called into question and the boundaries between the metadiegetic and the diegetic world are not clearly defined. As a result, different voices and stories overlap, making the film look like an accumulation of materials that are not complete and that clash with each other, consistently voiding them of their storytelling function. Fisher's voice-over in the frame story is dissociated from the projected events and gives the impression that it is the instigator of movement, as if the character is reading a script, which is actualized on the screen. There are moments that the voice-over blends the frame story with Fisher's revisualized memories, making it hard to discern the character's identity. Flashbacks inside of flashbacks join together and the authority of a sovereign point of view is undermined. This formula de-individualizes the narration, since flashbacks are used in such a way that access to character psychology is denied. Their function is not restorative or explanatory, as it is the case in a type of narration structured upon a cause-and-effect chain.

A reference to the deployment of flashback in classical narration demonstrates its complex function in the film. Pam Cook explains the flashbacks' function within a narrative, in which action springs from characters as causal agents.

> Flashback is a common way of articulating memory in classic cinema and its most usual form is a close-up on a character's face or eyes, suggesting that we are entering their head or thoughts, followed by a scene that represents their recollection of something that happened to them in the past. (2005, 103)

In classical narration, recollection becomes a form of "exorcism." The past is left behind and the individual is asked to move on, a formal choice that implies progress. One senses the difference between the paradigm described by Cook and *The Element*. Von Trier's employment of recollection does not place the narrator in a superior position of knowledge. The act of recollection is questioned and instead of reenacting an inner subjective moment, it is the very act of narration that is rendered unreliable. This formulation is telling because von Trier adopts the mode of the art cinema as a historical material—one senses similarities with Alain Resnais—and proposes that the art cinema meditation on issues of historical reference is potentially as suspect as any mode of representation.

Indicative of this practice is a scene in which Fisher reenacts Grey's trip to Friedingen. The camera remains stationary focusing on his girlfriend Kim (Me Me Lai). Meanwhile, Fisher's voice-over is delivered in the third person and informs us about Grey's trip and Kim's (Grey's former mistress) decision to join him. Here, the voice-over and the voice-on run concurrently. The audience is not aware whether it is the hypnotized Fisher in the frame story or the character in the main narrative who is speaking. The camera then moves away and captures Fisher, who is wearing different clothes and a hat with the initials H.G. Fisher looks at the camera lens saying, "Harry Grey," making us assume that he is restaging Grey's trip that took place three years ago. From then on, the voice-over is delivered in the first person. "I have waited half an hour for you. The bus is late." When he asks Kim whether she has missed him, she responds, "you know I like to see you." Fisher corrects her saying, "you know I like to see you Harry," something that she is asked to repeat.

Subsequently, the characters look as if they are quoting a script and the temporality of the plot is radically undermined. These transpositions from the third-person voice-over narration to the first one and then back to the plotline, where the narrative seems to be a self-conscious restaging of Grey's experiences, create a disjunction between the image-track and the sound track. The scene creates a distance between actors and characters, since the roles that they perform are complicated. Agency is problematized and one cannot ascertain whether it is Fisher or Grey who is the narrative agent. The prioritization of voices and images over concrete characterization and narrative is a formal choice that interrogates individual agency.

The fact that the characters give the impression of quoting a script confounds matters more. The topos of reading from scripts when they purport to illuminate the fictional characters' experiences raises questions with respect to identity and authorship. The characters speak as if their words are reported by someone else; and given that the film deals with recollection, one is asked to consider whether there is such a thing as a unified subject that can act as the locus of recall. On this account, the voice-over does not follow the logic of the omniscient narrator of the nineteenth-century novel, who can address a series of clearly composed events. When it comes to authorship, the audience is asked to rethink the validity of the text as a means of addressing the historical trauma and the role of the director as the person in the seat of knowledge.

Dialectical images

Not surprisingly, the crisis of authorship is a theme that preoccupies the film thematically. Osborne's text, *The Element of Crime*, appears quite often on screen, while Osborne himself is shown in televisual images advocating a scientific explanation of crime. In one of those moments, Osborne is accompanied by two men dressed in SS uniforms, a stylistic element that alludes to the European history of fascism. During a press conference, he proceeds to provide a scientific explanation of crime (figure 2.6) and explains, "*The Element of Crime* is a method based on a reconstruction of a known part of a criminal's life." The role of this commentary seems to be dual: It addresses the character Fisher and the audience at the same time, providing a tip-off for the film's interpretation. However, the unfolding of the narrative contradicts Osborne's scientific account and his text fails to provide an accurate explanation.

The crime that Osborne's method aspires to comprehend is an allegory for the European historical traumas. Evidence of this association is offered by the visual paraphernalia that evoke Nazi culture; there are also some unmotivated references to Auschwitz and Jewishness, particularly when Fisher visits a forensic surgeon to get evidence from the postmortem results and when he asks

Figure 2.6: *The Element of Crime* (1984).

a receptionist (von Trier) for a room in a third-class motel. But it is mainly the idea of Europe being a locus of traumatic memories which confirms the link between the crime and history. To return to Osborne's theory, the text's (*The Element of Crime*'s) failure opens up issues of representation and demonstrates the epistemological break between fiction and history. In the same way that Osborne's book fails to help Fisher understand and find Grey, the hints given by the story line are unable to connect with its visual actualization. In the end, the merging of the identity of the policeman with the criminal and the scientist points to a historical era of epistemological uncertainty. Science and authoritarianism are not shown as antithetical but as the two sides of the same coin. Out of all the perspectives that have appeared throughout the film's narrative, none of them is vested with validity. Fisher's humanism, Osborne's scientific reasoning, and Kramer's authoritarianism clash and are shown as equally problematic.

The result is that various levels of meaning and associations coexist, while none of them is privileged by the director. It is fair to conjecture that the failure of *The Element of Crime*—the text within the film—to provide an accurate explanation for the European trauma becomes a self-reflexive comment on von Trier's *modus operandi*. Fisher follows Osborne's method until the end, but the text and its scientific rhetoric do not succeed in offering a unified interpretation of the series of crimes. On one occasion, we see Fisher contemplating while the pages of the text are scattered around the landscape. The text in the film's narrative demonstrates skepticism regarding the understanding of the text—and as an extension of the author and the script—as the repository of truth. This point raises issues of authorial and epistemological uncertainty.

Uncertainty is strengthened by von Trier's prioritization of style over storytelling, which gives rise to a "cinematic-excess." This term has been developed by Kristin Thompson and refers to the ways style can be used to disorganize the unified narrative structure. Cinematic excess calls attention to form as a means of challenging the audience's perception of the object. Thompson quotes Roland Barthes' point that excess gives precedence to "the act of pointing" (which invokes Brecht's aesthetics of *zeigen*) over the commonplace understanding of representation as imitation. Excess is founded on the disruption of narrative causality and counteracts the unbroken unified Hollywood narrative structure.

> It [excess] suggests a different way of watching and listening to a film. It offers a potential for avoiding the traditional, conventionalized views of what film structure and narrative should be—views which fit in perfectly with the methods of film-making employed in the classical commercial narrative cinema. The spectator need not assume that the entire film consists only of the unified system of structures we call form and style; he/she need not assume that film is a means of communication between artist and audience. Hence the spectator will not go to a film expecting to discern what it is "trying to say," or to try and reassemble its parts into some assumed, pre-ordained whole. (1986, 140)

Thompson's discussion of cinematic excess invites for a different way of approaching film-viewing, which skips the equation of narrative with unity and authorial intentions. Attention to excess can lead to a more sophisticated awareness of an object's formal complexity, given that the audience accepts the arbitrariness of the narrative system.

Thompson's reasoning can help us appreciate von Trier's dialectical plenitude, which is devoid of a pregiven hermeneutical designation. This plenitude inundates the audience with a plethora of constellations that point to history, but do not lead to cognitive revelation. These constellations valorize excess over storytelling and generate *Verfremdungseffekte*, but unlike Brecht, the fragments are not used as a means of leading the audience to a reformed view of reality that is structured upon a specific doctrine of knowledge. The fragments crystallize antithetical elements that do not follow each other with dialectical precision. The various levels of narration do not cohere, a formal choice that demonstrates an inability to deal adequately with the trauma of history.

It is fair to suggest that the plot in the film comes as an afterthought, something that can be seen in some scenes where we expect an illumination of the events. Instead, the characters seem to quote lines without a storytelling function; one senses a complete dissociation between the speakers and their utterances. For instance, when Fisher goes to the crime scene to get information for the first murder, he meets with a group of kids that start reciting "Oranges and Lemons." This nursery rhyme is used in George Orwell's famous novel *1984* as a reference to issues of historical amnesia. Far from being accidental, this intertextual reference indicates the film's interest in issues of memory and the collective European history. Later, when Fisher meets Kim for the first time, she starts reciting "The House that Jack Built" instead of introducing herself, making the relationship between sound and image quite perplexed.

Consequently, language does not emerge in a verisimilar way from the story. Given that the film is concerned with Europe as a locus of traumatic memories, the outcome of the accumulation of disconnected materials demonstrates a preference for avoiding a unified historical narrative. What appear instead are fragments that subvert the story line and fuse different temporalities. Therefore, the clashes between images and words do not simply refer to the limits of the character's memory but to the inadequacy of representation to express the trauma of European history. History intrudes in the film's narration in the form of flashes, and one example can be drawn from a segment in which, while Fisher is laying the murderer in ambush, we hear someone whistling *Lili Marleen*, the German song that became popular during World War II, which von Trier also included in *Orchidégartneren*. The song is also an indirect reference to Fassbinder's homonymous film and demonstrates von Trier's hyperawareness of the European art house cinema tradition concerned with history.

Such a fragmented manifestation of history is firmly professed in a scene toward the end of the film. When Fisher assumes the identity of Grey and murders the girl, the camera exhibits its indifference to the professed narrative resolution and captures a narratively unmotivated suicidal ritual conducted by a group of skinheads. In the beginning of the sequence, this group is shown in a pool singing a military song. Later on, we see them being brutally attacked by a policeman. Meanwhile, a skinhead performs the suicidal ritual (figures 2.7 and 2.8). Here, the outwardly important story development is deliberately toned down; the ritual performs a determined pause in the narrative, which has a shock-effect on the audience.

This ritual does not develop the story line nor does it follow the rules of narrative continuity. The skinheads' appearance operates as an intrusion of the traumatic past, as hallucinatory fragments of European history. What makes the scene more problematic is that the arrangement of the images does not suggest historical reconstruction, but it points toward painful and chaotic memory. The images refer to the wounds of the fascist past. They are placed in a nonspecific landscape and are left to the audience to construct meaning out of them. At this point, the camera ignores Fisher's point of view, despite the fact that we are given

Figures 2.7 and 2.8: *The Element of Crime* (1984).

the impression that the mystery has been resolved. What occurs is a disturbance in the plot and once again the viewer is asked to reconsider who is the narrative agent.

The appearance of history as non-chronologically ordered images is interconnected with a historical reality, in which a systematic all-encompassing method, including the Marxist metanarrative (in the form of historical determinism), cannot account for the historical past and present. History is presented as an accumulation of fragments and heterogeneous elements that resist systematization and narrative order. The emergence of fragments that allude to the historical past is congruent with Benjamin's understanding of the dialectical image as "involuntary memory" that does not perceive history in a chronological arrangement. For Benjamin, the dialectical image valorizes sequential "disorder" so as to change the way the past has been inherited and its relation to the contemporary present. Benjamin's stress on historical discontinuity was intended to clarify the revolutionary potential of the present. In *The Element*, von Trier does not pronounce such a potential clearly, but what one shall retain from Benjamin when looking at the film is the understanding of the historical fragment as "a precise dialectical problem that the present is called upon to resolve" (cited in Buck-Morss 1981, 57).

The aesthetics of the fragment that resists unity and coherence poses problems in relation to issues of representation and spectatorship. In its proliferation of visual and aural signs, *The Element* requires a new mode of perception in which the audience is no longer required to reconfirm a predetermined theory or a specific scientific conclusion. They are asked to concentrate on the film's production of images, signs, and intricate constellations, which do not converge at a single point. Fisher's recounting of "the facts" fails, since neither he nor the audience manage to acquire specific information that leads to narrative closure. The plurality of voices and the intrusion of history in the form of disjunctive images and references deprive the narrative of an authoritative point of view.

The film exhibits a postmodern suspicion toward the ideology of presence, but this aspect does not necessarily set off an apolitical postmodern hermeneutics. In Chapter 1, I developed Brecht's idea that reproductive employments of the medium naturalize one's perception of social reality. Brecht did not see any merit in representing history as a closed series of events, because he was not concerned with offering a detailed portrayal of what happened in the past. He was rather more concerned with asking what could have happened in the past under different circumstances and how the past can be seen as historically specific, so as to make the audience explore the ways that the present can be changed. What Brecht's practice ruled out in principle was the reduction of history to mere surface, something that aligns him with German critical theory; characteristic from this perspective is Siegfried Kracauer's idea that "for history to present itself the mere surface coherence offered by photography must be destroyed" (1995, 52).

In *The Element*, von Trier shares an analogous mistrust toward surface historical reproduction. The accumulation of different voices and unconnected images from the European past, which are torn out of context, refutes the illusion of a self-contained historical world. Thus, in its refusal to reduce the traumatic European past to an ordered narrative, the film goes beyond the orthodox Marxist approach to historical evolution, which linked the representation of the past to human knowledge and emancipation. The audience is asked to coproduce so as to place the shown images in the present and work through collective repressed memories that cannot be enclosed within the fictive cosmos. The determining question here is whether von Trier's treatment of history proposes a *post-histoire* reading, or whether the film's valorization of uncertainty can be understood dialectically. It is thoroughly misleading to handle such a convoluted narrative as another "postmodern nostalgia film" (Simons 2007, 88), but in order to elucidate this line of argument, one needs to explain that the abandonment of the view of history as a completed whole does not necessarily imply a postmodern disappearance of history. History persists throughout the film, but not as a drama. The relegation of history to a dramatic narrative implies teleology, reconciliation, and historical determinism, which are the opposite of a dialectical view of history as an active process of perpetual transitions.

Literalization of the medium: The essay as film form

Epidemic, the second part of the trilogy, is also concerned with the chasm between history and its representation. This chasm is heightened by the film's quotation of its own making, which makes one rethink the relationship between history and dramaturgy. The film was shot without a crew and for the most part von Trier and Vørsel acted in front of an "unmanned" camera. The initial script was one-page long, and in a way, *Epidemic* foreshadows von Trier's fondness for a more ascetic aesthetics. As Schepelern explains, "Med sin prætention om at præstere stor kunst for begrænsede økonomiske midler og uden udfoldelse af kompliceret filmteknik foregriber filmen Dogme 95/Kyskhedsløftet med dets krav om en renselse af filmproduktion for alt kunstigt og forfængeligt" (*Epidemic*'s pretense in delivering art of limited financial means and noncomplex film technique anticipates von Trier's ascetic Dogme project) (2000a, 97). This preference for cinematic austerity is also strengthened by the Manifesto that accompanied the film's release, in which von Trier argues in favor of a naïve cinematic style that he equates with "the bagatelle" (Manifesto 2, Appendix). This Manifesto links naiveté with experimentation, something that brings us back to Brecht. For Brecht, as mentioned in the previous chapter, a naïve attitude is the synonym for an experimental approach toward art and reality that aims at rendering the "obvious" and the "self-evident" problematic. To return to *Epidemic*, the film's dramaturgical simplicity inaugurates von Trier's new approach toward dramaturgy and his preference for simple and less complicated narratives.

Drawing once again on metafiction, *Epidemic* merges dramaturgy with the process of its own making and reveals the means by which the filmmakers employ historical materials and anecdotes in order to complicate historical representation. The film starts with von Trier and Vørsel realizing that the script for *The Cop and the Whore* (reference to *The Element of Crime*), which they want to propose for funding, has been lost. From their dialogue, we get to know that they perform themselves and not fictional characters. Having mutually agreed that they prefer to make something more "dynamic," they decide to write a new screenplay called *Epidemic*, which deals with the Black Death that ravaged Europe during the fourteenth century. Thus, the filmmakers impersonate themselves. In this way, they are split in two. They act as characters in the story and perform themselves in the process of their filming.

The effects are dual regarding the narrative agents and the story. The characters fluctuate between being and not being the filmmakers, whereas the process of the filmmaking merges with the process of the filmmakers' quotation of themselves.[2] This contradiction pushes forward Brecht's understanding of acting, in which a historical subject plays an actor, playing a character. Here, the emphasis is on an acting "that shows" rather than on the actor's disappearance into the character (figure 2.9). But there are moments in which it is impossible to determine whether the pauses in the action, which show the characters thinking about their project, are acted or real. The defamiliarizing effect is heightened by the fact that von Trier performs Dr. Mesmer, the central character of the film within the film. Then again, certain formal elements, such as the employment of extra-diegetic music or the appearance of the film's title in the screen, destabilize authenticity.

In effect, the metalevel and the diegetic one collide. When it comes to the story, the effect is that the story development and the process of the film's construction are given equal weight. The interjection of the film within the film—the filmmakers' visualization of their work in progress—complicates matters more, since the "imagined" film appears without any introduction. Subsequently, the process of the production of the film within the film is blended with fragments

Figure 2.9: *Epidemic* (1987).

of its actualization on screen. The result is not a concrete fictive cosmos but an exploration of the ways in which the very act of representation takes place. We are clearly dealing here with what Gérard Genette defines as "narrative metalepsis" (1980, 235), which plays on the temporality of the story and the narrating at the same time. The film's emphasis on the process of its making reflects its treatment of history too. The illusion that we are able to formulate the question of historical representation objectively and from a superior position of knowledge is questioned.

A closer look at a sequence in the beginning of the film can clarify this argument. While researching for material regarding the fourteenth-century epidemic, the two filmmakers visit a museum, in which a Danish historian gives them some information regarding the specific historical period. Initially, the camera pans on the library shelves, while the historian's voice is heard saying:

> Fathers left their children. Wives left husbands. Brother left brother. For the disease attacked both through breathing and sight. Thus they all died. No one would bury them at any price. Family members dragged their dead to open graves without benefit of clergy, eulogy or tolling of bells. Throughout Siena mass graves were buried with victims. I Agnolo di Tura called the Fat one buried my five own children with my own hands. Some were covered with such a thin layer of dirt that dogs dug up their bodies and fed on them.

As the camera focuses on the library shelves, we can hear the historian's voice in the background, and later on the camera establishes a connection with the speaking subject through a close-up of his face. We come to realize that the historian is reading a letter written by one of the victims of the plague; therefore, he is quoting. The historian reads the letter in a very detached and de-dramatized way without, however, weakening the intensity of the delivered lines. This de-dramatization synopsizes the film's interest in avoiding a fetishization of history. Agency is again problematized, since the collection of historical witnessing and material becomes part of the film's thematic preoccupations. Correspondingly, *Epidemic* consists of many heterogeneous stories that join with the filmmakers' thinking process regarding their project.

The film's complex narrative structure defies dramatization in a manner that is analogous to Brecht's suspicion of the reconstruction of historical events for dramatic ends. Brecht's distrust of reconstructing historical events for the sake of dramatic purposes was predicated on the basis that such a practice separates the portrayed event from the audience's reception of it. Brecht's intention was to force the audience to think about "a subject" and not "within the confines of the subject"

(1964, 44). Critical theory has always been skeptical toward the plain dramatization of historical events and in particular of events that raise ethical questions, such as the Holocaust. From Theodor Adorno's condemnation of dramatizing the horror of history to produce empathetic identification with particular individual cases to Hayden White's point that reducing the past to drama leads to a "fetishization of history" (1996, 32; 1998, 101), the general consensus is that uncomplicated dramatization fails to point to the historical conditions that are to be blamed for the emergence of certain political attitudes. As Adorno argues, focusing on individual cases withdraws attention from the "terrifying totality" (1998, 101). The historical incidents are not historicized and the drama is given more prominence than any attempt to unveil historical processes and contradictions.

The key to historical understanding lies in a critical self-reflexive thinking which aims at questioning oversimplified polarities, so as to experiment with questions that canonical filmic accounts of history refrain from posing. This is the impetus for *Epidemic*'s central interest in using history as material for thinking the European present, and not as drama which purports to offer a set of incontestable truths. In its structuring of the diegesis as a work in progress, the film avoids placing emphasis on the dramatic narrative; it is more concerned with the medium itself and the ways that history can be portrayed. Most critics considered the film's interest in the process of its own making as uncinematic. The Danish Press suggested that *Epidemic* looks more like a "study" than a film, or like "style exercises" (Schepelern 2000, 95; Stevenson 2002, 46). To a large extent, these responses can be attributed to the fact that *Epidemic* avoids the reconstruction of a realistic *mise-en-scène,* in which all the episodes solidify. Even when the narrative moves from the story to the film within the film, von Trier denies a photographic reproduction of the horror caused by the epidemic.

For instance, the first scene of the film in process shows Dr. Mesmer facing animosity on the part of the scientific intelligentsia due to his decision to leave the fortified town so as to try to find a cure for the epidemic. The scene is exceptionally stylized and the actors deliver their lines in an extremely theatricalized way that points to the film's construction. Through this passage, we get to know the basic outline of the film within the film, which is the story of an idealist doctor who wants to help Europe find a cure for the epidemic, but he turns out to be the carrier of the disease. What is important for the audience is the contrast between the main story and the film in process. The first one is characterized by formal austerity and is shot in 16-mm film, while the latter is imbued with excessive artificiality—the product of Henning Bendtsen's (renowned for his collaboration with Carl Dreyer) cinematography. This first shift from the main story to the film within the film is also important because the director's historical research is followed by dramatization. In effect, the gap between the researched material and its dramatization is heightened, and one cannot avoid noticing the medium's limited ability to deal with traumatic historical memories.

The narrative of the film-within-the-film story remains incomplete, and it is by no means privileged in relation to the process of the film's construction. The filmmakers are not hesitant to capture themselves thinking about the making of their film. In one of the most provocative scenes, we see them discussing their project and von Trier recommends that at some point they should add some drama, because the audience will consider leaving the auditorium. Here, this sarcastic comment makes one consider the relations between dramaturgy and history, and whether dramatization serves the purpose of historical understanding.

The aforementioned scene brings profoundly into question issues of representation. The incorporation of the filmmakers' thinking process about the film in process invites the audience to think beyond the confines of the story and to adopt a more critical stance. The effect is that a certain "Literalization" of the medium takes place. Brecht introduced the idea of "literalizing the medium," which refers to a process committed to changing the apparatus. This "Literalization" intends to prioritize the changing of the institution of theater/cinema over its storytelling function. For Brecht, this change was of vital importance because, as he says, theater "theatres all down" to serve economic reasons, that is, to preserve an established apparatus (1964, 43).

The process of "Literalization" becomes a means of taking issue with the medium itself rather than with the very storytelling process. Brecht justifies this shift of interest on the grounds that the audience will be able to think beyond the limits of the story. To achieve this effect, Brecht advocated a playwriting that would resort to "footnotes and the habit of turning back in order to check a point" (1964, 44). His aim was to encourage a reading attitude in the auditorium, which would prevent the audience from being completely absorbed by dramatic action. In *Epidemic*, an analogous process occurs, because the discussions about the medium and von Trier's and Vørsel's commentaries on the filmmaking process are given the same importance as the visual elements. Both seem to take Brecht's suggestion word for word, since the structure of the film does not allow the audience to follow the story without considering how dramaturgy is constructed. Therefore, the minimization of dramaturgy makes film as medium and history the very subjects that the audience is asked to dwell on.

Brecht's ideas on the "Literalization" of the medium have found their expression in the essay film genre. This category of films is associated with directors such as Straub/Huillet, Alexander Kluge, and Harun Farocki, who have consciously adopted an aesthetics of resistance. As Anton Kaes observes, these directors blend different materials, such as sounds, images, dialogue, and acting, without integrating them into a coherent narrative that effaces the signs of its production (1989, 19). Following the Brechtian topos of self-reflexivity, essay films complicate the cause-and-effect linkage of the episodes with the view to introducing a level of imprecision that characterizes literary language. In Kluge's words, this practice aspires to use language and film in an "uncertain and open" way (cited in Koutsourakis 2011, 223).

Film theory has adopted many definitions of the essay film genre. Despite the different interpretations, the common argument is that this genre intends to go beyond the established film grammar and to downplay the rules of dramatic development in favor of questions that are addressed to the audience. The theoretical formulations of the essay film have been largely influenced by Adorno's view of the essay writing as an antisystematic form of writing that refutes the doubling of the existing reality. Adorno suggests that the essay is an incomplete artifact structured upon self-reflection. As Adorno says:

> Even in its manner of delivery, the essay refuses to behave as though it had deduced its object and had exhausted the topic. Self-relativization is immanent in its form; it must be constructed in such a way that it could always and at any point, break off. It thinks in fragments just as reality is fragmented and gains its unity only by moving through fissures, rather than by smoothing them over. (1984, 164)

Adorno's understanding of the essay-writing as dialectical is predicated on its emphasis on self-reflexive discontinuity that rejects any sense of absolute knowledge and totality. The essayistic writing is experimental and aims at viewing the object from various perspectives. Adorno's thesis that the essay is antisystematic is grounded upon the very idea of fragmentation. Fragmentation that fuses fiction and criticism is integrally connected to experimentation, as it does not strive for dialectical synthesis, but places emphasis on the process of assembling materials that defy compositional precision.

This dialectical openness is spelled out clearly by Noël Burch's commentary on the genre. Burch understands the essay film to be the dialectical fusion of fiction and nonfiction (1981, 159). The essay film takes its theme as the basis for the exploration of a set of ideas and not as a means of producing dramatic events, drawing equal attention to the filmic process and to the final object. Structuring the film as an essay serves also the purpose of changing one's perspective with respect to the past's relation to the present and of putting together different voices that challenge the narrative homogenization of a historical event. The result is a collage of different voices and agents. Michael Renov understands this multiple diegesis to be the outcome of a practice not concerned with dramatizing the phenomenal world. For Renov, the essay film is interested in representing the world and interrogating it too, and this practice results in a "pluralization of voices," which challenges every certainty and the director's authority (Renov 1989, 11).

This collage makes the audience acquire a distance from the portrayed events. The essay film pioneers a mode of filmmaking that thematizes the very act of representation, and questions the author's and the audience's positions and the medium of its own articulation. As Nora M. Alter explains:

> Like "heresy" in the Adornian literary essay, the essay film disrespects traditional boundaries, is transgressive both structurally and conceptually, it is self-reflective and self-reflexive. It also questions the subject positions of the filmmaker and audience as well as the audiovisual medium itself—whether film, video or digital electronic. The essay film is as international as it is interdisciplinary. The essay film can be grasped as an audiovisual performance of theory and criticism executed within and by the filmic text, thus producing a productive and/or inhibiting resistance to scholarly discourse, since it appears to have done the latter's work for it. Doubtless all films require us to resist becoming a mere *Sprachrohr* for the filmmaker's own positions (even or especially when we are in ideological agreement), but this resistance becomes essentially crucial with the essay film because—almost by definition—it offers the appearance of its own self-criticism, threatening to silence the critic's voice in advance. (1996, 171)

Alter's definition suggests that the fusion of film and "writing" problematizes the production of image and sound, and questions the director's superior position over her or his audience. The essay film collates a plurality of voices and arguments that expose specific tensions and not an authoritative voice that the viewer can identify with. The film's elements do not relate clearly to one another, producing a deliberate disunity, and the production of "unfinished material" introduces a hermeneutic imprecision that activates the audience's productivity.

As a genre, the essay film is liable to be misunderstood as a subjective expression on the part of an expert. However, taking our cue from Adorno's understanding of the essay as experimentation, Brecht's as *Versuche* (attempts/experiments), and given the essay's reliance on previous cultural artifacts, namely its dual function as creative work and criticism, one can apprehend that the essayistic writing/ filmmaking comes in stark opposition to the authority of an individual auteur. Timothy Corrigan describes this aptly when he says that "essayistic expression (as writing, as film, or as any other representational mode) thus demands both loss of self and the rethinking and remaking of the self" (Corrigan 2011, 17). Not surprisingly, filmmakers, such as Jean-Luc Godard, Kluge, and Harun Farocki, renowned for producing essay films assemble images alluding to other films/ texts, and words from literary or critical and historical writings that contest claims to originality and individual expression. Film segments, literary artifacts, and historical events are treated as historical materials.

In *Epidemic*, the Brechtian and Adornian understanding of the essayistic writing as experimentation is strengthened by the film's antisystematic form that incorporates fragments, which go beyond a goal-orientated dramaturgy and offer multiple perspectives on the historical past. For instance, in the third chapter of the film, the two filmmakers go to Germany to get some inspiration for their research. In the midst of a long-shot taking place in von Trier's car, the camera focuses on the landscape, without serving a strictly narrative function (figure 2.10). The "unmanned camera" captures images of factories, toxic waste, and of the motorway. These images of the European landscape are torn out of dramatic context and the audience is asked to make its own associations.

At one point, Vørsel starts listing the various cities they drive through. His voice accompanies the visual material captured by the "unmanned camera" and heightens the film's imprecision: "We are driving through Dortmund and Essen. Then Duisburg, Krefeld, Neuss, Dusseldorf. We will also be going through Remscheid, Solingen and Leverkusen." There is a sense of fascination with the

Figure 2.10: *Epidemic* (1987).

acoustic associations stemming from the pronunciation of those names. The succession of these names connotes an interest in the historical past and present and the cities' names act as signifiers that allude to collective memories that go beyond the speaking subject. Von Trier justifies his interest in the names of the cities on the grounds of the visual associations and the historical allusions that they create (cited in Björkman 2003, 48). The historical allusions are revealed in another scene that follows, in which the characters visit Udo Kier in Cologne. The visit in Kier's house makes clear the film's and the trilogy's interest in the traumas of fascism, since Kier tells them a story about the bombing of Cologne during World War II.

Again, a complete separation between art and reality is denied, since Kier performs himself. Moreover, the film's privileging of multiple diegeses and voices is intensified. One can also identify similarities with the tradition of Marxist filmmakers of the past, such as Godard, Straub/Huillet, and Kluge, who incorporated material not motivated by the diegesis as a means of breaking the narrative continuum. Kaes gives a remarkable explanation arguing that the reason for these interventions was the portrayal of history as a problem. These filmmakers act as "bricoleurs" who pick up anecdotes, fragments, images, and texts and portray history not as a "self-contained narrative," or as an auteurist vision, but as a heterogeneous process (1989, 118–119). *Epidemic* follows an analogous formal arbitrariness, and the episode with Kier is a germane example of the film's disintegrated narrative structure. Kier informs Trier and Vørsel that his mother has died and in her deathbed she confessed him some details about his day of birth, in which the allies bombed Germany with phosphorus bombs (figure 2.11). All through his description of the facts, we identify an indirect reference to the genre of horror movies. "My mother told me horrible things, one hand was sticking out of the water, it was only flesh, because the skin was burned." At one point, the camera ignores Kier and captures Raphael's and Raimondi's painting *The Massacre of the Innocents in Bethlehem* (1509) and invites the audience to make its own associations (figure 2.12). Kier finishes saying that all these people were not necessarily Nazis. In the beginning of his monologue, he remains emotionally detached, whereas toward the end he starts crying. Perhaps, this is the most emotionally intense moment of the film, which entails an ironic aspect if we consider that the story is fabricated.

But there is nothing that indicates the fictionality of the scene. The material here makes the audience identify with Kier's fabricated story, which complicates apparent authenticity with unacknowledged artifice and multiplies the perspective on the historical events that followed the German defeat in World War II. The specific episode has an unfinished/open character and forces the audience to

Figures 2.11 and 2.12: *Epidemic* (1987).

rethink the historical past and present beyond the ideological blinders of victims and perpetrators. Kier brings to the surface repressed memories on the part of the defeated and establishes a dialogic relation between himself as an agent and the audience. The scene remains incomplete, and nothing connects it causally with the previous material and the scenes that follow.

The material thus depends on the disposition of the recipient, and instead of a reproduction of a historical period, we are faced with fragments from different historical events which we are asked to assemble. This aspect of the film's form exhibits a valorization of the fragment as a means of formal experimentation. Von Trier juxtaposes different materials/anecdotes from European history, so as to view the object from different angles and to resist any all-embracing conclusions. Short scenes that reflect on the ways a film can dramatize history are not tied to a straightforward plotline. The narrative aligns antithetical materials and contradictions so as to expose the mechanics of filmmaking process. Therefore, the director's function is that of the "researcher." In other words, Von Trier and Vørsel do not embody authority figure roles, but they act as experimenters. This is intensified by *Epidemic*'s metafilmic dialectic, which deconstructs the process by which the filmmakers transform their historical research into filmic representation.

The film's foregrounding of the process of its own making, along with its episodic construction, the narrative digressions, which spring from the complication of diegetic and metadiegetic levels, and the capturing of documented material that seems unrelated to the story's progression, goes against the dominant understanding of cinema as a construction of a clear sequence of events. As such, there is a sense of an antistyle aesthetics that assigns value to the very process of exploration of the problems posed by the European historical past, rather than on a subordination of the contradictions to a unifying principle. Similar to *The Element*'s depiction of history, *Epidemic* treats the European historical traumas as constellations that do not solidify.

In many respects, history in *Epidemic* is shown as a question, and von Trier's refusal to simulate images of the historical past is in line with critical theory's mistrust of the photographic reproduction of historical events. If a crucial aspect of the dialectical thinking lies in the uncovering of contradictions and the revealing of historical processes, then one needs to challenge the tautological perception of history, according to which "the facts" are taken to be the meaning of a historical event. Hayden White's following comments are illuminating from this perspective:

> The distinction between facts and meanings is usually taken to be the basis of historical relativism. This is because in conventional historical inquiry, "the facts" established about a specific "event" are taken to be the meaning of that event. But the facts are a function of the meaning assigned to events, not some primitive data that determine what meanings an event can have. (1996, 21)

White's comments need to be seen in a broader historical context. Much discussion has been centered on the fact that human experiences have been transformed to visual commodities. From Guy Debord's excursus that social life has been replaced by the consumption of images to Jean Baudrillard's concept of the simulacrum as a copy that does not have an original, the overarching idea is that contemporary citizens have been reduced to the status of being spectators of history (Baudrillard 1994, 21; Debord 1995, 14). The simulation of history in films interested in the reproduction of historical facts reduces history to a museum piece and fails to reveal it as an active process that pervades the historical present. What renders these representations problematic is the fact that they strive for representational solidity and stability when it comes to issues that are many-sided. In their striving for unity and closure, they fail to implicate the viewers' role in the formation of history. Two pertinent examples are Steven Spielberg's *Schindler's List* (1993) and Margarethe von Trotta's *Rosenstraße* (2003), which depoliticize historical issues by treating them in moralist ways, as if fascism emerged ex nihilo, rather than being an historical and, as an extension, political end-product.

The task, therefore, of an oppositional/materialist aesthetics is to challenge the understanding of representation as replication of commodities, and to restore spectatorial responses toward the objects. The last scene of the film is suggestive of an aesthetics that invites further discussion touching on issues of film and historical representation. Having finished their script proposal, the two filmmakers invite their producer (Claes Kastholm Hansen) for a meal. To persuade him of the value of the project, they invite a medium (Gitte Lind), whom they hypnotize, and ask her to enter into the film's-in-process universe in order to make a vivid description of the project. The woman starts crying loudly and when the filmmakers attempt to calm her down they notice some plague buboes in her armpit. Eventually, all in the room realize that they are infected by a real epidemic.

In the sequence with the medium, what makes the scene more unbearable is that we see a woman crying and screaming without being able to get a visualization of her experiences. Unlike classical narrative, in which the cinematic screaming is the culmination of a sequence that functions as a machine built to give birth to a scream, here screaming is the outcome of a vision that is not accessible to the audience (figure 2.13). Michel Chion, in his analysis of "the screaming point," explains how cinema employs all the means available in order to reach that point and produce fascination. Screaming is justified by the plot and the film's action. As he says, "The screaming point is where speech is suddenly extinct, a black hole, the exit of being" (1999, 79). From Chion's comments, we can understand that the medium's hollers in *Epidemic* do not obey to dramatic realist rules, since there is no visual material that justifies it. What follows is the eruption of the plague and a general collapse. At this point, the horror is visualized and all certainties and demarcations disappear.

The scene turns into an Artaudian attack on the audience and the institution of cinema at the same time. Although I developed the Artaudian aspect of von Trier's aesthetic in the previous chapter, it is quite significant that *Epidemic* draws on the former's writings on the plague, which Artaud compared with an oppositional aesthetic of cruelty (1989, 129). Artaud's equation of representation with the plague is modeled in an understanding of cruelty as a violent disruption of the perception of art as a product to be consumed. In a like fashion, the

Figure 2.13: *Epidemic* (1987).

aforementioned scene turns into an act of aggression and challenges the audience's desire for reproduced images of historical catastrophe and horror. When the buboes appear on the screen and the plague is visualized, the film borrows stylistic traits from the B-movie horror genre. The initial fright is replaced by an excess of artificiality, which is offered through the cheap prosthetics used to suggest that a real epidemic takes place. As Howard Hampton explains, the eruption of the plague is a caustic comment toward artists who base their project on people's suffering. Here, the auteurs' sense of immunity is dissolved, and the audience's and the producer's wish for explicit images is satisfied, "instead of talking heads a bloodbath" (Hampton 1995, 46).

Subsequently, the unmotivated visualization of horror acts as a way of returning the gaze to the spectators; it challenges their security and violates the viewing contract. What is called into question here is dominant cinema's reduction of the audience to consumers of images and its treatment of the historical past as a consumable commodity dissociated from the historical present. This passage synopsizes the film's refusal to portray history as a mimetic mirroring of actions. It also gives us the chance to unpack the Brechtian connection regarding spectatorship. Brecht favored a type of representation that would place the audience into history and would defamiliarize their habitual understanding of historical incidents as being inevitable. A necessary step on this direction was the metacritique of the recognized representational paradigms.

The film's favoring of disorientation, its valorization of the fragment, and its placing of the audience at the center of the action are along the lines of this metacritique, but it is also liberated from an ideological totality. This practice remains dialectical given that the interjection of historical material stemming from von Trier's and Vørsel's research and its transformation into drama in the film within the film make visible the functions that insert themselves between historically formed reality and its representations. This method shifts the audience's attention from the imitation of actions to the film's assembly of materials that question the homogeneity of the fictive cosmos, and the view of history as a homogeneous series of events.

History as transition

This heterogeneous representation of history in the *Europa* trilogy is accentuated by von Trier's treatment of historical time, which posits history very much as a dialectical question rather than a deterministic answer. Different time sequences mix together, undermining the narrative temporality and dramatic linearity. We may further cement the dialectics of these temporal disturbances in *Epidemic* and *Europa* by looking at them along the lines of Brecht's *Historisierung*. While the former film employs a complex narrative structure that piles up fragments from the European history of violence, *Europa* has a more discernible narrative. Yet both objects problematize the linear understanding of historical time so as to transform our understanding of the European present.

Brecht' theorization of the *Historisierung* is hugely influenced by the fluid shifts of historical time in epic poetry. Epic poetry's reliance on narrative over plot gives the author the possibility to blend different time sequences and move from a historical period to another. According to Brecht, the intermixing of past and present intends to show the potential for change in the future and thus, to reveal the historicity of human relationships.

> Historical incidents are unique, transitory incidents associated with particular periods. The conduct of the persons involved in them is not fixed and universally human; it includes elements that have been or may be overtaken by the course of history, and is subject to criticism from the immediately following period's point of view. The conduct of those born before us is alienated from us by an incessant evolution. (1964, 140)

Brecht's *raison d'être* is based on the Marxist idea that analyzing the historical forces of the past can show the present as changeable. In this sense, the intermingling of different time sequences evokes the impermanence of human relations and of the social structure too.

In theater, the historicizing effects rely upon acting techniques that estrange the portrayed actions. Paradigmatic of these acting techniques are the actors' transposition into the third person, which dissociates them from the characters and their actions, the reversal into the past, and the quoting of the stage directions (Brecht 1964, 138). As Fredric Jameson explains, the aim of such a defamiliarized acting is to reveal the positive effects that might occur by training people to think historically. "What history has solidified into an illusion of stability and substantiality can now be dissolved again, and reconstructed, replaced, improved, '*umfunktioniert*'" (1998, 48). The *Historisierung*, therefore, reflects a modernist anticipatory hope of radical revolution. That said, the intersection of different time sequences operates as prolepsis of a progressive reality in process. However, cinematic treatments of the *Historisierung*, which negate the closed form of the Brechtian *Fabel*, have confirmed that the materialist treatment of historical time can be treated in ways that do not necessarily take progress for granted.

The major example of such an approach is Straub/Huillet's *Not Reconciled*. In this film, unanticipated temporal ellipses connect different private stories saturated with historical memories. The shifts in historical time are so rapid that the audience is disorientated and cannot easily distinguish between the pre–World War II years that refer to the main character's childhood and the postwar ones. Straub/Huillet's intention was to analyze the continuum of history, so as to indicate that the fascist experience in Germany cannot be dissociated from the present, and the remnants of fascism can be observed in the postwar capitalist reality. Straub/Huillet's film draws on the *Historisierung* to disclose the historical transitions and exhibit at the same time the historical present's reliance upon the past historically formed relations. In the same way, von Trier's practice questions the closed form of the *Fabel*, and the merging of historical temporalities offers a nightmarish vision of European history, according to which the traumas of the past are repeated in the present. Concomitantly, the films' merging of the past with the present negates the Enlightenment narrative of progress.

In *Epidemic*, historicizing effects are created by the complex narrative structure, in which the present state of Europe is contrasted to wisps of historical narratives of the past. These narratives derive from the filmmakers' collection of historical material, the appearance of the metafilm in the main narrative, and the insertion of unrelated material into the story line (for instance, Kier's personal recounting). A very crucial moment in the film is when von Trier and Vørsel discuss their future project while traveling to Germany. They agree to add a dramatic moment, in which the first person to die of the plague will be Dr. Mesmer's girlfriend (Cæcilia Holbek Trier). Her death shall follow the fate of other victims of the plague, who were thought to be dead and were buried alive. At this point, the film cross-cuts to the film within the film and we see Mesmer's girlfriend waking up inside her grave and trying to escape (figure 2.14). The "plague" here becomes the metaphor, in the literal meaning of the word, namely transition, for the repeatable history of violence in Europe. Later on, the filmmakers visit Kier in Cologne and here the linkage with the fascist past becomes evident. Caroline Bainbridge mentions, for example, the parallel between the Black Death of the fourteenth century and the debauchery of Jews, who were accused of having plotted the epidemic. Bainbridge explains how this moment of European history is linked with Kier's recounting of his "experiences" that unfolded in a historical context when another massive persecution of Jews took place (2007, 34).

Figure 2.14: *Epidemic* (1987).

Thus, the bombardment of the audience with material stemming from the European vicious circle of violence leads to an interrogation of the contemporary historical reality. The narrative places into doubt the perception of history as an evolutionary process leading to progress and prosperity. The progressivist philosophy of history characterizes Western thought from the very first historiographical attempts until the Enlightenment optimism. What this tendency introduces is the usefulness and the *telos* that sensible individuals can attribute to history. According to it, individuals can learn from the mistakes of the past and deal with analogous situations that confront them in the present (Callinicos 1995, 58).

Such a perception of historical maturity deriving from the knowledge of the past permeates the classical Marxist theory and Brecht himself, as someone committed to it. Von Trier's treatment of historical time in *Epidemic* creates clashes between the past and the present that expose the historical transition in a manner similar to Brecht's. Then again, these clashes seek to redeem European history as a nightmare, a vision of history analogous to Benjamin's conception of it as a catastrophe which keeps piling wreckage upon wreckage. On this account, the cross-cutting from the main story to the film within the film presents us with incomplete stories from the past and the present, offering a Benjaminian moment of recognition, in which past and present illuminate each other. The mixing of different historical temporalities illuminates connections and interweaves images and narratives from different centuries. The result is a dialectical critique of the narrative of progress itself. The conflict between the European past and present shows the transitory nature of history. What is disputed is that the mistakes of the past have reformulated the present for the better.

Similarly, *Europa* defies the post-1989 neoliberal thought, according to which history is a narrative of progress, liberty, prosperity, and equality. The film is engaged in a critical project of providing images that challenge such a liberal optimism. *Europa* offers a view of history which is counter to European and Hollywood portrayals of it at the risk of appearing Nazi-friendly. The role of the allies in the postwar West Germany is demystified to the point that there is a sense of reversibility of roles between victims and perpetrators. Former Nazis collaborate with the Americans; a Jew (von Trier) testifies in favor of Max Hartmann—an ex-member of the Nazi Party; and Leopold Kessler, an American visiting Germany with the best intentions, ends up causing a massive disaster.

The film's indifference toward historical authenticity is evidenced by the fact that back projections and superimpositions replace authentic images of the German space. Rosalind Galt, citing Elsaesser's discussion of the importance of the ruin in postwar German films, argues that the absence of ruins and rubble betrays the film's mistrust toward the West German de-Nazification and historical progress (2006, 188). Moreover, the use of back projections transmits an intentional feeling of uneasiness with respect to the characters' relationship to the diegetic space. This uneasiness gives the impression that the characters do not belong to the temporal reality under which they operate. The difficulty in distinguishing the borders between the past and the present is heightened by the fact that the film starts with a voice-over asking an unidentified "you" to go back to *Europa*. When the story starts and we see Leo in the postwar Germany, we cannot easily determine the diegetic from the metadiegetic level. Given that the voice-over constantly intervenes to interrupt the action, which is meant to take place in the past, one notes that temporal demarcations are quite slippery.

The voice-over connects the viewer with the contemporary historical reality from which the past events are seen. Leo's story motivates the enactment of fragmented stories that appear within the film's narrative and refer to the past. On his first journey, Leo comes across a German Jew, who asks him to calm his wife and ensure her that Wöldstat has not been inflicted by the bombings. When Leo enters the compartment, he meets the Jewish woman who cries "Palestine." This is followed by the man's frustrating response: "We are Jewish, but we are German, but we are Jewish." Later on, during a dinner party in Max Hartmann's house he witnesses through a window the allies' demolition of the German cranes in Westhafen. Larry Hartmann (Udo Kier) questions their motives, explaining to him that many companies that flourished during the war were owned by Americans. Thus, Leo acts as the link that connects many

Figure 2.15: *Europa* (1991).

heterogeneous stories that dispute the official historical narrative. The past appears in the form of unmotivated references to it, which connect his story to the broader historical reality of the fascist and the postwar West Germany. But the most problematic withholding of temporal orientation in the film occurs in a scene where Leo walks toward the train's exit and reaches a compartment full of emaciated people who are reminiscent of familiar pictures from the Nazi concentration camps (figure 2.15). Here a radical break occurs in the chronological order of events. Suddenly, there is a feeling that we have returned to the reality of World War II.

Undeniably, the scene does not function as a temporal ellipsis. Its role is the production of collision and not that of narrative transition, something that can be understood by the fact that it does not have any effect in the articulation of the plot. After, exiting the carriage, Leo follows Larry Hartmann (Udo Kier) and the story unfolds as if nothing has happened. As Serge Gruzinski says:

> This destabilization of the imaginary is all the more unsettling in that it applies to bits of the past that are sufficiently vital to be easily reactivated. As it plows across the Germany of the post-war years, the train of *Europa* transports visions stolen from the world of the concentration camp: skeletons in convicts' rags, piled up on pallets. The post-war and Nazi parts are articulated like the compartments of the train. They confuse the spectator about the meaning to be given to these false archive scenes. (1997, 510)

Gruzinski's confusion can be understood if we scrutinize the different temporalities that intermingle in the particular scene. The voice-over speaks from the contemporary historical time and addresses Leo saying, "you are led through carriages you never knew existed." The images that Leo sees belong to the fascist past, while Leo himself participates in the narrative actions that take place in the postwar German reality. The result is that this scene fails to affirm a logical, spatial, and temporal connection with the narrative content.

This linkage of heterogeneous elements creates historicizing effects that call into question the homogeneity of historical time. The distinction between Brecht's use of the *Historisierung* and the effect created here is more than apparent, since the presentation of historical discontinuity defies the evolutionary resolution of historical conflict. Even so, what is Brechtian here is von Trier's concern with the richness emanating from the opposition between unrelated historical materials. Brecht's *Historisierung* served the purpose of making people aware of the historical contradictions and the repeatability of the terror of history, so as to conceive themselves as active historical subjects and think of alternatives to the repeatable historical oppression. To relate this point to the aforementioned scene, of particular interest is that the voice-over responds to Leo and the audience simultaneously. Evidently, it is not simply Leo who is accused of being ignorant but the collective in the extra-filmic reality too.

The audience is challenged on the grounds of its ability to consume and objectify such an image. Crucial here is the reproduction of Leo as a spectator, as an observer of the largest historical narrative of the postwar reality. His actions do not instigate the narrative, but he is shown as simply witnessing events, as if he is a spectator in a film instead of a narrative agent, a point to which I shall return below. His passive status is linked with his decision to remain neutral and choose not to side with anyone. Von Trier explains that:

> Katarina Hartmann in *Europa* also illustrates an interesting theory, when she suggests that it's the people who haven't made up their mind, the neutrals, who are the real villains. Looked at in that light, you can see most humanists as villains, because of course, they maintain a neutral position. (cited in Björkman 2003, 129)

Von Trier's comments are important because they establish a link between history and political interests, and help us oppose the denunciation of the film on the grounds of postmodern relativism. One of the charges leveled at postmodernism lies in the subordination of politics to seemingly universal ethics. Thus, a historical event such as the Holocaust fascinates the public simply because it is reduced to an "excess of evil," an apolitical crime. The relegation of such a political issue to a matter of "preposterous evil" serves as a way of further depoliticization of history, which refuses to understand that fascism was, as Alain Badiou says, "a political sequence" (2001, 65), namely the product of conflicting interests, and not the outcome of madness or excessive malevolence, as official history tends to allege.

As opposed to such an apolitical treatment of history, von Trier wishes to divide the audience by means of dialectical contradictions. These contradictions oppose the clear-cut distinctions between right and wrong, and historical past and present, and most importantly they negate the very notion of historical progress. Like Brecht, the film's treatment of this problematic historical reality does not strive for a collective unity in the auditorium "on the basis of the common humanity shared by all the spectators alike" (1964, 60). But this division is once again an act of returning the gaze to the audience, of politicizing the material instead of assessing this complex part of European history in terms of facile moralism.

On film voyeurism

This positioning of the audience at the center of the action explicitly associates film voyeurism with historical irresponsibility, in view of the fact that all the films in the trilogy create a comparison between cinematic voyeurism and historical apathy. In *The Element,* the therapist's look at the camera in the frame story reproduces our own gaze as cinematic voyeurs. The film finishes with a song titled *Der Letzte Tourist In Europa* (*The Last Tourist in Europe*). The lyrics operate as an ironic comment on Fisher, who remains a simple observer of the nightmare of history despite returning to Europe with the best intentions. In *Epidemic*, the main characters become voyeurs of their own film in process. The effect is more apparent in *Europa*, a film that starts with a prolonged shot of railway tracks that are similar to a film reel (figure 2.16). In all the films, the question that arises is how much the characters are ready to witness before they act. When asked about the connection between voyeurism and history, von Trier responded in a laconic way: "Of course, being a spectator can be tantamount to being a criminal! If you are a spectator of a crime" (Interview, Appendix). Certainly, a parallel here exists between cinematic fascination and historical latency.

Figure 2.16: *Europa* (1991).

This inference can be illuminated by referring to some examples from the film. By the time Leo arrives in Germany, the narrative communicates his voyeurism through short scenes that demonstrate the character's interest in witnessing images of history. During his first night in Germany he opens the dormitory's curtains to see what is outside the window. Suddenly he is told off by his uncle (Ernst-Hugo Järegård), who prevents him from accessing the reality outside the train. Later on, while on duty he looks past the window and faces hundreds of wretched people asking for help. Again, his uncle intervenes and closes the curtains justifying his act on the basis of the working rules and regulations. But Leo throughout the film insists on looking from the windows. Here the window becomes a metaphor for the cinematic screen. As Christian Metz explains, "If characters in a film are watching something from the window they reproduce my own situation as a spectator and remind me both of the nature of what is going on—a film projection, a vision in a rectangle—and the part I am playing in it" (1991, 754). In reducing Leo as a spectator of the larger postwar narrative, von Trier proceeds to confront the audience and argue that the mere fact of being a spectator is not enough. Not unlike Brecht, the renunciation of spectatorial passivity addresses issues that go beyond the film's universe and in particular issues of historical responsibility. Years ago, Guy Debord had warned that the more one acts as a spectator, the less he acts in the social sphere (1995, 23).

Nonetheless, the film connects spectatorial passivity with historical inactivity without resorting to a radical situationist critique of the spectacle, as we can see in Debord's film version of his book *The Society of the Spectacle* (*La Société du Spectacle*, 1973). By contrast, von Trier criticizes voyeurism from within, that is, by employing the spectacular aspects of the medium. At some points, the female body becomes the metaphor for the spectacle that distracts the character's attention from the historically loaded environment. This idea is manifested in Leo's first encounter with Katarina. We see Katarina from Leo's point-of-view shot, while her image in the foreground is in color, set against the black-and-white image of Leo in the background. Katarina is framed in an extremely aestheticized way that alludes to the *femme fatale* of the film noir genre (figure 2.17). This antithesis between foreground and background generates a feeling of visual excess. Leo's view of Katarina reproduces our situation as spectators and Katarina appears more like a self-conscious quotation of cinematic material instead of a character in the film's universe. At this point, we assume Leo's point of view and the idealized female image addresses both the character and the audience. The overtly dramatic extra-diegetic music in the background becomes ironic and heightens the feeling that the image develops into a palpable quotation of materials.

Figure 2.17: *Europa* (1991).

The connection between the female body and cinematic voyeurism is also substantiated in a scene that takes place after the burial of Max Hartmann. Leo enters the car of a Nazi sympathizer, who blackmails him with Katarina's safety so as to force him to help the Nazi partisans in a terrorist strike. Suddenly, the camera captures Katarina, who appears in the foreground, while the background frame is in black and white (figure 2.18). This color antithesis intensifies Katarina's depiction as a cinematic material instead of a character. Again, very dramatic extra-diegetic music cuts in and the camera cross-cuts to Leo, who is framed in black and white. Another cross-cutting from Leo to Katarina follows, and when the camera returns to the former he appears in color, while the German next to him is in black and white.

As the frame fades out, Leo's face is still visible in color and behind him an image of railway tracks is superimposed (figure 2.19). The tracks in the background—which look like film reels—as well as Leo's semihypnotic state turn the image into a metafilmic comment. Leo has turned to a consumer of illusion and this segment acts as a commentary on the link between spectacle consumption and social apathy. The character's attention is once again diverted from the historical threat; the scene exceeds the limits of the diegesis so as to address the collective in the auditorium.

One commentator understands the film's fondness for these multilayered images as a postmodern trope *tout court*. He argues that von Trier implies that

Figure 2.18: *Europa* (1991).

Figure 2.19: *Europa* (1991).

the medium cannot deal with history. All we are left is "layers upon layers of faulty perspectives" (Greenberg 2008, 47). Unlike this postmodern relativism, I want to consider Schepelern's point that "Leo er den første turist i det sønderknuste Europa" (Leo is the first tourist in the stricken Europe) (2000a, 126). To understand his argument, it is useful to consider the role of the train and the metaphor of travel, which can be equated with the very cinematic experience: not only because cinema and the steam locomotive are emblems of modernity but also because the allegory of the subject as tourist/observer has preoccupied critical theory. The state of being a tourist and a spectacle consumer are comparable because in both cases the subject cannot really alter the reality facing her or him (Elsaesser 1987, 76).

Emblematic from this point is the scene after the assassination of Ravenstein, a German who collaborates with the Western allies. The camera cuts to Leo and stays still. His face remains in the foreground retaining the same expression, whereas in the background images of railway tracks come into view. The background eventually dissolves and then a new layer is attached, which establishes a new spatial connection and shifts the narrative to Hartmann's house (figure 2.20). Throughout this spatiotemporal change, Leo's face remains passive and stares at the camera as if he is a spectacle

Figure 2.20: *Europa* (1991).

consumer. The character remains unaffected, a mere observer of the historical narrative.

This emphasis on multilayered images thematizes the very act of filmic projection and complicates the distinction between the diegetic and the metadiegetic cosmos. Gilles Visy has offered an analysis of the three different spatial levels that can be identified in the film. The first dimension is the fictional universe, the second one is Leo's conscience, which is extra-diegetic, and the third one is a *peridiegetique*, which blurs the boundaries between the two previous spaces discussed. According to Visy, the latter dimension aims at producing a "meta-level" which simultaneously addresses the audience and the character (2008). It is in this *peridiegetique* universe that cinema becomes the metaphor for the role of the individual in the formation of history. Passive consumption of spectacular images is equated with historical irresponsibility. This "meta-level" manifests itself clearly in the last scene of the film, in which we see Leo dead but the voice-over asserts: "you want to wake up to free yourself of the image of *Europa*. But it is not possible." Here, the voice-over's function becomes extra-diegetic and addresses the collective in the auditorium and not just the character. At the same time, the commentary loses its authoritative function, since it denies hermeneutical orientation and follows a formula that could be summed up like this: "It is all yours now."

The fatalistic ending of the character who becomes mere voyeur in the broader historical narrative raises questions with regard to the audience's historical agency. Thus, by problematizing narrative agency, historical temporality, and clear-cut ethical distinctions, the film raises questions that cannot be resolved within their diegetic borders. The pessimistic tenor of the narrative in the trilogy as a whole proposes that as long as the collective continues to perceive itself as a spectator in the larger historical narrative then the remnants of fascism are still strong and omnipresent. In the postmodern media reality, in which the boundaries between historical images and artifice are not quite straightforward, the question of fascism and image consumption becomes a matter of political importance. Thomas Elsaesser has brilliantly captured this point when arguing that the most important issue raised by Nazism is its aptitude to spellbind the public using excessive visuals as well as "to create a public sphere, a mass audience" (1982, 136). Following this point, one can see the film's equal interest in history and the medium itself not simply as postmodern exercises in style, but as a way of pointing out that historical responsibility requires that subjects perceive themselves as producers of history and not as voyeurs. In this context, the *Europa* trilogy challenges the institution of cinema and the audience, so as to bring to the fore a set of questions dealing with the dialectics between the individual and history. Not unlike Brecht, formal complexity aspires to transform the audience and its position toward the object as well as to make them question the current historical circumstances.

The *Europa* trilogy references one of the major historical traumas of European history, which is fascism and the Holocaust, so as to open a set of questions with respect to the future of Europe. The trilogy is completed in the post-Wall Europe, a period in which the European nations were optimistic that Europe moves forward and leaves the animosities of the past behind. The European integration was predicated upon the citizens' duty to remember past catastrophes so as to avoid the repetition of the same mistakes. The right to remember the Holocaust implied Europe's responsibility to implement policies that respected values, such as diversity, human dignity, and tolerance. Consequently, the Holocaust became a point of reference for a common political European identity. Lothar Probst explains that "the commemoration of the Holocaust—as an event which gives meaning—is not only a source of symbolic legitimacy, but also of political action and values, such as the rejection of racism, anti-Semitism and xenophobia" (2003, 53). Today, the current economic crisis has reanimated past traumas and mistakes that question the whole project of European integration along with the values that Europe stands for. Neoliberal policies have torn the social fabric in various European countries, leading to the reemergence of fascist and xenophobic groups in the UK, Greece, Hungary, France, and Italy. The insistence on dubious economic courses of action along with the Weimar-like weakening of democracy in favor of the markets negates the idea that historical knowledge has been the route to political maturity.

With these in mind, the *Europa* trilogy's idea that Europe is in a state of crisis needs to be seen in its own historicity. The current uncertain political reality in Europe makes evident that the citizens' duty is not simply to "remember" past catastrophes but to act to prevent similar phenomena too. Consistent with Brecht's Benjaminian-like motto that "die Jetztzeit wird zur Historie" (history is in the present) (cited in White 2004, 96), the trilogy's core point is founded upon the important proviso that as long as the collective continues to perceive itself as a spectator in the larger historical narrative, then fascism is an unfinished nightmare. The films' formal abstraction and their radical portrayal of different historical sequences propose that the trauma of history persists and without practical activity our contemporary present appears as the compulsive repetition of past events. Their antiheroic portrayal of history does not propagate clichés regarding historical improvement, but aspires to historicize the present, so as to place the audience into history, rather than offering a fetishized image of the past to be consumed.

Notes

1   I refrain from referencing all the intertextual references given that this has been repeatedly done so far. For a detailed discussion of intertextuality in the films, see Schepelern 2000a, 78–83, 102–103, and 120–129. Caroline Bainbridge, Linda Badley, and Jan Simons have also covered this ground.
2   A similar point is made by Barton Byg in his discussion of Straub's and Huillet's appearance in their Schoenberg films. See *Landscapes of Resistance: The German Films of Daniele Huillet and Jean-Marie Straub* (Berkeley, Los Angeles, London: University of California Press, 1995), 46.

3

The Primacy of the Apparatus

Back to the 1970s? Dogme 95: Realism and anti-illusionism

Any discussion of politics and representation cannot exclude the very question of realism, which has preoccupied cinema from its very inception. Fascinated by the new medium's ability to engage with the "real," modernist thought hinged on the contradictory idea that the very systematization and rationalization produced by the modernized historical environment may stimulate different modes of perception that can undermine the very capitalist hierarchies that modernization sought to establish. This politicization of perception was contingent on the materialization of processes that can make the individuals question the obviousness of their everyday reality. Cinema's relation to "realism" centered on the emergence of what Brecht called the apparatus, that is, of the machine, through which one could register the characteristics of social and historical reality that elude people's awareness. It is cinema's ability to document something and, at the same time, to debunk fixed and ordinary ways of viewing the world that synopsizes the modernist understanding of the very issue of realism. From Siegfried Kracauer's idea that the utopian aspect of the film medium relies on its capacity to capture the historically and materially contingent, to Brecht's understanding of film as a document of its time, and André Bazin's celebration of film as an art form not dependent on individual expression, the general consensus was that film's reliance on mechanical reproduction can defamiliarize our habitual understanding of social reality, by offering us a direct access to the materiality of the historical environment.

The question that arises is what happens when changes on the technological level reduce the medium's dialogue with the external material and social reality and adopt representational strategies more in tune with the art of painting?

This is very much one of the major challenges leveled by von Trier's critique of the new media technology via the Dogme 95 project, which nodded to some "unfinished" debates of the past. This return to the past operates as a means of rethinking aspects of interactive cinematic activity in a different context, that is, examining the ways that the medium can give rise to connections that derive from the dialectic between the act of filming and the filmed material/social reality. Before proceeding to a discussion of Dogme 95, it would be useful to consider an unfinished experimental project initiated by von Trier and Vørsel titled *Dimension*. This experiment prefigures some of the major realist aims of the Dogme project, such as the connection between realism and the accident and mainly Dogme's interest in the intrusion of chance aspects of reality into the narrative. The project was ignited by an interest in filming the historical changeable European environment and observing the temporal transitions and their mark on the European landscape, as well as on certain individuals. According to the original plan, the filmmakers would start shooting from 1991 until 2024 with a plan for a premiere on April 30, 2024. The film was not tied up to a script; there was no dramaturgical scheme other than a very loose mock-gangster theme. Von Trier and Vørsel explained the film's objectives in a Manifesto published on October 5, 1990.

> Our idea is to make a feature film, with the march of time as its all-prevailing undercurrent. A film that not only presents, in "documentary" form, the march of time as inherent to the action it decorates, but also as a suspense-creating element—"the pursuer of all living things". In order to visualize the march of time in the actors and their surroundings as concretely as possible—that is to say, without the aid of the medium's characteristic use of illusory effects—we have decided upon a production time of about 30 years with premiere in 2024. In other words, we intend to concentrate a span of about 30 years into a feature film of about 100 minutes (the present normal length) and produce a good 3 minutes of effective running time per annum. As to how people—their situation, surroundings and products—will change, and what they will change into by the year 2024, as the result of political, economic, technological, climatic, linguistic and other developments, no one, as we all know, can tell us. Nor do we know which of us will still be alive in 10, 20 or 30 years' time. (*Dimension* Manifesto, Appendix)

Dimension was left unfinished after 1997, but it is very important in order to grasp the challenge that von Trier posed toward the media and the cinematic institution via the Dogme project. In August 2010, the Danish magazine *EKKO* released a bonus DVD with Nordic short films, which included a version of the filmed material. All the scenes were put together using the raw unedited sound recordings. Among the actors who participated are some familiar faces from previous films, such as Eddie Constantine, Udo Kier, Stellan Skarsgård, Jean-Marc Barr, and Katrin Cartlidge.

Having access to this unfinished project gives us the chance to identify some of the motifs that spread through von Trier's Dogme and post-Dogme practice, such as the minimal dramaturgy, the intrusion of reality into the fiction, and his tendency to manipulate the borderline between the character as a fictional persona and as an actor. *Dimension* was meant to be a collection of nonsequitur scenes, a "European collage" that would be communicated via a pseudogangster story. The first episode is shot in Cannes in 1991 and shows the arrival of a senior gangster played by Eddie Constantine, who is received by two younger ones (Udo Kier, Jean-Marc Barr); he gives them a package, telling them in a dramatic tone that they will never meet again. But while this obscure plot line leaves the viewer perplexed in terms of dramatic understanding, the film achieves to capture spatial, temporal, and corporeal changes in a depersonalized way that puts forward the primacy of the apparatus. The following scene shot a year later in Germany sets this forth very strongly. In this passage, we see the gangster played by Eddie Constantine (who was seriously ill throughout the shooting), and the scene here is an index of the marks of time on the actor's body (figure 3.1). Constantine died a few months later and, as Peter Schepelern remarks on this scene, "Tiden har sat sine ubarmhjertige spor. Man mindes Godards påstand om, at film er at se døden i arbejde" (Time has left its ruthless mark. One is reminded of Godard's claim that a film shows death at work) (2010a, 49). Later on, in a scene shot in 1993 in Copenhagen, we see the characters played by Barr and Kier looking themselves persistently in the mirror to identify marks of time in their faces, which leads to a question that will preoccupy me in my following discussion of *The Idiots*: Are the characters' or the actors' responses captured by the camera (figure 3.2)?

Posing this question may help one understand how this way of filming demotes the primacy of the script and focuses more on the process rather than the final product. The act of filming turns into an active process of engaging in a dialogue with the very material, social, and corporeal reality, so as to develop the tension between "real" time, fictional time, and the double space between reality and fiction. In these terms, *Dimension* prefigures von Trier's Dogme practice, which merges a long-take realist tradition with an investigative attitude that generates tensions between the scripted material and

Figures 3.1 and 3.2: *Dimension* (1997).

the filmmaking process. Unless we revisit the question of realism, which needs to be rethought in the current post-photographic age, we cannot understand the historicity and the politics of the Dogme 95 movement, as well as the formal intricacy of *The Idiots*.

One of the major debates regarding realism and the cinema was brought about by the 1970s film theory which was largely influenced from Brecht's writings. Critics writing for the French journal *Cahiers du Cinéma*[1] and the British journal *Screen* considered that a materialist, anti-illusionist cinema based upon Brecht's critique of empiricism could not be reconciled with the very notion of realism introduced by André Bazin's postwar writings. This incredulity toward realism permeated the writings of numerous film commentators, such as Jean Narboni, Jean-Paul Fargier, Colin McCabe, and Stephen Heath, who opposed Bazin's theory as an uncritical appeal for reproductive realism (1986, 301; 1971, 138; 1974, 12; 1974, 125). The basis of this argument was that realism gave an illusionist view of the world, that is, a static and unchangeable one, which was not in line with Brecht's call for representations that could demonstrate the historicity of human relationships.

One important contradiction is noteworthy here. These critics conducted an exploration of a Brechtian/materialist cinema against the Hollywood paradigm, which they rejected on the grounds of being illusionist. Yet, as Thomas Elsaesser has pointed out, European Cinema has always distinguished itself from Hollywood "on the basis of its greater realism" (2009, 3). Thus, the association of realism with illusionism during the 1970s did not make a distinction between dramatic realism and realism as a filmmaking process that clings into indexicality—the material connection of representation with its referent—in order to incorporate unforeseen incidents and materials within the film's narrative.

Dramatic realism refers to the causal linkage of a sequence of events, which consist of a series of coherent psychological motivations. This emphasis on psychology as the motivating element of actions is busy portraying changes in moral and psychological attitudes and fails to show individuals as part of a larger sociopolitical frame. However, realism as a filmic process that registers physical reality and interacts with the captured environment allowing for unpredictable moments to enter a film's dramaturgy is a *modus operandi* that has marked the practice of European art cinema. Such a practice does not simply reproduce the external environment but interacts with it so as to question it. A major example is Italian Neorealism, whose fictional narratives are placed in "real" historically formed environments. Indexicality in this case complicates matters since the captured images are not simply narrative laden but are indexes of the social and historical reality of the time.

Dogme 95 constitutes a cinematic movement that holds onto a realist filmmaking process, and a study of its theoretical and formal principles may help us reevaluate some of the 1970s debates and rethink the germaneness of the very subject of realism in the current historical circumstances. A close examination of the Manifesto as a text demonstrates that Dogme's realist filmmaking method is not tantamount to pure mimesis and can assist us in placing the movement in a historical context. Dogme started as a collective of four filmmakers—Lars von Trier, Thomas Vinterberg, Søren Kragh-Jacobsen, and Kristian Levring—who shared the belief that cinema could be resuscitated by establishing certain rules and restrictions that would determine the operations of the filmmakers and their crew. The Dogme Manifesto voices some anxieties and thoughts about the future of the cinema, but the films shot under the particular rules are not characterized by formal or thematic uniformity. The rules impose certain restrictions on the filmmaking and the postproduction process, but they do not intend to produce similar types of films. One should also acknowledge that, despite the movement's collective character, the Manifesto was written solely by von Trier and Vinterberg, whose films were probably the most committed ones to the project.

Dogme's employment of rules and restrictions derives from the work of the Danish filmmaker Jørgen Leth, who was named as the "papa" of the movement by the Dogme brothers (Lundtofte 2004). Leth's filming method strived to interrogate the frontiers between reality and fiction and to employ restrictions that could lead to unplanned sequences. As he says:

> I allow chance some leeway in my films, during shootings, but often during editing, too. In various ways, I invite chance to join in the game. Rules provide

an important working principle for me. I invent rules. A new set for each film—most often with the purpose of delimiting my technical possibilities. What the camera is allowed to do, and what it is not. What the editing can do, and what it cannot. This restrictive discipline is of crucial importance to my work. It is like making mental optics with which things and events in life may be viewed in a particular way. It is a way to create order out of chaos. (Leth 2002, 3)

Leth's "anti-illusionist" practice springs from an aesthetic that engages with the filmed environment in a productive way. But most crucially, his recurring use of long-take realism was accompanied by a modernist experimentation with sound and image. Leth's reconciliation of a realist aesthetic with a metacritique of representation found its foothold in Dogme, which revisited the realist debates of the past. A closer look at the Manifesto's pronouncements can illuminate things further. In the opening paragraph, the Manifesto distinguishes itself from the 1960s and the Nouvelle Vague and dismisses the concept of the auteur cinema as "bourgeois" and states quite emphatically that "to Dogme 95 cinema is not individual" (Manifesto, Appendix).[2] Dogme presents itself as a counterstrategy to the individual film and expresses a belief in the productive potential of the new technologies, which can lead to "the ultimate democratization of cinema." The movement proposes a set of strategies that resist the illusionist filmmaking and the predictability deriving from dramaturgical clichés. The rules proposed by Dogme are location shooting, direct sound, and hand-held cameras. Furthermore, postproduction manipulation is prohibited, while genre films and the director's crediting are not allowed. Finally, the Manifesto asserts that for Dogme "the instant is more important than the whole" and the director's ultimate aim is to "force the truth out of the characters and settings."

The Manifesto itself constitutes an important piece of writing that verbalizes its concern regarding the medium's radical aspirations in the current historical circumstances. The Manifesto, as a form of writing, attaches itself to the earlier cinematic avant-gardes and their furious production of texts and pronunciations, and demonstrates an awareness of the importance of theory as a means of exploring the possibilities for the foundation of political cinema. In light of this, Brecht and political modernism can enrich our understanding of the movement and help us answer a set of questions regarding Dogme's anachronistic language and the politics of "realism." Such a reading can make us appreciate Dogme beyond the conventional perception, which sees the movement as a postmodern parody. Implicit in Dogme's rhetoric is a self-conscious engagement with the political modernist filmmaking rhetoric to the point that one senses a self-mockery of the project's originality. Illuminating is D.N. Rodowick's definition of political modernism. According to him, the movement was dedicated to the production of radical/political objects that emphasize the material aspects of their representation and assume the form of an "auto-critique" (1998, 12). Rodowick's definition refers to a variety of filmmakers, such as Eisenstein, Vertov, and Godard.

Dogme's rhetoric echoes mainly early political modernist practices, such as that of Vertov and Brecht. Both expressed their enthusiasm over the film medium and equated technology with productivity. For political modernism, questioning the dominant cinematic language was heuristic to modifying the audience's habitual spectatorship with the aim of offering them an alternative view of social reality. The troubling paradox in Dogme's case is that the political modernist rhetoric is accompanied by a call for ascetic realism and a disciplined "avant-garde." By implication, the Manifesto itself seems to go beyond the 1970s binarism—materialist versus realist cinema. The rules that advocate location shooting, direct sound, ban on extra-diegetic music, hand-held camera, and avoidance of gratuitous action clearly articulate a preference for a realist aesthetics. Yet the Manifesto's belief in the new technological means of production, the rejection of predictable dramaturgy, and the dismissal of the concept of the auteur cinema resonate with a political modernist style.

The rules imposed by Dogme are redolent of Italian Neorealism's preference for real locations rather than studio settings, unaffectionate acting, and for an aesthetics of reality that undermines the role of the script in favor of the presentation of fragments of concrete reality. As Bazin says in his discussion of Neorealism, the script and the plot of the Neorealist films are of less importance. For it is the script's adherence to an aesthetics which offers fragments of the historical reality that renders the films unique, and not their dramaturgy, which, as he explains, does not differ from "moralizing melodramas" (1971, 21). Bazin's reading of Neorealism as a movement that undermines the role of the script for the fragments of concrete reality, as well as his conviction that the Neorealist aesthetics leads to the disappearance of dramaturgy, is key to illuminating Dogme's reconciliation of a raw realist aesthetics with an anti-illusionist one.

The anti-illusionist rhetoric is the outcome of Dogme's rejection of predictable dramaturgical tricks and its preference for the "instant rather than the whole." These rules foreground the movement's interest in an episodic, paratactic style, in which each scene does not necessarily move smoothly from and toward the scenes before and after it. Furthermore, this emphasis on the "instant"— the fragment—evokes Brecht's writings on film. Brecht sees film practice as a process of compressing the dramatic process into independent scenes that do not necessarily serve dramatic ends.

> Their [the independent scenes'] sequencing and combination, arrangement and plausibility are contained only implicitly in the original film text. They obey their own principles, which are different from those of the verbal drama and distinct as well from those of pure stage mime. It is the responsibility of the film director not only formally to stage this, but also, in a certain sense, to transpose all of these indispensable things into reality. (2001, 186)

Brecht's privileging of a fragmented film form aims at focusing on the exposition of arguments and counterarguments instead of establishing dramatic situations. The camera's investigative attitude is the prerequisite for the formation of an anti-illusionist aesthetics, which is not interested in reproduction, but in the presentation of a set of contradictions. Such an emphasis on the fragment rather than the whole also serves the purpose of overcoming the bourgeois notion of art as mimesis and the perception of the artist as the creative "genius."

The devaluation of the role of the artist is part of an aesthetics concerned with assigning a more productive role to the audience. Dogme's dismissal of the auteur cinema and the rule that forbids the crediting of the director clearly recall the political modernist arguments of the past, according to which the author/director is not in a privileged position over her or his audience. From Brecht's understanding of the author as a person who produces work "from the materials of history" (Wright 1989, 17) to the Dziga Vertov group's mockery of the director's individuality, the common argument is that the value of artistic practice does not rely on the communication of an "individual vision" (Wollen 1982, 83). In Dogme's case, this devaluation of the director coincides with a technological development that leads to the "democratization of the medium."

Technology and productivity

Again, this view of technology as productivity aligns Dogme with political modernism and fashions a metacommentary on film as medium, since the movement explores counterhegemonic forms of representation.[3] Thus, the movement can be seen as a call for a productive instead of a reproductive use of the new technologies. It is this distinction between production and reproduction that clarifies the movement's opposition to the use of digital technology for the production of special effects and "cosmetics." This distinction demonstrates the movement's lack of interest in using technology as a means of reproducing a perceptually realistic dramatic cosmos by means of postproduction manipulation. Antithetically, Dogme's imposition of rules on the filmmaking and the postproduction process summarizes a will to retain the medium's indexical nature.

Herein lies the main similarity with the political modernist rhetoric and its view of technology as productivity. The heightened realism afforded by the developments in technology is seen as a motivating element in producing radical effects and renewing the audience's perception. For Brecht and political modernism, realism is grounded in the camera's ability to merge the portrayed reality with the process of copying/reproducing that reality. Brecht considered this overlapping between process and product analogous to the defamiliarizing effects he aimed to achieve in the theater. As Wolfgang Gersch explains, "Es sind zwei Dinge, die Brecht beim Film hervorhebt: die durch die optischakustische Technik mögliche dokumentarische Abbildung der Wirklichkeit und die dieses Ergebnis bedingende und vermittelnde Handlung der Apparate" (There are two things that Brecht points out in film: the potential of the documentarist depiction of reality through the optical acoustic technology and the mediating intervention of the apparatus) (1975, 79). The revolutionary potential of the medium hinges on its ability to abstract concrete images from reality and expose the process of mediation. The ultimate aim of this method is the revelation of processes of social mediation that are confounded in the everyday life.

Brecht thought that the "gestic camera" produces "realism" in the Marxist sense of the word, that is, "die Wiedergabe typischer Menschen unter typischen Umständen" (the portrayal of typical people under typical circumstances) (Engels cited in Berlau 1952, 432). His understanding of realism comes in contradistinction to what he considered as naïve naturalism, that is, "Kunstrichtung, die bei der Wiedergabe der Naturerscheinungen nach peinlichster Genauigkeit strebt, jedoch bei der pedantischen Anhäufung zufälliger Details oft alle Sinnzusammenhänge zudeckt" (the reproduction of natural appearances with fastidious accuracy, which, however, often conceals meaningful contexts by pedantically accumulating random details) (Berlau 1952, 433). In this context, the gestic camera's role is not that of the invisible observer of actions. By contrast, the camera points to the process of constructing a copy of reality and the audience is asked to coproduce and not simply to consume a dramatic narrative.

Brecht's approach toward cinema invokes the political modernist enthusiasm over the medium, which was based upon the latter's capacity to go against the notion of the individual being at the center of the world. One well-known example is Dziga Vertov's valorization of the Kino-eye (seeing through the camera) over the human eye. Vertov's argument is grounded in the premise that the Kino-eye can give the audience access to processes not visible by the human eye. Vertov's interest in capturing processes over unified drama downplays the role of the director in favor of the cameraman. A similar practice was followed by Thomas Vinterberg while shooting *Festen* (1998), since as the director of photography—Anthony Dod Mantle—recounts, "one of the odd rules was that the director should not have any artistic opinion whatsoever" (cited in *Don't Try This at Home: From Dogme to Dogville*, 2006). The cameraman, therefore, was given an unprecedented freedom vis-à-vis the shooting process. To return to Vertov, the Kinos (the cinematographers working under the principles of the Kino-eye) are primarily constructors and not artists. For Vertov, the bourgeois artistic cinema is a remnant of the "old world" and needs to be replaced by a cinematic practice based on "coolness and distrust." As he says, "Film Drama is the opium of the people" (1984, 71). The ultimate aim of the "new cinema" is the filming of the everyday life, so as to use the recorded material to educate the audiences.

The mediated reality deriving from the intervention of the camera can make the audiences discern processes not distinguishable in the empirical reality. To achieve this learning effect, Vertov denies dramaturgy and the praising of artistic individuality, proposing that "the departure from authorship" can liberate cinema from the mainstays of bourgeois aesthetic, "the poser-actor, fairy-tale script, those costly toys-sets, and the director high-priest" (1984, 71). Vertov's downplaying of dramaturgy is predicated upon a preference for an aesthetics that refuses to dissociate the recorded objects by the very process of recording itself. The crucial aspect of the learning effects he wants to achieve lies in the self-reflexive movement of the camera, in which the copy and the original overlap with each other, so as to bring to the surface the hidden aspects of reality. Vertov describes this process as "filming life unawares," in which people are captured by the camera lens unaware of being filmed (1984, 41). The cameraman observes people's activities without impeding them. Vertov's *modus operandi* establishes a linkage of shots deriving from the ontological authenticity of the images with dynamic montage sequences that aim at developing constructive effects.

The liberated camera advocated by Vertov is equivalent to Brecht's valorization of the "gestic camera," whose role is explorative and revelatory. These approaches to filmmaking—that is, the privileging of the machine, the camera, over the director's individuality and over dramaturgy—summarize the political modernist idea that the emergence of cinema needs to establish a redefinition of art. Brecht thought the same, and his dissatisfaction with the film medium derived from the industry's understanding of the cinema solely as a dramatic medium. Dominant cinema's employment of character point-of-view shots and its commitment to the creation of dramatic effects led the audience to identify with the camera, an effect totally irreconcilable with Brecht's perception of it as a sociologist. This identification with the camera provided the audience with finished objects, without giving them access to the process by which the objects were produced. The result is that the camera loses its performative/productive function, and the very ideas of artistic individuality and dramaturgy, which the new medium wished to oppose, are perpetuated.

For Brecht, these tendencies failed to change the medium of their own articulation, and here it is important to recall his argument that it is not enough to produce for a medium but to change it too. Walter Benjamin has captured the intent of this argument in an essay hugely inspired by Brecht, in which the author is equated with a producer. As Benjamin explains, Brecht introduced the term *Umfunktionierung* (refunctioning) to describe "certain works that are not so much intended to represent individual experiences (to have the character of finished works), as they are aimed at transforming certain existing institutes and institutions" (1998, 93). Benjamin expands Brecht's argument and explains that technical progress can become the basis for political progress because the artist can shift his or her attention from the products (the finished works) to the very means of production. In this context, the work of the author/producer becomes a model of "an improved apparatus," which familiarizes the public with the very production process and turns the readers or spectators into collaborators.

Analogously, Dogme equates technological progress with a film practice that questions the cinematic institution and the understanding of filmmaking as an individual expression. This faith in technological development clearly references the political modernist axiom that emphasis should not be placed solely on the product but on the very means of production too. Von Trier has made that quite clear in an interview given after the completion of *The Idiots*, in which he explains that the new technologies give the filmmakers a chance to focus on the very filmic process, and to rethink the cinematic rules.

> Film has become very much like magic tricks—you're not supposed to know how it's done, which is also very old-fashioned, especially if you think about the new techniques, the new cameras, and how everybody can produce their own films, which I think is fantastic. So it's about time there was a real debate. Nobody has really talked about film form or film content, not for many, many years, and the arrival of these techniques makes it very good time to have that discussion. (cited in Kelly 2000, 144)

The small cameras that have emerged out of the digital revolution offer filmmakers the opportunity to shoot scenes in long-takes without worrying about the price of film stock. Von Trier suggests that these cameras can downplay precision in favor of indeterminacy. The director is deprived of absolute control and the final cut contains the filmmaking process and the product at the same time. This formulation resonates with the Bazinian preference for long-take cinematography and with Brecht's call for a self-reflexive and investigative camera movement. In both tendencies, knowledge about the world and reality is associated with the knowledge about the process of capturing that reality on screen.

The point of rupture between von Trier and the aforementioned modernist and realist rhetoric is that the very process of exploration is valorized over any concrete educative effects. According to von Trier, there are two different ways of working with the camera: framing and pointing. The framing process involves a passion for perfectionism and absolute control, whereas the pointing one privileges realism and loss of control (cited in Schepelern 2005b, 11). Certainly, this view of realism has little to do with dramaturgical and compositional consistency. By contrast, the pointing process opens itself to the contingent and encourages the director to discover things from the surroundings instead of imposing his or her ideas to the audience. Von Trier's dialectical understanding of the medium's investigative potential can be seen in the following quotation. "Truth is about searching an area in order to find something, but if you already knew beforehand what you're looking for, then it is manipulation. Maybe truth is finding something you're not looking for" (cited in Knudsen 2003, 122). Von Trier's comments summarize Dogme's call for an ascetic aesthetics that aims at breaking the conventional way of filmmaking and film-viewing. The director and the audience have to adopt a more interrogative/productive attitude toward the camera's engagement with the concrete reality. On this basis, Dogme's idea of unveiling the truth does not imply a reductionist revelation of preexisting ideas, but the restoration of responses of astonishment to the processes of recording and perceiving reality. Evidently, all these ideas are not new and one senses that Dogme theatricalizes its own belatedness.

This view of technology as productivity recalls the political modernist anxiety regarding the use of technological development in a revolutionary rather than a reproductive way. Access to technology was seen as a prerequisite for motivating political change. In Brecht's words, "The technology that triumphs here, and appears to be condemned to nothing more than guaranteeing the profits of some dinosaurs and thus of barbarism, can achieve very different things in proper hands" (2001, 195). Brecht's interest in using technology for the production of radical effects is symptomatic of his forward-looking politics, which sees technology as the synonym of change. Technology signifies the new and heralds the coming of the new society, which will emerge out of the old one. The contradiction that arises with respect to Dogme lies in the fact that the movement appeared in a historical moment when there is no such thing as a tangible political alternative to accompany the productive use of the new technologies.

The question that arises then is why Dogme returns to the past to "rescue" cinema from its "decadence." My proposition is that Dogme's employment of a political modernist rhetoric, the privileging of austerity, and the movement's enigmatic commitment to truth can be seen as a desire for orientation in a historical period in which the experience of the world is media constructed. I want to illuminate this point in reference to two later Manifestoes written by von Trier, very much inspired by the Dogme one. I am talking about the Defocus Manifesto (2000) (published prior to the film he codirected with Leth—*The Five Obstructions*) and the Dogumentary one (2002). While the former one manifests its commitment to a filmic process that is dedicated to the investigation of something between fact and fiction, the latter one is concerned with the exploration of a documentary form that goes beyond the established "documentary and television reality" (Dogumentary, Appendix). Moreover, the point of convergence between these two Manifestoes and the Dogme one is a filmmaking process, in which technology is not "the goal itself." All these Manifestoes valorize the process over the finished product and set as a prerequisite the use of technology as a means of discovering things instead of achieving dramatic perfection. Von Trier argues in the Defocus Manifesto that instead of reducing everything to plot, "the ultimate challenge of the future— to see without looking: to defocus!" (Defocus, Appendix). This quotation synopsizes an interest in a film language that is not keen on the mere duplication of a story. It is rather a call for a practice that encourages the registration of unforeseen incidents and materials not firmly controlled by the film's narrative and the director.

One needs to highlight that there is a robust antirepresentationalism in this interest in engaging with the material filmed reality with the purpose of avoiding the conventions of the preplanned filmmaking. Endemic to this idea is an interest in using technology at the service of a camera work concerned with the search for the object and not with the creation of a unified locus dramaticus. This is evocative of the modernist critical theory debates that gain new potency in the current context of the digital revolution. Walter Benjamin in the 1930s forewarned that a productive use of the medium needs to sidestep aesthetic conventions that produce "anestheticization" and paralyze the individual's social agency. Benjamin's Brechtian critique of the medium advances the thesis that technology can be used in productive ways under the stipulation that it provides an "empowering" relation to the external social milieu. For Benjamin, this relies on film's ability to double social interactions and "de-familiarize them" as long as technology is not used as fetish (Buck-Morss 1992, 17; Hansen 2012, 156). This returns us back to the core issue of the primacy of the apparatus and its ability to register material not firmly regulated by human intervention. Alexander Kluge describes this as "blind-shooting" in the sense that the filmmaker allows the apparatus to connect with the object of representation without imposing her or his ideas (Koutsourakis 2011, 224).

Currently, the employment of digital technology for the production of spectacular effects has led to a separation of the represented objects from any material social context. Lev Manovich observes that cinema has returned to the "pre-cinematic practices of the nineteenth century" and is no longer an indexical medium, but "a sub-genre of painting" (2001, 295). This development valorizes human intervention and the mastering of every single pixel to the detriment of the apparatus' capacity to capture the contingent. But what merits more attention is that the massive production of Hollywood films without indexical reference heralds a filmmaking practice devoid of social reference. This separation of art from life can have adversary effects, and pertinent here is Elsaesser's reference to *Avatar* (2009) viewers suffering from depression after returning back to a social reality that seemed mundane compared to the virtual and aestheticized environment of Cameron's film (2011, 252). Consequently, in a historical period in which the simulations of the real coexist with the reality we experience, the restoration of the investigative aspect of the medium and of its dialogue with the material reality is of political importance.

The aforementioned comments elucidate Dogme's anachronism, which can be strengthened with reference to Laura Mulvey's analysis of cinema's role in a new technological age. Mulvey explains that a prospective dialogue between "the old celluloid cinema of the past" and the new digital technologies can make us return to the old left visions and the modernist aspirations. Through a historical study of the medium and its relation to political radicalism, Mulvey describes the modernist belief in cinema coming together with a belief in political change. The medium's evolution became tantamount to the Marxist belief in progress and the view of time as an evolutionary process of historical advancement toward a new society. This belief in the medium's radical aspirations terminated during the 1980s with the appearance of the neo-right, which "captured the dynamic of the new," a gesture that demonstrates its differentiation from the conservative right, which used to act as the safeguard of the past. Mulvey sees that as the crisis of Marxism, which, after the historical defeat of socialism, is forced to seek progress into the past.

> The problem of fissure, gap, loss of continuity faces the left. Its failed aspiration becomes another corollary to the contemporary sense of separation between "now" and "then." This imaginary of left history needs to be challenged, in the first instance by returning to question the significance of the modernity and left politics that seem to have got lost on the other side—the "before," the "then." Now that the idea of progress is relegated to the past, it may be time to look further back, into what is now history, the past of modernity and the radical aspiration. (2004, 151)

Mulvey proposes that cinema is faced with the same challenge. Returning to past cinematic practices and the political modernist debates can help the medium appropriate the revolutionary potential of digital technology to radical ends. The prerequisite for revolutionizing technology is to rethink its function and to go beyond its ability to simulate.

Digital imaging offers the possibility of simulating images of convincing realism, whose lack of reference fails to give the audience access to the process of their own making. This lack of indexical reference annuls one of the political modernist objectives, what Brecht defines as the moment in which the audience recognizes itself in the film's reality and becomes conscious of the social reality as a construct (Silberman 2009, 242). In opposition to the use of technology as simulation, Dogme rejects accounts of the digital that associate it with figuration/painting and nonindexicality and holds onto indexicality as a means of registering contingency and the plurality of the real. Correspondingly, Dogme's dialogue with the past is motivated by a will to reinstate the revolutionary aspect of the medium, which does not lie in the construction of reality effects, but in the very questioning and rethinking of the filmmaking and film-viewing process.

The Idiots—"Performant" function and performative camera

Integrally connected to Dogme's anachronism is a valorization of the process over the finished product. Exemplary from this point of view is von Trier's film *The Idiots,* which reduces the narrative to the bodies of the actors and commits itself to the filmability of the performative contingent. This formal austerity along with the film's thematic emphasis on performance creates a tension between the presence of the actors and the embodiment of their roles. The film's back-to-basics form invites the audience to question the ways dramaturgy shapes one's understanding of the "real," and the whole idea of "reality" itself.

The Idiots was the second film shot according to the Dogme rules, the first being Thomas Vinterberg's *Festen.* The script was written in four days and retains a simplicity that is associated with von Trier's understanding of the story line as a material for exploration. The film tells the story of a group of young people who pretend to be mentally disabled and perform "idiotic" happenings in public spaces. Their provocative performances intend to challenge middle-class values and conformity. The film starts *in medias res*, showing Karen (Bodil Jørgesen), a working-class woman, enjoying herself at a fair. This is followed by a scene in an expensive restaurant, where she meets up some people who pretend to be mentally handicapped, in order to challenge the clientele and avoid paying their bill. When Stoffer (Jens Albinus), the leader of the group, approaches her performing the idiot, Karen spontaneously follows them and eventually becomes part of the collective.

The group inhabits an old villa in Søllerød, a wealthy suburban town outside Copenhagen, which belongs to Stoffer's uncle. Despite the collective character of the project, Stoffer seems to be the leader of the idiots and the one who challenges them to go beyond their limits. At times, he reproaches them when he feels that their performances are not genuine and challenges them to explore their "inner idiot." Apart from Karen, all of them have the chance to go back to their everyday lives, and, in the course of the narrative, it can be seen that most of them are well-functioning and career-focused individuals. The group disintegrates when they realize that the whole project cannot be reconciled with their careers and their private lives. In a last attempt to save the group's integrity, Stoffer challenges them to go over their limits and "spass" in front of their families and their career environments, an effort that comes to naught.[4] Surprisingly, Karen, the only person within the group to explicitly dispute the objectives of the project, decides to "spass" facing her family. We come to realize that she has recently lost her child and her appearance at the film's beginning, in terms of the story order of the film's fabula, had directly followed her disappearance following the child's funeral.

The story in the film is an epiphenomenon; what merits more consideration is the ways that form complicates the boundaries between the actors performing their roles, the characters performing an "idiotic identity," and the moments when the film hovers between dramatizing a story and the process of its own making. There is certainly a dialogue between von Trier's Dogme practice and performance art, and evidence of this connection is given in a documentary directed by Jesper Jargil, in which he follows von Trier's conceptual project *Psychomobile 1—The World Clock*. The project started a few months after the publication of the Dogme Manifesto and is a combination of cinema, performance, and installation art. A mobile camera filmed images of an ant colony in New Mexico and the images were broadcasted live in the Art Society Building in Copenhagen. The images triggered light changes on a stage which consisted of nineteen rooms and fifty-three actors. Changes in the light were accompanied by changes in the disposition of the actors/characters. The actors' responses were pretty much improvised given that they did not have a script to memorize and they were only given a schematic description of their characters' traits by von Trier. At times, von Trier's collaborator—Morten Arnfred— intervened and asked them to justify their characters and their decisions, while the distinctions between actors and characters eventually collapsed.

This emphasis on performance as an object of investigation infiltrates *The Idiots* as well, as the film stresses its "performant" function over the storytelling one. My understanding of the term "performant" function is informed both by film and theater studies. In cinema, the medium's "performant" function pertains to a deictic style favored by Brecht and described as the "presentational style of early films" by Miriam Bratu Hansen (2012, 80). This "presentational" style is antithetical to the classical cinema's representation of a closed diegetic cosmos filled with psychologically motivated characters. Film in these terms is understood as *Spiel* (play) and performance and not as a cohesive dramatic narrative (Miriam Bratu Hansen 2012, 86). In theater studies, Jean Alter singles out the difference between the "referential" and the "performant" function of theater. The first one aims at the communicating of signs and the transmission of information, while the "performant one" stresses the event itself and the physical aspect of it (1990, 32). These arguments signal an important point in approaching the film. *The Idiots'* formal organization as *Spiel* refers to a process of doing and undoing the narrative, which blurs the boundaries between filmic and nonfilmic reality, allowing for certain unpredictable and antisystematic moments to enter the film's universe. The "performant" function of the film is also stressed by a shooting style—to which I shall return—according to which technology adapts to the acting and not the other way around. The effect is an unconventional dramaturgy, which constantly defers unveiling Karen's enigma and places emphasis on the group and its performances. As von Trier stated during the shooting of the film, "This is the kind of film they teach you not to do in a film school; because the point is not revealed until the end. And when it is, we need a violent reaction" (cited in *De Ydmygede*: 1998).

This privileging of the "performant" over the storytelling function indicates a different understanding of dramaturgy, according to which the film is not a stable object that communicates a certain amount of information to the audience. This *modus operandi* downplays dramatic realism in favor of a process that places emphasis on the act of quotation as a means of estrangement. The film dramatizes a story and the process of its own making and activates an acting style in which the characters are in-between (in and out of character), while the story is based upon the characters' performing of other characters— the idiots. Formally and thematically, the film brings together the represented actions and the very act of representation, and, as Anne Jerslev rightly remarks, it complicates the very ideas of "the real" and "the performative" (2002, 56). But while Jerslev understands this complication as an avenue of creating emotional identification with the characters, what needs to be underscored is the ways that the object exposes the performativity of its performance to the detriment of plot.

A starting point for exploring the film's privileging of its "performant" function is von Trier's employment of the camera. Peter Schepelern explains that Dogme 95 constitutes a milestone in von Trier's career, due to the radical break with his past work that paid detailed attention to the visual compositions. This attention to detail denied the films from any great measure of spontaneity and aimed at predetermining every movement on the part of the actors. For instance,

Europa's (1991) shooting was based on a "visual storyboard" that provided a detailed description of the optical connections between the scenes. According to Schepelern, after Dogme von Trier employs the camera in ways that the director is deprived of absolute control (2000a, 233). In a way, the release of the Dogme Manifesto coincides with von Trier's different approach to filmmaking that shows a preference for a less stylized acting, which incorporates filmic and extra-filmic responses.

The first film that initiated the new *modus operandi* was *Breaking the Waves*. This movie drew upon some of the Dogme rules, such as the handheld camera, location shooting, and direct sound. Then again, the manipulation of melodrama, the use of optical filters, and the nondiegetic music are some traits that prevent the film from being classified as a Dogme one. The crucial aspect of the film was the preference for long-takes and its disregard for conventional editing. According to the cinematographer, Robby Müller, the actors were not aware of whether they would be in the shot or not. At the same time, von Trier's preference for protecting the spontaneity of the performances made him skip detailed rehearsals and use, in many cases, the first takes so as to avoid artificiality. This way of working led to an acting style that foregrounded the very act of performing rather than a psychological impersonation of the roles. As Müller explains:

> Lars wanted to have this Cinema Scope feeling because it adds an extra dimension to people when you are so close to them—studying them in the center of your frame, as you would when you are already talking talk to them. But Lars wanted to get rid of the compositions you usually see in the widescreen movies. There was to be no extra stuff—only the actors. And that was very exciting, because it forced us to rediscover looking at things innocently. (cited in Oppenheimer 1996, 18)

The process described by Müller does not favor the enactment of a coherent, psychologically complex character but the production of *Gestus,* which exploits the split relationship between the actor as an individual and the personification of her or his role. Therefore, the actors do not simply concentrate upon emoting specific reactions that justify the characters. Quite the opposite, they are captured in the process of embodying their roles and reflecting on them. Reflecting on *Breaking the Waves*, von Trier suggested that this "liberated acting" derived from the fact that the actors were caught unawares and given a freedom of movement without having to follow a specific plan (Oppenheimer 1996, 19).

Katrin Cartlidge (Dodo McNeill in the film) explained that von Trier encouraged the actors to make mistakes, allowing them a more productive participation in the filmmaking process. Put simply, dramatic perfection was discarded in favor of a borderline acting that benefited from gestures/responses that confused the boundaries between acting and nonacting. As she said, "Lars wanted the technical machinery of the film to be as light as a feather" (cited in *Tranceformer: A Portrait of Lars von Trier*: 1997). The latter comment along with the whole process of filming employed in *Breaking the Waves* epitomize in a laconic way one of the basic interests of Dogme, that is, that technology needs to adapt to the acting and not the other way around. Accordingly, the role of the script is reassessed, since the director and his crew use it as material for investigation rather than reproducing it faithfully on screen.

As such, the acting style produces an effect of interruption and not a seamless reflection of responses to the stimuli. When I asked von Trier whether this shooting style makes the actors act out of character, he responded that challenging the borderline between the character and the actor is one of his central aims (Interview, Appendix). The connection with Brecht is more than apparent. Brecht argued in favor of an acting method that would turn the actor into a demonstrator and an observer at the same time. This formula compels the audience to assess the various fragments and reconcile them with the preceding and the following ones. Hence, this acting style establishes an interruption of action and character and negates steady representational development. The aim is to bring to the surface the contradictions that are smoothed over within a framework of representation based upon imitation. As a result, the audience, like the actors, is drawn inside the story and pushed away into a critical appreciation at the same time.

For Brecht, this method aimed at the production of concrete and calculating *Gestus* that would create contradictions deriving from the actors' showing of themselves and the event at the same time. On the contrary, von Trier's valorization of the actor's relative autonomy to create more than what lies in the script is related to a whole shift from acting to performance, which demarcates the Brechtian from the post-Brechtian. Whereas orthodox Brechtian aesthetics strived to externalize the characters' actions and place them in a social context, post-Brechtian performance-based practice prioritizes the very act of "showing" over the represented object, since the produced material does not provide a "reference system" offered in orthodox Brechtian practices. As David Barnett says, there is still a link between the individual and society, but performances "are offered as signs of behaviours" (2011b, 346). To connect this point with von

Trier, it is important to discuss his camera work. His employment of the handheld camera adds a sense of mobility, which changes the relationship between actor and director along with that of actor and character, since the final image is the outcome of material not necessarily premeditated. The effect is that the entire process generates variations from the script that transcend distinctions between staged and "real" events.

Von Trier's use of the handheld camera poses questions regarding the script and its performance, questions that deny the unproblematic fusion of the two elements within the film. Jesper Jargil's behind-the-scenes documentary *The Humiliated* (*De Ydmygede*, 1999) has captured this tension quite eloquently. The documentary shows that von Trier avoided very detailed rehearsals for the majority of the scenes. Rehearsals were replaced by collective discussions that aimed at investigating how the characters and their "idiotic happenings" could be presented in a more plausible way. These discussions transmit a theater ensemble feeling, which is reminiscent of theater groups of the 1960s, such as The Living Theatre and The Open Theatre. Furthermore, Jargil's documentary shows that despite some moments that required a certain degree of perfection (for instance, the last scene in Karen's house), von Trier preferred to keep shots that incorporated moments not necessarily scripted, an approach that is compatible with his perception of the handheld camera as a productive rather than a reproductive tool. At one point in the documentary, we hear von Trier's voice referring to a scene that Stoffer explodes into a verbal tirade against a member of the local council who tries to entice them with money provided that the group abandons the area. As he says:

> It is interesting that there are so many improvisations. Everything we filmed today are far from the original idea and the script. Basically these are things the actors could have done. They lead up to something and they don't follow it up for some reason. (cited in *De Ydmygede*)

One of the reasons why von Trier's practice privileges improvisations over the detailed script is that he uses the hand-held camera in a way that neither the director nor the actors know in advance where the camera movement starts and where it ends. Von Trier justifies his fondness for using hand-held cameras (he occasionally operates them himself) on the grounds that "a hand-held camera tells you more, while a camera on the tripod tells you less. A hand-held camera is like hand-writing" (Interview, Appendix). The captured material elides fiction with a reflection on the process of its construction.

Von Trier's technique relies on the filming of long scenes that are not overrehearsed, and this grants the actors a certain degree of performative freedom. Consequently, the camera becomes a provocateur and not simply an apparatus that records dramatic actions. This is a principle that characterizes the films of the godfather of Dogme—Jørgen Leth—as well as of American Independent filmmakers, such as John Cassavetes and Shirley Clarke. Particularly, Leth's approach to filmmaking was inspired by a will to reinstate an amateurish approach to reality, so as to keep away from the conventions of documentary and fiction filmmaking. Leth took advantage of the impoverished conditions of his films' production and merged documentary with fiction using the camera as a provocateur of gestures and responses that blur the boundaries between performance and real life. For Leth, openness to the filmed "accident" is a key to a new cinematic language which revolts against the moralizing conventionality and the "suffocating professionalism" of mainstream filmmakers (Leth 2009). In his films, his camera work is not concerned solely with the reproduction of actions, but is interested in the dialectic between the captured actions and the material produced by the camera itself. This mobility contributes to an uneven representational aesthetics that demonstrates the camera's ability to construct an image of the real. The notion of the camera as a provocateur of actions is key to our understanding of von Trier's *modus operandi* in *The Idiots*. The camera is used as a performative tool that foregrounds the performance of the actors and highlights the process of transforming the profilmic body into represented material.

Interrupting the narrative

The Idiots' privileging of the film's "performant" function is made evident by the interview sequences that offer contradictory and non-clarifying evidence regarding the causal sequence of events. The film's narrative flow is interrupted by interview sequences with the characters, which are conducted by von Trier and aim to clarify the past events. Von Trier remains offscreen, and it is mainly the Danish audience and perhaps some art-house cinéphiles that can clearly understand the identity of the person conducting the questions. The reason is that von Trier enjoys a celebrity status in Denmark and his voice can be easily distinguished by the Danish audience. Thus, the metaeffect is much more obvious for those who can recognize him as the man behind the camera. However, the fact that an interviewer poses questions regarding the value of the project produces ruptures in the film's linearity. These ruptures clearly complicate the boundaries between the diegetic and the metadiegetic universe.

The only characters that do not appear during the interview sequences are Stoffer and Karen. The first interruption of the narrative takes place straight after Karen's joining the group at the beginning of the film. Jeppe (Nikolaj Lie Kaas), Henrik (Troels Lyby), Josephine (Louise Mieritz), and Ped (Henrik Prip) comment on Karen and the reason that led her to become a member of the idiots. What is important here is that this first interruption does not follow the question-and-answer format, and one cannot ascertain whether the characters are being interviewed or whether they address the audience reflecting on their past. The effect is very disorientating given that the chronological unfolding of actions is suddenly broken down by a shift in time and space.

During this interview break, all characters set out Karen's story as an enigma and offer contradictory responses that complicate, instead of clarifying, the story line. The interviewed individuals succeed one another in a frenetic way, which makes narrative orientation problematic. They are the only sequences in the film where von Trier employs intense montage successions. In the first interview, none of the characters manages to establish a unanimous agreement over Karen's participation in the group.

JEPPE: Karen was the last to join the group.
HENRIK: She was really nice. It wasn't that. Karen was really nice, but she was also … I think that she'd have joined everything.
JOSEPHINE: I don't know how she came to the factory but she did. I don't know. I don't know what she thought.
PED: She was right when she said "you're poking fun". Yes, we were poking fun.

Despite the fact that the interviews are seemingly interested in establishing a causal explanation of the whole project, their function in the narrative becomes more complicating. This disorientation can be attributed to the fact that the sequences appear randomly and without having a cause-and-effect linkage with the preceding episodes. The second interview sequence, for instance, comes after a scene in Stoffer's house, in which the group reflects on their previous idiotic happening. The scene is suddenly cut and the temporality changes. The location is now Axel's (Knud Romer Jørgensen) flat. Von Trier's voice is heard in the background, asking him to give a quick summary of the project. Axel's response is followed by von Trier's point that he has already heard seventeen different versions that fail to give a clear explanation of their motivations. Axel's failure to give a concrete answer is followed by Katrine's (Anne-Grethe Bjarup Riis) argument that the whole project was initiated by Stoffer, a statement that denies his version. Jeppe, the next to be interviewed, asserts, "It was my idea ... But it was Stoffer who wanted to do something about it." Von Trier responds ironically, "That's funny. None of the others say it was your idea. How come? None of them!" The last person to be interviewed in this sequence is Susanne (Anne Louise Hassing), who states that Stoffer took the whole thing seriously, but it was nothing but a game.

The interviews bring to the surface the film's dialogue with itself about its own scope and efficacy. Their intervention within the narrative operates as a linkage of the episodes that constitute the film's loose dramaturgy. The contradictory answers given by the characters problematize the audience's quest for a diegetic motivation of the actions. Furthermore, it is important to note that these interviews break the chronological unity of the narrative and make the audience step out of the story and reflect on it. Their function in the film is problematic because they hover between being part of the story and a reflection on it. Their unclear position in the narrative is heightened by the fact that the interviewer's (von Trier's) position in the diegetic world is quite ambiguous. We can hear his voice but he is in-between; that is, he hovers between being part of the diegesis and an external agent too.

Yet there are moments that these sequences become argumentative; that is, they aim at modifying or undermining the originality of the project or the characters' reliability. One prime example can be seen in the sixth interview break, in which von Trier asks Axel, if he holds some anti-middle-class ideas. Axel responds positively.

INTERVIEWER: Katrine says that you held some very anti-middle-class views
                or ideologies.
AXEL: I do. (Plays with his baby). How are you darling?
INTERVIEWER: Based on what? Your ideologies?
AXEL: Anti-middle-class ideologies?
INTERVIEWER: Yes.
AXEL: Mainly that there is something more than meaningfulness and
                purposefulness.
INTERVIEWER: Oh! She made it sound as something that has to do with family.

Axel's response to the first question is problematized by the image that follows, which shows him embracing his little child in a middle-class flat. Here the scene operates as an ironic commentary. The scene also prepares the ground for the subsequent one, in which Katrine visits Axel at his professional environment in order to embarrass him and challenge his antibourgeois rhetoric.

Consequently, the narrative interruptions produced by the interviews tighten the film's loose narrative structure, which is based on a repetitive pattern. We see the characters preparing to embark on their idiotic provocations, their ensuing idiotic happenings, and their discussions/reflections on them. By systematically interrupting the narrative, the interviews aim at stimulating the audience's critical alertness. Their role is not to soothe and confirm but to challenge the viewers' conventional forms of perception. This emphasis on interruption serves the role of combining analysis and demonstration. The actions are interrupted, the viewer can notice the episodic format of the film's structure, and she or he can step back and reflect on the represented material. This structure can be aptly characterized as Brechtian. For Brecht, interruptions constitute an essential aspect of his work in theater and film. In theater, he argued for a knotting of the episodes in a way that could be distinguished by the audience. As he explained, such a structure could provoke different responses that would not lead to a seamless linking of different materials. The audience would be forced to acquire "a disconcerting look," which would develop their analytical skills (1964, 201). Similarly, his cinematic work strived for the breaking of "total visibility," in order to deconstruct the portrayed incidents and reveal the social conditions of their construction. Indicative of this practice is the repeatable biking sequence in *Kuhle Wampe*, which places the individual story in a historical context.

The interruptions have a bearing on the acting as well, which is concerned with the act of demonstrating and analyzing specific incidents and actions. Walter Benjamin, in his discussion of the role of the narrative interruptions in Brecht's work, explains that this methodology shifts the focus from the unfolding of the actions to a representation of the conditions that lead the characters to acquire certain attitudes (1998, 18). Accordingly, the audience's capacity for identification with the characters is undermined and they are asked to seek the meaning beneath the surface of the actions. In a like fashion, the breaks caused by the interviews in *The Idiots* give the audience time to think and reflect on the portrayed actions. This interruptive strategy has become commonplace in mainstream filmmaking and even in television advertising, but there is a major difference. In Hollywood and in advertising, this strategy creates an incoherence that does not strive for narrative complexity. Incoherence in these paradigms operates as a means of minimizing ambiguity, and, as Geoff King brilliantly expounds, incoherence in mainstream cinema is "a symptom of offering something to everyone" (King 2000, 105). In other words, the looseness of contemporary Hollywood narratives and their manipulation of interruptive techniques is a means of facilitating the consumption of the product and not of reflecting on the depicted reality. This simple comparison provides the impetus to understand how the interview sequences in *The Idiots* obfuscate rather than simplify the narrative. They merge various viewpoints on the whole project, calling into question a direct correspondence between actions and reality. They also disrupt the audience's desire for action and voyeuristic consumption of the material, compelling us rather forcibly to respond, rather than consume a "message." Therefore, these narrative interruptions value the "non-reproductive" aspects of the medium, implying that film-viewing is an interactive and playful process and not one based on exchange value. They are ipso facto consistent with Trier's metareflection on film as medium, proposing a more productive and playful spectatorship in line with Brecht's idea that "unsere Fähigkeit des Erzeugens macht uns Vergnügen" (our ability to produce gives us pleasure in itself) (*Schriften* 7, 289).

It is also noteworthy that the interviews problematize the relationship between actors and characters. This practice recalls analogous deconstructionist devices on the part of other European directors. Ingmar Bergman in *Passion* (*En Passion*, 1969) and in *Autumn Sonata* (*Höstsonaten*, 1978) employed similar techniques that unsettled the narrative. His aim was to bring extra-diegetic material stemming from interviews with his actors, who offered their hermeneutical approach toward the characters they performed. Similarly, Jean-Luc Godard has employed parallel tropes in films, such as *Masculin Féminin* (1966), so as to foreground a different type of filmmaking, which he loosely described as "survey film." Godard's practice combines fictional material with a cinema direct reportage that aimed at freeing film narrative from a conventional reliance on plot (Haycock 1990, 64). Von Trier goes beyond these practices and his interview sequences have a degree of novelty. For instance, in Bergman's case, the interviews are clearly distinguished from the rest of the narrative. They operate as a "break in the diegesis" but this break marks itself clearly from the fictional narrative. In Godard, the interviews are conducted by the main character and they are part of the story. What renders von Trier's interview sequences innovative is the fact that their placing in *The Idiots*' narrative plays a dual role; that is, they are part of the narrative and combine material that exceeds it. In a way, these sequences are self-critical explorations of *The Idiots* project on the part of the filmmaker and the cast. When asked about their placement in the film, von Trier outlined their defamiliarizing effect and explained that they were added after the completion of the main filming, because they were not scripted.

They [the interviews] were completely improvised. The actors answer for their characters, and at the same time they defend their characters. You can't write those sorts of answers beforehand, because they'd look false and constructed at once. The breaks caused by the interviews have a kind of a distancing effect. But they are also an affirmation. This whole idea of a few people running round playing as being idiots gained a whole other significance because of the interviews. If the members of the cast could sit down afterwards and talk about their experiences, then it must have meant something to them. And that validates the interviews, as well as giving impetus to the plot and the film as a whole. (cited in Björkman 2003, 214)

The fact that the interviews were shot long after the completion of the main film adds to the film a semidocumentary aesthetics about its own making, since the actors are not in the position of retaining a continuity of character.

Furthermore, their improvisatory aspect allowed for the intrusion of moments, in which the boundaries between characters and actors collapse. This is clearly confirmed in all these sequences, in which the characters are separated from their previous roles as idiots, and the actors are somewhat separated from their fictional roles. As it has been evidenced in an interview with Anne Louise Hassing, von Trier gave the impression that he addressed himself to the actors rather than the characters, a choice that created confusion for the performers involved in these scenes (cited in Oxholm and Nielsen 2000, 28). The achievement of these split identifications through the interviews shifts the interest from the finished object and draws the audience's attention to the dialectical interplay between the object and its performance, that is, its interpretation. Consequently, these interruptions do not simply question the group or the characters' motives, but they deny the authority of a finished object, opening the preceding and the ensuing scenes to the audience's hermeneutical activity. Reflecting on the film's practice, the interviews defy an unsophisticated understanding of "truth" and suggest that one can reach "truth" by means of experimentation.

Performance as form

The film's pseudo-documentary form accumulates three different representational levels: the reality of the story line, the reality of the characters, who pretend to be mentally disabled, and the reality of the movie's filmmaking process. Such a complex narrative structure deprives the audience of a psychological in-depth access to the characters, since for the most part the film's dramaturgy is concerned with the performing of a nonauthentic identity. In effect, the performing of the performance becomes the film's thematic interest and the prolonged scenes of "spassing" are shorn of a clear dramatic dimension or an illustration of the characters' psychological state.

What renders these scenes more problematic is the combination of a realist/long-take cinematography with an acting style, according to which the actors are not asked to deliver for the camera. As von Trier says reflecting on the film's shooting, "the handheld camera follows the actors, which allows them to concentrate on acting with each other, and not acting towards a big monster of a camera" (cited in Simons 2007, 48). This method dates back to the practice of the Danish filmmaker Henning Carlsen, who gave his actors a freedom of expression and asked them not to think of the camera while shooting *Hunger* (*Sult*, 1966). In *The Idiots*, this practice privileges a gestural acting, which is not solely concerned with the communicating effect, since the camera captures the "real," and here the "real" stands for the process, the documentation of the actors' performances. Brecht aimed for the same result when he argued in favor of a camera movement that would not aim at capturing emotions and psychology, but at revealing the relationship between reality and its representation. The difference is that he aimed to solve the problem via an interjection of montage sequences. Mark Silberman's writings on Brecht's understanding of the role of the camera can help us establish the connection:

> The camera's operation of registering physical reality—objects and gestures rather than emotions and psychology—in other words its *Von-Aussen-Sehen* (seeing from the outside) becomes the cornerstone of an aesthetics of making visible *das Sichtbarmachen*. Finally, in the cinema the perception of the image undergoes a disintegration of visual perspective with the levelling of difference between the image and the original. Aura is no longer attached to the photographic or cinematic image as material value, but to the process, to the functioning of the reproduction. (1987, 151)

This process favored by Brecht acknowledges an important difference between cinema and theater. In cinema a very important element in the production of empathetic feelings is the camera itself, whereas in theater, identification, which Brecht aimed to abolish, is produced by means of the acting technique and the actors' portrayal of their roles.

In *The Idiots*, empathy with the characters and the action is problematized through the very process of the film's production, which combines an emphasis on the materiality of the performances with a handheld camera movement that points to the very practice of recording. Since performance is the thematic core of the film, the camera is concerned with the capturing of a contradictory process, that is, the registering of the characters' simulations in real time. Thus, the film becomes a film about performance and identity, and while this aspect develops into a finished object that is contained in its dramaturgy, there are moments when performance becomes a process of self-discovery. A prime example of this process can be observed in a moment when the camera registers the cameraman and a sound technician. At this point, the diegetic and the metadiegetic level collide, and once again the film incorporates the process of its own making in the final object. As the film employs the trope of performance to rethink the boundaries between "self and other," this scene incorporates the basic media of the film's own articulation as a means of challenging the boundaries between inside and outside. Thus, in copying the copying of its own making, the film questions the very idea of its own originality and the very idea of a concrete "real."

This self-exhibitionist strategy explores the thin boundaries between identity, performance, and social construction. There is a moment in the film that merits particular attention: The scene takes place in a forest and shows Karen and Stoffer discussing the objectives of the project. Karen asks Stoffer for their motives, and while the latter starts his ardent tirade, the camera pans away and captures some members of the group "spassing" (figure 3.3). Then, it returns back to Stoffer and Karen, capturing only the lower part of their bodies to end up in a close-up of their faces (figure 3.4). During their discussion, images of the "spassers" intervene, making clear that this is not a point-of-view shot (figures 3.5 and 3.6). Here the camera plays a dual role: On the one hand, it manifests its presence and the immediacy of the event; on the other hand, the camera's consciousness of the process of representation is not demystificatory. On the contrary, the staging

Figures 3.3 and 3.4: *The Idiots* (1998).

Figures 3.5 and 3.6: *The Idiots* (1998).

makes a self-mockery of the immediacy of the event, since what is presented is inauthentic, that is, simulations on the part of fictional characters. Thus, the ontological status of these images crumbles into performance.

During Stoffer's and Karen's discussion the camera pans away, and for a moment Katrine's head appears completely out of focus. Then again, instead of returning to the characters, the camera registers minor details. Stoffer's voice is heard in the background, but we do not see his face. What appear on screen are fragments from the idiotic performances and minor details from the forest that do not enhance the dramatic aspect of the scene. When the camera returns to Stoffer, Karen asks him how one can justify their game given that there are people that are truly handicapped. Stoffer replies laconically, "you can't." This scene and the short dialogue sequence between Karen and Stoffer indicate that their role is not just to advance dramatic and narrative forms of progression. Here there is a sense of performative excess on the part of the camera and the actors, since the scene aims at discovering the moments that cannot be contained within a conventional narrative.

The film, therefore, is in constant dialogue with itself, and such a manipulation of the materiality of the actors' bodies renders performance—as a thematic and as a formal element—its principal referent. This facet of *The Idiots* evokes Ivone Margulies' discussion of "corporeal cinema." Margulies discusses Chantal Akerman's cinema taking into consideration Neorealism's and direct cinema's "investment" in the concrete reality, and their simultaneous acknowledging of cinema's artificial nature. "In this cinema, in fact, the quality of presence wavers precisely because of its materiality, because of the excess produced in it by hyperbole and redundance" (1996, 20). Margulies explains that by investing in this borderline situation cinema produces an "extramateriality, a surplus" of corporeal connections, a point that aptly describes *The Idiots*, since the camera registers the process of the actors' embodiment of a role and the very embodiment itself as contained in the film's dramaturgy. In line with this configuration, the film is paragon of an aesthetics that "shows the showing," that is, breaks the material into performative fragments, so as to open them up to analysis instead of fusing them under the aegis of a unified storytelling pattern.

This emphasis on performative rather than strictly referential connections derives also from the film's dramaturgy. What characterizes the group's idiotic provocations within the film is not a desire to communicate a message. They understand their role to be of political importance, but their happenings do not intend to enlighten but to provoke. Accordingly, they do not provide resistant political messages, but their political effect derives from their challenging of certain aspects of living (that they are also part of it) and their refusal to provide any explanations for it. Stoffer's view of the idiot as "the person of the future" in the aforementioned scene with Karen is not convincing.

What von Trier omits is an elucidation of the characters' motives, and to an extent his film acts as a performative provocation toward the audience, similar to the provocations conducted by the group toward the people they meet during their happenings. The restaurant scene, which activates the narrative, demonstrates this characteristic solidly. The "spassing" in the restaurant starts unexpectedly after Karen has ordered her meal and the camera has established a rudimentary narrative orientation. Suddenly, the camera points to another table and we see Susanne trying to feed Stoffer and Henrik. When her attempts fail, Stoffer and Henrik burst into hyperactivity, typical of mentally disabled people. At this point, the captured material, which focuses on the idiotic performances and the customers' uneasiness, creates feelings of empathy with the "idiots." These feelings are frustrated a few minutes later, when Stoffer and Henrik burst into laughter and the former one says, "What the hell could we do? That lunch would have cost a fortune." We get to realize that this was just a performance and like Karen, the audience feels distanced and the question that arises is why?

The story of the group's performing of an abject identity can be seen along with the historical changes provoked by the establishment of capitalism and the decline of the social movements after the late 1970s. The following formation of various groups, who asserted the unique and intense aspect of their oppression, aimed at increasing visibility for individuals with marginal identities. This emphasis on "identity politics" led to the gradual exclusion of class questions from the political movements that followed (Callinicos 1995, 198). Performance art and avant-garde film practice posed questions concerning the boundaries between "normative" and "deviant" identities. Their objective was to raise issues that could give public voice to individuals who remained in the margins of society and, as Rebecca Schneider explains, to underscore that "certain markings of identity bear the historical weight of privilege and others the historical weight of disprivilege" (1997, 21).

Yet the contradiction that arises when watching *The Idiots* lies in the fact that with the exception of Karen none of them could be seen as representative of a marginal identity. They are all middle class, heterosexuals, and white, and none of them has a mental disability. Their emphasis on mimicry, as a form of "political radicalism," creates a gap between the characters and their intentional feigning of a marginal identity. This gap is heightened at moments when their nonperformative identity predominates over the idiotic one. One example can be drawn in the scene that they dine eating caviar. Initially, they all refrain from wasting it, and they seem to enjoy it. It is only when Stoffer senses that the whole thing does not differ from the bourgeois lifestyle that they mock, that he provokes them shouting, "at least eat it the way they eat caviar in Søllerød," and starts spreading it all over their faces.

This performative struggle generates contradictions and raises questions regarding identity. The question that arises is what it means to assume an abject identity. Is it just a matter of performative choice or a choice based upon the capitalist model of exchange value? Thus, *The Idiots* puts forward the conjecture that identity politics can be quite problematic in a historical period in which radicalism can be reappropriated and thus commodified. Schneider's writings on the mimicry of "disprivilege" in contemporary capitalism offer an implacable autopsy of this latent commodification of difference.

> The rampant mimicry of disprivilege across emaciated bodies dressed in extremely expensive clothing compels questions about the envy of disprivilege in a culture of insatiable accumulation. Perhaps, the imagining of despair, violence and loss attempt to appease anxiety about reality effects-claiming ownership or control over the signs of wreckage in the wake of capitalism's progress—turning them into artifacts of privilege. Appropriating such images to the dreamscape may reassure the consumer with one of postmodernism's dictates: that even the most troubling "reality" can be considered masquerade, hype, sham. Such tragedy is not "really real." Impoverishment becomes a choice one can buy into, wearing its signs like blackened eye-shadow, re-appropriating fear of the disenfranchised "other" into the belly of high-cost consumptive desire. (1997, 22)

These observations help us understand the historicity of the film's interest in the simulation of "disprivilege." Is political emancipation simply a matter of mimicry of an abject identity? The film's ending with Karen "spassing" in the presence of her family points to the tensions and contradictions of class and gendered relations within an oppressed working-class environment. At this point, the incommensurability between being someone and performing someone becomes clear, since Karen's performance points to states of marginalism and oppression that cannot be reduced to a masquerade, or to a postmodern surface reality.

Characters as bodily effects

Von Trier lays these contradictions bare, and his semidocumentary treatment of the material does not facilitate the audience's involvement in the fiction. There is one particular scene which draws upon the Brechtian concept of Gestus and makes one rethink the idea of identity as difference. In a noteworthy scene, von Trier utilizes a gestic acting which exhibits varied Haltungen so as to question the group's happenings and the very conflict between the individual and the mimicry of an abject identity. While the group performs their happenings in a swimming pool, the camera focuses on Axel, who performs the idiot (figures 3.7 and 3.8). After receiving a professional phone call, he adopts different postural attitudes. At this point, he assumes a different identity, setting himself at a distance from the performing happenings (figure 3.9). As a result, the actor is split in two and the *Gestus* offers an embodiment of a social contradiction that renders Axel's participation in the group problematic. Here, *Gestus* is used as a means of setting at a distance the character as an impersonator of an abject identity, and as a social being that is part of the very reality he negates.

Figures 3.7, 3.8, and 3.9: *The Idiots* (1998).

Subsequently, subjectivity is characterized by disunity. While this scene illustrates a concrete antiphasis, there are moments in the film in which the characters' physical attitudes pose stronger questions vis-à-vis identity and offer contradictory possibilities of interpretation. Let me support this last proposition with reference to two scenes. The first one involves Josephine and Jeppe, who engage in a private sexual intercourse, while the other members of the group are having an orgy. The couple's sexual activity is not separated from their performative identity, namely the idiotic one. In a prolonged sequence, the camera captures the couple, which starts their performance in a kind of biomechanic way (figure 3.10). The effect is that there is a constant tension between distance and affect that creates confusion for the audience, which presumes that the whole thing is a simulation. Eventually the two characters come closer to each other and the scene culminates in a dramatic moment, which hovers between being part of their idiotic performance and part of the character's "real identity." The happening concludes in a very forceful way, when Josephine falls into tears and tells Jeppe that she loves him. Subsequently, the characters move from their performing to their social identity. Later on, uncertainty is heightened when Josephine is forced by her father (Anders Hove) to leave the group because she suffers from a mental illness. Her father says in an acrimonious way, "This might be a game to you and good luck. But it takes nothing to make Josephine seriously ill."

As a result, the interplay between performing and being raises questions about performance and identity. This aspect of the film has been acknowledged by Ove Christensen. As he says:

> Basically the film is about role playing and being. What does it mean to be someone and what does it mean to pretend to be someone? Is being a consequence of acting or does acting make a disguise of an individual's character? Is the

Figure 3.10: *The Idiots* (1998).

individual a persona or a mask? This concerns the status of fiction in relation to art. (2000, 40)

Christensen's questions can be clarified by my discussion of the previous scene, in which the individual disintegrates into gestures that cannot be attributed to a unified character. This disintegration connects the scene with post-Brechtian employments of *Gestus*, in which the body does not simply flatten and clarify the contradictions, but crosses the boundaries between its physical presence and its transformation into material. As in Brechtian practice, signification is limited in favor of simplification, but without offering unitary hermeneutical points of reference (Barnett 2011b, 341).

A similar effect occurs in the last scene of the film, in which Karen "spasses" in the presence of her family. Earlier, the audience becomes aware of her recent bereavement. During her "spassing," what makes the scene emotionally intense and complicated is the gestic camera which avoids establishing a clear origin of the shots. The camera alternates between Karen and her family, capturing different gestures and reactions, and generates abstract responses that hover between critical distance and engagement (figure 3.11). Like the character, the camera is in-between; that is, it constantly shifts from a semidocumentary observation to a direct involvement with the material, which cannot be reduced to a pure reproduction. The audience is given space to analyze the material and identify at the same time with Karen as a character. Yet Karen's convincing idiotic performance splits her in two; it becomes psychophysical, in the sense that it is a simulation and a response to her trauma at the same time. The camera and the story have her reduced to bodily effects, but her body is not simply transformed

Figure 3.11: *The Idiots* (1998).

to a locus of dialectical explication. The process becomes dialectical the moment the body crumbles into performance and the boundaries between inside and outside cannot be determined.

This clash between performing and being advances a hermeneutical approach, according to which performance becomes the precondition of identity and not the other way around. Furthermore, the significance of Karen's performance corresponds with the film's skepticism toward verbal communication; this reduction of action to performative *Gestus* takes us back to the roots of early film language, whose tendency to externalize the characters' actions instead of offering a direct equation between behavior and expression fascinated Brecht. Karen's performance shows the very act of performing; it is not an expression of an inner essence. She shows the actor in the process of acting the character, and the character in the process of performing an act, which is also provoked by the oppressive domestic working-class milieu. The quotability of her performance operates as a means of metareflection both on the very issue of social oppression and on the film as medium as well. Effectively, the crisis of communication holds a special place in the film's narrative, since the privileging of performative fragments over verbal communication poses the very issue of the relationship between language and ideological structures, from which Karen momentarily escapes when she performs the idiot facing her family. As Antje Flemming says, the question one needs to think is "Wie drückt man sein Unbehagen an einer Welt aus, in der die herkömmlichen kommunikativen Wege ins Nichts führen?" (How expressive can somebody be of her or his discomfort in a world where the conventional channels of communication lead nowhere?) (2010, 68). Therefore, the film's confusion of "reality" and "performance," in a narrative fiercely occupied with "reality" and "performance," turns into a revisiting of some of the modernist experiments dedicated to the interruption of predictable dramaturgical strategies in favor of analytical rather than reproductive forms of communication. As Silberman underlines, what connected Brecht with Kafka, Breton, and Artaud was a search for "a more genuine language of physical movement that connects thought and world" (2006, 327). Revisiting this pursuit of an authentic "language" that connects representation with social reality is a precondition for evading the reproduction of simulations that fortify the existing power structures. In these terms, Karen's spassing operates both on the artistic and on the social level; it simultaneously connects the individual with society and proposes a more "polemical" film language. But it is an act of negative resistance and not one that puts forward a "universalist" empathy with the underdog, which can be easily co-opted by the social and cultural apparatuses.

Performing out of character

Anthony Dod Mantle, who acted as a cinematographer in three Dogme films (but not in *The Idiots*), has given a summary of *The Idiots'* aesthetics and argues that the interesting aspect of the film is that the audience is faced with a "sudden experience" of not knowing whether the object is "real or unreal" (cited in Kelly 2000, 107). This ambiguity stems to a large extent from the manipulation of the body of the actor as a presence. Jens Albinus attributes this uncertainty to the acting style, which does not allow for much preparation and for the actors' complete identification with their roles. As he says, "Even though Dogma might look like method acting, it is something else. You cannot prepare yourself for the part; the fiction can only take shape here and now" (cited in Oxholm and Nielsen 2000, 24). This lack of preparation described by Albinus favors the moments in which reality intrudes, and the performer oscillates between acting as an actor and as a character.

Such an example can be drawn from the film's most provocative scene, in which the characters meet up with some people who are truly mentally disabled (the people performing them are people with disabilities) (figure 3.12). Here the responses on the part of the characters (or the actors?) heighten the ethical dilemmas and undo the viewer's certainty regarding the fictionality of the portrayed events. Jargil's behind-the-scenes documentary contains a moment in which von Trier recalls the making of the specific scene. As he explains, during the first shooting none of the actors could remain in character. They also forgot their fictional names and used their real ones (cited in *De Ydmygede*). Yet even in the final cut, one senses this clash between reality and fiction that makes the actors act out of character.

Figure 3.12: *The Idiots* (1998).

This ambiguity is accentuated by the fact that the Down syndrome sufferers do not act, but literally perform themselves. At this point, the film moves from the symbolic to the literal, since von Trier shifts the focus from the bodies of the group, who imitate a fake identity, to the bodies of the disabled people, who perform themselves. Schneider, in her writings on contemporary performance, identifies a preference for an aesthetics in which the literal, that is the physical presence of the bodies, downplays their symbolic function. As she says:

> To render the symbolic literal is to disrupt and make apparent the fetishistic prerogatives of a symbol by which a thing, such as a body, or a word, stands by convention for something else. To render literal is to collapse symbolic space, "leaving no room for the signified" (Kristeva). It is to pose borrowing Benjamin again and noting his allegiance to Brecht a "direct threat" to the naturalized social drama of "comprehensibility." (1997, 6)

An analogous suspension of coherent meaning occurs in the aforementioned scene, in which there is a shift from representation to presence. It should be noted that dramaturgically the specific scene has no connection with the episodes before and after. There is only a brief allusion by Henrik in an interview preceding it.

HENRIK: I thought they were all very nice. Jeppe was ...
INTERVIEWER: Interesting to hear they were nice. The idea does not seem
                 polite.
HENRIK: No but ... No you could put it that way.

The scene's placement within the film is quite arbitrary. At this point, dramatic realism is abandoned in favor of a materialist realism in the literal corporeal sense, given that one cannot affirm whether the parts played by the Down syndrome sufferers are acted or not. The spontaneity that characterizes them intensifies the feeling that these people do not perform but appear in the film's universe as themselves. Their physical presence undermines the film's fetishistic aspiration to become as realistic as possible, simply because the characters' preceding simulations and the disabled persons' "real" behavior fuse reality and fiction within the film's narrative. This conflation of illusion and reality operates as an act of aggression against the audience. Von Trier is committed to an aesthetics that attacks the unproblematic consumption of images and the pleasure stemming from the certainty that the represented material is illusory and not real. Here, the intrusion of the material corporeal reality of the disabled people becomes a defamiliarizing effect that interrupts the viewer's concentration on the narrative. Von Trier questions the limits of the medium itself, and, in placing an excess of reality within the film's diegesis, he does not simply create a scene but activates medium awareness and points to the medium's ability to intermix the illusory and the real.

This oscillation between illusion and reality forces also an awareness of the audience's voyeurism, which is made abundantly clear in another provocative scene, in which the group decides to have an orgy. Throughout the orgy, there are moments that the camera captures the male actors' erections, and, at this point, the distinctions between the bodies of the actors and the bodies of the characters, who perform the idiots, collapse. The scene documents sexual actuality and fiction, an effect that characterizes films of sexual adult content. By mixing actuality and fiction, the scene blurs the boundaries between sexual activity and simulations of that activity. When the camera registers Stoffer's and Henrik's erection, the actors shift from states of acting to not-acting; the effect is that separations between actors and characters, and film and nonfilm are constantly placed into doubt.

This scene does not derive its power solely from the presence of the naked bodies and the sexual activity but from the coexistence of images of real penetration within a context of artifice, since the characters perform the idiots during the orgy (figure 3.13). This coexistence is rendered more problematic because of the camera's uninterrupted capturing of the action, which adds to the film a sense of "liveness." In effect, the simultaneity of "real" sexual activity and simulation valorizes the very process of making a scene rather than the finished product. For this reason, the audience participates in a different way, which mobilizes its ability to assess the material critically and activate affective responses at the same time.

Figure 3.13: *The Idiots* (1998).

Illuminating from this viewpoint is Brigitte Peucker's discussion of cinema's ability to incorporate the real through the corporeal presence of the body. Peucker explains that certain portrayals of the body within a film's narrative may provoke material-somatic responses on the part of the audience and challenge the subject and object relationships. She sets as an example Michael Haneke's cinema, which derives its power from an emphasis on austere images that provoke the viewer intellectually and create affective responses too. Haneke's shocking images of implied violence create feelings of irritation, feelings that are not solely intellectual but somatic too (1995, 167). Peucker's analysis draws attention to certain film practices that valorize the performative aspect of the medium rather than the representation of a reified product. Similarly, von Trier's incorporation of moments in which the actors are in and out of character creates a split in the represented material and the mode of its representation. The audience is neither totally distanced nor in complete identification with the characters. The incorporation of truly mentally handicapped people and real sexual activity in the film's diegetic world makes one oscillate between distanced scrutiny of the material and somatic participation; this participation is expressed through responses of anger, disgust, and/or stimulation. As a result, the film coerces the viewer to respond, and to engage in a process that perceives the filmmaking and film-viewing process as a resistance to the consolidation of the movie into a consumable object. But it is exactly through this interactive process that the film becomes realistic, in the sense that it provokes dynamic questions that intend to divide the audience. Furthermore, Dogme as well as *The Idiots* draw our attention to the fact that realism in art is a set of conventions (e.g. meaningful dialogue and goal-orientated dramaturgy) that may have nothing to do with "reality." Von Trier revolts against these conventions, and his utilization of the Dogme rules leads to an oppositional realist practice that is not structured upon the empirical reproduction of reality. *The Idiots* is rather a justification of unconventional art forms resonant with Brecht's argument that "Realistische Kunst is kämpferische Kunst" (Realistic art is polemical art) (*Schriften* 7, 315).

Reflections on the primacy of the apparatus: Post-Dogme developments, rules, and Automavision

In his renowned "performance" at the conference "Cinema in Its Second Century" in Paris in 1995, von Trier said in an idiosyncratic tone, "it seems to me that for the last twenty years ... ok let's say ten then, film has been rubbish" (cited in *De Lutrede*: 2003). In a rather performative way, von Trier, via the Dogme project, expressed very strongly the need to produce objects which do not efface the film's performativity, the traces of their mediation, and the medium-specific ability to engage with the "real." One needs only to compare Dogme with James Cameron's radically different view of the medium, expressed the same year that the Dogme Manifesto was published.

> We're at the threshold of a moment in cinematic history that is unparalleled. Anything you imagine can be done. If you can draw it, if you can describe it, we can do it. Anything is possible right now, if you throw money at it, or enough time. We have the right tools or we can combine tools, to do anything. (cited in Griffiths 2003, 12)

Cameron's perspective embodies the filmmaking procedure that Dogme opposes, that is, the ability to manipulate images in order to enhance a scene's realism at the perceptual and the dramatic level. Yet this type of filmmaking advocated by Cameron is dedicated to the erasing of all traces of cultural and political mediation. The pseudopolitical neutrality that permeates the narratives of the blockbusters commits itself to the oversimplification of social and historical issues, in view of the fact that politicization endangers a film's marketability. Producing something "for everybody" entails a will to treat complex issues in a monolithic way. It is in this respect that one can understand the employment of dogmatic rules as a means of freeing oneself from the conventions and the clichés of the industry, and, as Schepelern rightly suggests, this is especially prominent in *The Idiots*, where the film's formal *Verfremdungseffekt* is combined with a social experiment that questions normative behavioral patterns (2000a, 232). Von Trier's Dogme experimentation with the social norms is predicated upon the very valorization of the apparatus, what David Trotter defines in his discussion of cinema and modernism as "film as medium before film as art" (2007, 4).

As mentioned earlier, the valorization of the apparatus is founded on the condition that the medium reveals the signs of its mediation so as to engage with the real and involve the audience productively, show social reality beyond the limits of dramatic inevitability, and capture the "real" not for the sake of reproduction, but as a means of questioning the world. This was clearly the case in the collective project *D-Day*, initiated by von Trier and the Dogme brethren and based on an unprecedented form of interactive TV narrative. On the Millennium New Year's Eve, the Dogme brothers organized an interactive project shot in real time, in which four characters' stories overlap. The directors instructed their actors through radio broadcasting from a control room, while the unedited sequence was simultaneously broadcasted by Denmark's main TV stations, giving the audience the chance to zap and create their own versions of the material. This project put forward very strongly the notion of the social aspect of the apparatus, since, as Mette Hjort observes, story is downplayed in favor of "the very setting—and worlds—that location shooting captures"; not surprisingly this engagement with the social reality is combined with a departure from artistic individuality striving for "the momentary transformation of mere consumers of TV fiction into coproducers" (2005, 74, 75). While the final outcome was something between chaos and dramaturgical collapse, what the project clearly exposed was the production apparatus involved in the filmmaking and meaning-making process. In capturing contingent fragments from the material reality and in involving the audience in the final editing, *D-Day* exposed the conditions that shape filmmaking, clearly proposing that meaning is also contingent and the outcome of a social interaction and not an individual activity (figure 3.14).

D-Day baffled and confused the audiences (Schepelerna, 240; Stevenson 2002, 142), but despite its incoherence it remains an important document of an object which does not simply adopt an oppositional aesthetic, but openly explores and rehearses its own strategies of subversion. It entails a utopian aspect which is very much consistent with the political modernist project, what Brecht outlines as "Der Blick des Films ist der nahe Blick des Beteiligten" (the film's gaze is close to the parties involved) (cited in Gersch 1975, 81). What Brecht implies is that

Figure 3.14: *D-Dag* (*D-Day* 2000).

the exposition of the technological traces of mediation is a way of understanding social mediation too, a point that *D-Day* presses on quite convincingly. Yet the project's failure unfurls the very productive aspect of failure as a conscious artistic strategy devoted to the exploration of things that cannot be unified into a finished product.

This is certainly the case in *The Five Obstructions*, which von Trier codirected with Jørgen Leth. The film accomplishes the Dogme objective to produce films that are not solely fictional narratives but act also as treatises on filmmaking process itself. Von Trier assigns Leth the task of remaking his avant-garde film *The Perfect Human* (*Det Perfekte Menneske*, 1967) in five different ways, each time with different formal and production obstacles. But what the film clearly articulates is that what matters is not what one represents but how form affects the content and the ways we understand an object. Pushing further Leth's idea of rules as the path to productivity, the film's experiment indicates the ways understanding is contingent upon technological and social processes that skip authorial singularity. Reflecting on the original version of the film, Leth expounded that:

> Curiosity matters in the kind of cinema I make. My basic idea is: I know nothing, but I would like to know. That's my approach. My premise. Curiosity is an engine. Searching, fascination, framing. Discovering, seeking to understand. Not knowing in advance, not proving, not illustrating, certainly not arguing, but showing. (2009)

Leth's valorization of an aesthetics of "showing the process showing" as a method of discovering things returns us again to the primacy of the apparatus, in the sense that the camera is in active engagement with the environment not strictly for dramatic purposes. Uncertainty is an inherent part of an aesthetic concerned with bringing contradictions to the fore without solving them. This practice allows for the intrusion of "uninvited" elements in the narrative universe (Interview, Appendix).

The most prominent examples in this regard are the first two versions of the film that adhere to obstruction one and two, respectively. In the first one, Leth is asked to shoot the film in Cuba and each shot has to be in less than twelve frames, but what is noteworthy is that the process of preparing the film is prioritized over the final object. Throughout the film, we see neither the entire original version of *The Perfect Human* nor the complete reworked ones, but we have access to material from the film's preparation. In one of the most challenging scenes, we get to see Leth choosing women for the first version, which takes place in Cuba, clearly exposing the problematic gendered issues involved in the filmmaking choices, as well as the fact that his presence there is in a way a form of cultural intrusion. By drawing attention to the process over the final outcome, Leth consciously or unconsciously incorporates within the narrative forms of cultural, political, and social mediation that are flattened out in more conventional forms of narration. In the second version of the film, von Trier asks Leth to shoot it in "the worst place in the world" and the latter chooses the red-light district in Bombay. Prior to showing the final version, Leth spends plenty of time engaging with the social environment. In one emblematic scene, we get to see a woman with a skinny baby begging for change and to Leth's credit he does not cut these moments that call into question the very purposes of his own work (figure 3.15). In the finished form of the second version, Leth performs *The Perfect Human* in front of a transparent frame that captures a plethora of underprivileged locals who cannot control their reactions. We can see them in the background staring at Leth and the crew with astonishment and even boredom (figure 3.16).

Figures 3.15 and 3.16: *De Fem Benspænd* (*The Five Obstructions* 2003).

In allowing for the intrusion of moments that are not preplanned, Leth counteracts directorial intentionality, generating what Mette Hjort defines a "loss of style" (2008, 16). This loss of style prevents the spectator's complete absorption into the story and invites the audience to focus on the very performativity of the medium as well as on the dialectic between staged and "real" events. The camera's attentiveness to material deriving from this dialectical collision valorizes the apparatus over the human eye, and the final object turns into a metacommentary about the limits of human perception. Of considerable critical interest is also the fact that this will to relinquish control is accompanied by a self-criticism which questions the very role of art-cinema experimentation. Can someone in the name of art completely discard social questions? Leth seems very uncomfortable eating his opulent meal and drinking champagne in front of the impoverished Indian residents, but nonetheless he does not abstain from using von Trier's obstructions to interrogate his own practice.

The question of ethics is firmly posed by von Trier's semi-Dogme film *The Boss of It All*, which also proposes a filmmaking method that prioritizes the apparatus over human intervention. The film is shot using a process that von Trier named Automavision. The images were initially framed by von Trier, but camera movement, such as zoom, pan, and close-up, was determined by a computer. Von Trier described this method as "a principle of shooting developed with the intention of limiting human influence by inviting chance in from the cold" (cited in Badley 2010, 137). This process certainly invokes the modernism "will-to-automatism" (Trotter 2007, 11), which aimed at using technology to challenge canonical representational regimes. Indeed, this is exactly what the film achieves, and it is noticeable that this productive manipulation of the "accident" is once again combined with a subject matter that revisits issues of performance and performativity.

The film starts with a preamble by von Trier, who says that "this film is a comedy, therefore harmless. Just a fun way to spend time. Why not make fun of artsy fartsy culture?" This Brechtian introduction is followed by a brief explanation of the film's story, which is again about identity and acting in the social sphere. Kristoffer (Jens Albinus) is an actor who is offered a job by Ravn, the owner of an IT firm (Peter Gantzler). His task is to feign to be the senior manager who ostentatiously resides in the United States, and whom Ravn blames for all his unpopular decisions. Ravn wants to sell his company without taking the blame from his employees and thus he assigns power of attorney to Kristoffer. The latter takes up the task of impersonating "the boss," but he does not conceal his moral reservations. After a few failed attempts to sign a contract with the Icelandic buyer—Finnur (Frdidrik Thor Fridriksson)—and having feigned that he is subordinate to another fictional boss, who is above "the boss of it all," Kristoffer forces Ravn to reveal his true identity and cancel the transaction. But when the infuriated Finnur states that this is "more absurd than Gambini" (Kristoffer's favorite avant-garde playwright), Kristoffer, fascinated by this reference to his hero, signs the deal on the condition that he performs in front of them Gambini's "masterpiece" *The Hanged Cat*.

While the film employs many mainstays of comedy, what makes it remarkable is exactly the automatism of the camera which collates different shots "with continuous dialogue (in gappy duration)" (Bordwell 2006). The effect is that the produced material is characterized by a deliberate instability that fragments the characters, and following the Dogme trope of *The Idiots* renders the individuals as performative constructions. In the first meeting between Ravn and Kristoffer, the whole business deal is posed in terms of performance. Kristoffer asks for guidance regarding his role and even poses the question whether he can divert from the text that Ravn has prepared for him. The camera's arrangement of a plethora of unconnected fragments challenges conventional point-of-view shots, creates a discontinuity in duration (figures 3.17 and 3.18), and dissociates the characters from their lines. At times, the sudden and unanticipated camera movements eschew, framing the speaking subjects, and capture material of no dramatic importance. This *modus operandi* becomes a self-exhibitionist foregrounding of the apparatus, which has its effect on the narration; the camera confuses both the actors regarding their position in the frame and the audience, whose capacity to follow the narrative is challenged. For the most part, characters are framed obliquely and the endless cutting disrupts dramatic continuity,

Figure 3.17: *Direktøre For Det Hele* (*The Boss of It All* 2006).

Figure 3.18: *Direktøre For Det Hele* (*The Boss of It All* 2006).

making the characters look like parts of broader systemic relationships. Linda Bandley remarks that "Automavision corresponds with the corporation as capitalist machine" (2010, 138) and her point is illuminating in the sense that the portrayed individuals are reduced to segments of the corporate apparatus. One senses the nexus between the mechanized camera movements and the mechanized social relationships, and this once again returns us to Brecht's view of technology as the key to understanding processes behind surfaces.

Without a doubt, the film is far from being "harmless and non-political," as von Trier states at the beginning. Conversely, von Trier's deployment of Automavision is compliant with the Brechtian desire to historicize signs of behaviors, since the characters' attitudes are denaturalized and exposed to be part of multifaceted relationships that point to the contemporary corporate reality. The audience cannot keep away from noticing how the business structure affects and stage-manages the characters' actions, and this is communicated through the camera movement which frequently has the characters framed off-centered, capturing nondramatic driven material, for example, the white walls and office-related paraphernalia; this engenders a "clinical" and impersonal depiction of their interactions. Confronted with the full gamut of fragments deriving from the process of Automavision, the audience can get a dialectical understanding of the relationships. This is also enhanced by the film's references to the art of theater and performance. The constant playing with the identity of "the boss" has humorous and farcical effects, but also makes one see the corporate reality as more "impersonal," and focus on structures which seem to involve individuals in a larger "theatre play," in which their agency is ambivalent. Ravn and Kristoffer repeatedly discuss about theatrical strategies prior to their meetings with the Icelandic businessman or with the employees of the company. Typical of the theatricality of the corporate structure are the scenes where the business unschooled Kristoffer utters some industry jargon only to perplex and frighten the firm's employees.

Thus, as in *The Idiots* the limits between performance and life are blurred so as to point to dialectical contradictions. This also functions as a metacommentary, something that is clearly illuminated toward the end of the film. Kisser (Sofie Gråbøl)—Kristoffer's former wife and Finnur's lawyer— advises the former to employ conventional theatrical strategies, "chamber-realism and sentimentalism," so as to prevent the completion of the firm's sale which will lead to redundancies. Kristoffer gathers all the staff around the round table and voices sentimental clichés that break Ravn and make him cancel the deal. Ravn turns out to win the employees' applause and this sudden change dissatisfies the young actor's vanity. "You don't jump from hell to happy ending," he says, and when the Icelandic businessman manipulates his passion for Gambini, he signs the deal for the sake of performing the latter's one-act play. Like *The Idiots*, the film finishes with a performance (figure 3.19). But whereas Karen's performance provided a metacommentary on the Dogme project and operated as an act of resistance that combined an interrogation of "normative" behavioral patterns and "normative" film language, Kristoffer's performance of Gambini's experimental play becomes a metacommentary of another sort. It implies that artistic experimentation without social objectives can end up reproducing the existing institutions and being devoid of any social impact.

Figure 3.19: *Direktøre For Det Hele* (*The Boss of It All* 2006).

Notes

1   In his book, *Bertolt Brecht, Cahiers du Cinéma and Contemporary Film Theory* (Ann Arbor, Michigan: University of Michigan Research Press, 1982), George Lellis rightly maintains that Brecht was influential on a large amount of critical work produced by the *Cahiers du Cinéma* in the 1960s and 1970s.

2   From heretofore, for all the quotations from the Manifesto see the Appendix.

3   This challenges Berys Gaut's point that the Manifesto does not intend to call attention to film as medium. See Gaut, "Naked Film: Dogma and Its Limits" in Mette Hjort and Scott MacKenzie (2000) *Purity and Provocation: Dogma 95*. London: BFI, 89–101.

4   The word "spass" is used throughout the film to describe the characters' activity of pretending to be physically impaired.

4

Dogville and *Manderlay*: Experimentation and Dialectical Negations

Representation as an experiment

What I'm saying is that the victims' stories can sometimes be controversial. They can be dark. We're convinced that we know ourselves so well. We say we would behave differently in this or that situation. Before coming to such a conclusion we should put ourselves in the actual situation. It's too easy to think that you wouldn't do the same.

Liliana Cavani

The above-mentioned quotation by Liliana Cavani is taken from an interview in which she discussed the starting point of her controversial film *The Night Porter* (1974). The film has been very influential on von Trier's earlier films (e.g. *Menthe—La Bienheureuse*) and on his more recent filmmaking ventures (Schepelern 2000a, 40, 124); it tells the story of a concentration camp survivor (Charlotte Rampling) who visits Vienna with her husband only to discover that Max (Dirk Bogarde), her former tormentor and protector at the same time, is currently working as a night porter in the hotel she checks in. They resume their ambiguous sexual relationship at Max's former SS comrades' disapproval. Fearful of any further revelations of their past roles, Max's former Nazi comrades commit themselves to terminating violently the couple's affair. The film's intricate texture lies in its refusal to offer fixed positions to the victims and the perpetrators, implying that victims are not necessarily innocent. While this suggestion forces the audience to look more intimately into the past and understand the depicted relationships politically instead of morally, the critical reception of the film has either downplayed the broader political implications of its form and subject matter, conducting personal attacks on the filmmaker or reducing the whole issue to an exploration of sadomasochism. Kriss Ravetto mentions certain critics who refuse to consent to the film's proposition that complex political issues cannot be understood using the standardized binaries of victims and perpetrators (2001, 181). He cogently observes that the film's challenging thesis is that "bourgeois culture fomented fascism and continues to harbor such extreme ideologies—racism, sexism and a sadistic form of moral puritanism" (2001, 160). Critics tend to downplay this object as the outcome of Cavani's caprice; and by insisting on an ambiguous moralist rhetoric and a moralistic assessment of the characters' actions, they avoid dealing with the film's central premise, that is, how the moralization of a complex political problem serves the purpose of overlooking its social causes and burying the collective guilt.

This atypical introduction to the last chapter of this book aims at conducting a similar experimental gesture which sets out to draw a parallel between criticism's reception of Cavani's film and of von Trier's *Dogville* and *Manderlay*. The critics' tendency to interpret the latter objects by resorting to the directors' personality, his supposed anti-Americanism, or the moralist condemnation of these films results in the depoliticization of the objects, that is, the refraining from examining the ways they present social relationships in ways that make us think beyond the limits of ideological obviousness and banality. But most importantly, this "personalization" of objects that are complicated diverts attention from their political critique. In this chapter, I bracket the very issue of experimentation both in terms of form and content so as to rethink the films' politics and innovations and press on their dialectical open-endedness. I want to place these two films together so as to identify their connecting elements and the ways that their ascetic form politicizes the depicted relationships and the audience's responses.

Dogville and *Manderlay* are the only films by von Trier that have been consistently discussed in relation to Brecht; and resembling Cavani's aforementioned object, they refuse to offer fixed delineation between victims and perpetrators in order to examine broader social/political relationships and conditions that generate particular attitudes. The two films comprise a trilogy still incomplete—titled *USA Land of Opportunities*—and share thematic and formal similarities. Both theatricalize a social experiment which is dedicated to exploring how an act of solidarity and compassion can lead to animosity, punishment, and retaliation. *Dogville*, as the offscreen narrator informs us, is the sad story of a small American town in the Rocky Mountains. Set in 1932, it comprises a prologue and nine chapters. The people living in the town are hard-hit by the Great Depression and live under adverse conditions. As the narrator says, "most of the buildings were pretty wretched, more like sacks frankly." After being given a brief introduction to the characters, the offscreen narration focuses on Tom (Paul Bettany), a young self-appointed intellectual, who organizes regular meetings with his fellow citizens, aiming at the town's moral "re-armament." When he meets a young fugitive, Grace (Nicole Kidman), chased by a bunch of gangsters, he protects her and decides to accommodate her in Dogville. To do so, however, he has to gain permission from the people. Therefore, Tom decides to use Grace as an "illustration" for his argument that Dogville is not a receptive town and its people have forgotten how to receive unconditionally. Grace will be their chance to prove that they are committed to community values. The people accommodate her, and Grace for her part, and at Tom's suggestion, volunteers to help the citizens of Dogville with any errands that need to be done. Initially, nobody accepts her services, but eventually people consent to let her do things "that they do not really need," but can make their lives better.

The people decide that Grace is entitled to stay, but when they realize that there is a large amount of money offered to anyone knowing of her whereabouts, they start abusing her in various ways. Grace is coerced to work more hours and to accept a pay cut; she eventually becomes the victim of sexual assault on the part of the male population. In the last chapter, the citizens of Dogville decide to deliver her back to the gangsters. The "big man" (James Caan) turns out to be her father, and after a brief conversation between them, we learn that the two of them had disagreed about his brutal methods. The reason that Grace left him was because of her willingness to prove that human beings are essentially "good." Now that her experiment has failed, her father offers her the possibility of sharing his power with her. Initially, Grace hesitates but eventually she accepts his offer and orders the gangsters to burn the town and execute its citizens.

The second part of the unfinished trilogy elaborates loosely the same thematic motif and is told in eight straight chapters. Grace (Bryce Dallas-Howard), her father (William Dafoe), and his group of thugs travel through Alabama and stop briefly outside a plantation called Manderlay. Suddenly, a woman appears and cries for help, explaining that one of the slaves is about to be whipped for having stolen a bottle of wine. It turns out that slavery still persists in this part of America. Disgusted, Grace feels that as American citizens "they owe something" to these people and decides to liberate them. In the same evening, the Mam of the house (Lauren Bacall) dies and prior to her death she begs Grace to burn a book titled

Mam's Law, which provides a "psychological division of the Manderlay slaves" that simplified the masters' task. After witnessing the remaining family's attempt to trick the former slaves into signing debatable work contracts, Grace decides to stay in the plantation to ensure the peoples' smooth transition from slavery to freedom. Her father tries to make her reconsider, but Grace persists, taking with her a unit of gunmen and her father's lawyer (Teddy Kempner), whose presence in the plantation will facilitate her liberal task.

Throughout her stay in Manderlay, Grace teaches the black community lessons in democracy and American citizenship, so as to train them to behave as active citizens. Initially, the former slaves are baffled by the new conditions and the fact that there are no set rules that they have to follow. This passive mentality has its harmful effects on the town's harvest, but eventually Grace manages to make them work collectively and sell their reaped cotton at a competitive price. Eventually, she falls for Timothy (Isaach de Bankolé), who was classified as a "proud nigger" in Mam's book, without realizing that he has gambled the community's profits from the harvest. Going back to the Mam's book, Grace is shocked to realize that the book was cowritten by the community's eldest member Wilhelm (Danny Glover), while others were also aware of the book's psychological divisions. Looking at it closely, she also discovers that Timothy belonged to the category of "the pleasing nigger," that is, the one who can change one's behavior at any time, so as to please his or her beholder. Determined to return to her father, Grace is asked by the community to assume the role of the former Mam and punish Timothy for his misconduct. Knowing that her father is waiting outside the plantation, she criticizes the people of Manderlay, and her denunciation of the community concludes with her whipping of Timothy. Passing through Manderlay, her father witnesses Grace's act and decides to leave, assuming that his daughter has managed to put the community in order. The film ends with Grace being aggressively chased by the former slaves who cannot forgive her refusal to become their new Mam.

Von Trier has promoted both films as aesthetic, political, and moral experiments that aim at challenging the established cinematic language and the audience's film-viewing habits of uncritical consumption. But it is exactly because of their experimental form that these films have baffled critics struggling to find "concrete messages and morals." Part of the problem in using Brecht to understand these two films is that critics' reference points designed to elucidate the films' Brechtianism have managed to obscure their formal and political complexity. One of the main reasons for this lies in the fact that critics overemphasize von Trier's anti-Americanism, and by doing so, they avoid looking at the broader political implications of the films' experimental form. It is far from my intentions to offer a detailed account of the films' reception, but briefly it is noteworthy that both films have been discussed under the rubric of anti-Americanism in ways that their very "Brechtian" form has been flattened out. *Dogville* has been consistently seen as a "didactic piece" which targets America and its president of the time, that is, George W. Bush, while other critics have drawn attention to its religious undertones (Bainbridge 2007, 141; Badley 2010, 103; Helmke 2006, 50). Similarly, *Manderlay*'s questioning of the racial divisions in America has led to discussions that defy the film's intricacy, implying that the narrative justifies reactionary ideas and is indicative of right-wing cynicism. For instance, Brian Goss suggests that *Manderlay* "allows the Right-winger" to avoid interrogating "his fanatical idealism with the rigor that is directed at other von Triersian protagonists across his corpus," while Mette Hjort argues that the film's provocative subject matter is "a source of harm and offense in any context where slavery is an issue" (Goss 2009, 161; Hjort 2011).

Along the same lines, the Grand Jury at the Cannes film festival accused *Dogville* of being "anti-humanist," while after the official screening of *Manderlay* in Cannes, numerous people protested that it is inconceivable to think that the victims can collaborate with their despots to facilitate their own oppression. These lines of argument prioritize moral questions without, though, questioning how morality is ideologically "contaminated" by the hegemonic social conditions, something that both films investigate. Even Jacques Rancière tends to read *Dogville* in moralist terms. He suggests that the film manipulates the Brechtian fable of *Saint Joan of the Stockyards,* in which Joan Dark wanted to impose Christian morality within a capitalist system of exploitation, only to realize that Christian ethics serve the very capitalist interests that produce inequality and unfreedom. Rancière argues that unlike the politicized Brechtian narrative, *Dogville* is characterized by a cynical amoralism. "'Only violence helps where violence rules' was the Brechtian lesson. Only evil repays evil is the transformed formula, the one that is appropriated for consensual and humanitarian times" (2006, 8).

Things became more complicated for von Trier after Anders Behring Breivik referenced *Dogville* as one of the films that have inspired his actions. Breivik was the neo-fascist perpetrator of the 2011 Norway attacks that took place in Oslo and Utøya on July 22, 2011. Considering Islam, Marxism, feminism, and multiculturalism as Europe's rivals, Breivik bombed government buildings in

Oslo, which led to the death of eight people. He then went to the island of Utøya and shot to death 69 people, who were participating in the Labour Party youth camp. On Breivik's Facebook account, *Dogville* was listed among the films that had inspired his actions. When asked to comment on the incident von Trier replied: "Jeg har det vanvittig dårligt med at tænke på, at 'Dogville,' som ellers i mine øjne er en af mine mest vellykkede film, skulle have været en slags drejebog for ham. Det er rædselsvækkende" (I am mad to think that *Dogville*, which I consider as one of my most successful films, acted as a script for him. It is horrific) (cited, in Thorsen, 2011). When the journalist asked von Trier whether the Norway massacre made him regret having directed the film, he responded: "Og så kan du spørge, om jeg er ked af, at jeg har lavet filmen. Og ja, hvis den har givet sig det udslag, så er jeg ked af, at jeg har lavet den. Men det er klart, at jeg også har et pædagogisk sigte med mine film, selv om jeg nødig vil være ved det, og mit sigte går i hvert fald i den stik modsatte retning af Breiviks handlinger" (And then you ask if I am sorry that I have made the film. And yes, if it was pivotal for his actions, I am sorry that I have made it. But it is clear that I also have a pedagogic purpose with my films, although I would not like to be in it, and my aim is certainly in the opposite direction of Breivik's actions) (cited in Thorsen, 2011).

Von Trier's aforementioned comments provide a productive line of argument that can help us go beyond the oversimplistic tendency to equate a filmmaker with his characters. Eliding the director with his characters is certainly an oversimplistic and questionable way of analyzing a film, which does not bother to read a film's contradictions beyond the limits of the story or to identify the link between the contradictions within the narrative and the historically formed environment to which the object refers to. But it is also quite risky for the state of scholarship itself, given that if we tend to reject films that do not subscribe to easily identifiable morals and meanings, then we backslide to Aristotelian truisms that call for clear-cut moral conclusions, without questioning the very frame of representation or the relationship between ethics and ideological hegemony.

Before tackling a set of questions concerning the films' contradictions, let us analyze their experimental form and particularly their references to other arts and media. Here Brecht offers a fruitful paradigm particularly in light of the fact that both films have obvious Brechtian references. Both utilize a minimalist aesthetics and they were shot in a hangar located in a Swedish town, Trollhättan. The hangar is used so as to resemble a theater space where chalk marks are used to define scenography. The actors act realistically in a set which is far from being realistic. Despite the stylization that stems from the spatial simplicity, sound effects are used to substitute the lack of frames so there are moments that we hear door-knockings even though there are no visible doors or houses in the set. Equally important is that the lack of detailed scenography places the characters in a specific context, asking us to dissect the relationships and analyze more closely their physical attitudes. The story in both films is told by an offscreen narrator (John Hurt), who pares away with the inessentials of plot and intervenes to comment on the action, as well as to pose questions to the audience. Consequently, the narrator might be omniscient in terms of story development, but when it comes to the broader contradictions generated by the narrative, he does not pretend to hold the answers to the questions; at times he expresses his own uncertainty, with the view to forcing us to respond and question the material on screen.

Evidently, both objects merge cinematic, theatrical, and literary elements and in an interview given after the completion of *Dogville*, which was the first film to introduce this experimental fusion of different elements, von Trier explained that the film's aspiration is to challenge any stereotyped ideas regarding film form. As he says:

> The most reactionary attitude to art has always been the question "what is art?", followed by the statement "This isn't art". Limiting it, labelling it. In the same way, people have tried to contain and limit film—and literature too for that matter. I'm trying to challenge that now by creating a fusion between film, theatre and literature. That doesn't mean filming a performance in a theatre though. *Dogville* lives its own life, according to highly specific value criteria within the genre which, as of now, can be called "fusion film". It's important not to get bogged down in questions of what is cinematic or not cinematic, because it seems like we've reached a position where everything is possible. The cinematic has been purified to the point where it has all become completely lacking in interest. There, a bit of cinema philosophy! (cited in Björkman 2003, 241–242)

Von Trier's argument that "film has been purified" emanates from an acknowledgment of the cinematic institution's tendency to reduce film-viewing to a process of commodity consumption, minimizing the viewers' capacity for critical reflection. Similarly, in a recent interview hosted at the official site of *Melancholia* (2010), von Trier points out the ways film narrative has been standardized and how cinema can benefit by engaging in a dialogue with literature. "And it is an interesting point. Why the hell films have to be so stupid?

Why do all lines have to be about something? When books have a red thread, they only brush it momentarily. Whereas a film is completely tied to the plot. It could be fun to take some of the novel's qualities" (cited in Thorsen 2010). In light of the previous comments, one of the aims of this minimalistic aesthetics in *Dogville* and *Manderlay* is to experiment with a variety of media so as to challenge medium specificity and transform a set of conventions with respect to film language and film-viewing habits of uncritical consumption.

This aspiration helps us to expose the idea of experimentation as production instead of reproduction. Here, one recalls Brecht's understanding of experimental thinking as a means of changing a medium's function. For Brecht, the experiment is a synonym of a new method of production which is not satisfied with perpetuating the institution of theater/cinema. In this way, one should aim at challenging the established institutions that resist any modification in their function. Brecht's intention to change the cinematic/theatrical institution is in accordance with his view of the dialectical process as a way of confronting certain established ideas by means of practical activity. With Brecht's comments in mind, one can see von Trier's experimentation in *Dogville* and *Manderlay* as a means of resisting the commodification of the medium. What is also a Brechtian gesture *tout court* is the synthesis of materials from different media as a means of encouraging a more productive spectatorship. To clarify this point, one has to recall Brecht's argument concerning the process of "literalization," which I have discussed in Chapter 2. According to Brecht, the "literalization" of the theater refers to a process in which the medium experiments and makes contact with other institutions so as to produce "complex seeing." The term "complex seeing" describes a dialectical engagement with the material that is not concerned with transmitting a single-minded message. By contrast, the audience adopts a "reading attitude" that guarantees a freedom of thought as opposed to the theatrical institution's tendency to homogenize the audience's perceptions and reactions. This "reading attitude" invites the audience to experiment with the material, and as Brecht says, "illusion is sacrificed to free discussion" (1964, 39). This "new attitude" can make the audience question "the present form of society" and transform certain institutions from places of reproduction to places of productive communication and discussion. For Brecht, this "reading attitude" is tantamount to an experimental thinking that sees reality as open to transformative practice. Endemic to the idea of experimentation is the debunking of any fixed ideas that provide secure points of reference.

In a like fashion, von Trier's formal organization of *Dogville* and *Manderlay* as filmed theater, the chapter structure, and the omniscient narrator invite a reading response that valorizes the role of the audience in the construction of meaning. While Annette Bühler-Dietrich argues that this theatricality provides a unity of signifier and signified and of thought and action (2008, 78), a closer look at the films' form reveals that there is a separation of elements that negate the singularity of meaning. The fusion of image, narrated text, and fixed narrative space shows the represented material via representation, a process that is not dedicated to the production of a seamless narrative. Moreover, the offscreen narrator interrupts the story and delivers it to the audience to analyze it; this method reinforces the film's interest in encouraging discussion. The crucial corollary of this method is that it challenges the cinematic institution and the understanding of the medium as a consumable reflection of reality. In a way, the ascetic set turns into a laboratory that aims at reactivating the relation between production and reception.

The model of the laboratory in both films is interconnected with the austere setting. By restricting the action in a bare stage, the films aim at preventing the audience from being completely absorbed by the story. Instead, the viewers are urged to focus on the examination of the portrayed relationships, and their susceptibility to change. Giorgio Agamben said once that "in the cinema, a society that has lost its gestures seeks to re-appropriate what it has lost, while simultaneously recording that loss" (1978, 137). Given that Agamben's point was formulated at a moment in history that cinema took advantage of the photographic possibilities of the apparatus, we might rethink the currency of the argument in a period that developments in cinematic technology lead to the production of objects that fail to provide an analytical examination of social relationships. As stated in the previous chapter, the prioritization of technology as an end in itself downplays cinema's function as a medium and becomes "a reality in its own right" (Elsaesser, Hagener 2010, 12). In these respects, the minimalist aesthetics of *Dogville* and *Manderlay* and their impoverished conditions of production are the logical continuation of von Trier's critique of the cinematic institution through the Dogme project. These two films push further Dogme's aspiration to reinstate the social function of the medium, by placing the stories in a theatricalized *locus dramaticus* that allows us to single out the contradictory social *Gestus* and *Haltungen*.

In both films, the minimalistic set simplifies the story line and this simplification invites a more scrutinized observation of the social relationships.

The connection between experimentation and simplification is another important Brechtian gesture. Referring to experiments in the art of theater, Brecht mentions that "Die Versuche führten zu einer großen Vereinfachung in Apparat, Darstellungsstil und Thematik" (the experiments led to a great simplification of the apparatus, of the representational style and subject matter) (*Schriften* 3, 103). Taking a cue from Brecht's argument, one can see the relationship between simplification and politicization, and in *Dogville*'s and *Manderlay*'s case this is obvious given that the references to the art of theater have their impact on the film's portrayal of the characters, since the limited diegetic space demonstrates the dialectic between the individual and society. The characters' reactions and attitudes are shown as the outcome of particular social relationships and not as actions motivated solely by psychology, something that preoccupies me in the subsequent sections of this chapter. Aleksey Govozdev mentioned once enthusiastically that "Piscator is not afraid to bring theatre and movies together" (cited in Meyerhold 2005, 23). A similar conclusion can be drawn by von Trier's practice in *Dogville* and *Manderlay*, with the exception that in this case it is the film medium that benefits from the art of theater.

The productive aspect of film's reference to the art of theater and the idea that such a method produces an "anti-spectacle effect" that can make the audience focus on dialectical contradictions have been acknowledged by Stephen Heath. For Heath, the "theatricalisation of cinema" leads to a fusion of theatricality, textuality, and cinematic narration. This fusion of different media produces heterogeneous effects, which challenge the dominant cinematic language and disturb the film's representational flow. The result is that this practice favors formal and thematic indeterminacy that leads to provisional and nonauthoritative conclusions. "Reality can only be theoretical, the theatricalisation of representation in its forms; film theatre, critical cinema, a cinema of crisis and contradiction" (1974, 121). Heath draws his conclusions mainly from films directed by Straub/Huillet, whose work resists the mainstays of character and plot and is radically different from *Dogville* and *Manderlay*. However, what merits consideration is Heath's point that this practice disrupts canonical film-viewing habits by turning film spectatorship into a reading process that does not facilitate the production of unequivocal conclusions. It appears that his argument hinges on the idea mentioned earlier that film's reference to the art of theater leads to a simplification of the actions and the set, forcing the audience to think beyond the drama and theorize, that is, to experiment with the most obvious ideas that are taken for granted.

Experimentation as pedagogy

The ascetic set in both films is symptomatic of the obvious Brechtian references, though Jan Simons suggests that the film's abstraction in regard to the characters, the setting, and the objects is anti-Brechtian, because this abstraction intends to stimulate the audience's imagination (Simons, 157). Despite his anti-Brechtian reading, his terms coincide exactly with Brecht's idea that formal abstraction makes the audience productive/imaginative and this productivity generates change. Brecht brilliantly formulates this when he says that "Es ist ein Vergnügen des Menschen, sich zu verändern, durch die Kunst wie durch das sonstige Leben und durch die Kunst für dieses" (it is a pleasure of man to change oneself, through art and life, and therefore through art) (*Schriften* 7, 288). In simple terms, both films' abstraction resonates with Brecht's idea of experimentation, and at this point, one needs to draw attention to the method in order to understand experimentation in Brechtian terms, that is, as a dialectical process. For Brecht, experimentation, that is, the application of dialectics, provides a methodology that intends to complicate form so as to force the audience to perform dialectical connections. This view of experimentation does not necessarily need to reach categorical conclusions. As seen above, the films' lack of clear morals and ethics has puzzled various commentators of both *Dogville* and *Manderlay*, who may identify the obvious Brechtian references, but not the method, while some of them more or less infer that both films are reactionary objects. The following quotation by Brecht clarifies this idea of experimentation as a dialectical process:

> In reality, processes do not reach conclusions. It is observation that requires and imposes conclusions. By and large, of course, decisions are made (and encountered), certain formations change or even lose their functions, qualities decay and the overall picture changes jerkily. Seek out the situations in which the statements in question might appear. From what quarter might they appear, and for what purpose might they be uttered. Application of dialectic to destroy ideologies. Axiomatic tables: what are the consequences, what lies behind it. Asocial behaviour (2003, 106)

The examination of relationships via the dialectical method in von Trier's unfinished USA trilogy aims exactly at the dissolution of ideologies and, in particular, liberal democratic ideologies based upon the oversimplistic principle that moral and ethical changes can lead to the overcoming of social and historical contradictions.

This line of reasoning is communicated by von Trier via a thematic experiment taking place in both films. In *Dogville*, the pioneers of the social experiment are Tom and Grace. Tom suggests that Dogville is a community structured upon individualism and self-deception. The young fugitive becomes "an illustration" that can cancel out his argument and reveal the town's potential for something else. Grace, on the other hand, disagrees with her father's practices and flees from him to prove that a mode of conduct based upon unconditional generosity and forgiveness can make individuals show their best qualities. Throughout the film, Tom's and Grace's experiments raise contradictions that do not solidify to a concrete resolution. For instance, Tom's willingness to make Dogville a community based upon values of openness and acceptance leads to Grace's exploitation and suffering. Eventually, Tom adapts himself to the community's treatment of Grace and ends up delivering her to the gangsters. Equally problematic is Grace's behavior and her shift from a stoic acceptance of her abuses to a violent retribution. This change acts as a provocation toward the audience that has been fooled to identify with her throughout her misfortunes.

Similarly, in *Manderlay* the film experiments with the whole idea of liberalist goodwill that turns out to produce antithetical effects. The pioneer of the experiment is again Grace, who naively believes that the empowerment of the former slaves will automatically end their oppression. Eventually, the community is led to its self-destruction, because the former slaves use their "democratic rights" to satisfy individualistic desires rather than collective ones. The problem starts from Grace's sense of integration: She erroneously assumes that people raised in different historical circumstances can be easily adjusted to the same value system which produced their oppression. Her paternalistic attitude is also substantiated in the third chapter of the film, in which she offers the former slaves lessons in democracy. These lessons clearly hint at the fact that the liberalist "respect for the other's right to difference" assumes that the latter must conform to a set of ethical concepts that are taken for granted. Not surprisingly, Grace, who was shocked to see Timothy being whipped in the first chapter of the film, ends up flagellating him herself toward the end of the film. Thus, the central question posed by the film's experiment is whether the overcoming of social oppression can be brought about by those in power. In other words, is it enough for the suppressed subjects to conform to different coercive structures, which have been introduced by their former rulers? In this regard, the film's questions go beyond the racial problem and delve into thorny social issues, implying that moralist concepts based upon abstract notions of "humanity" and "social contracts" are far from being innocuous, but they are also the product of particular social interests.

The overarching idea is that social crises are political crises and not ethical ones, a point that returns us to Brecht. In both films, von Trier follows Brecht and employs "the negative example," in order to frustrate any easy decision-making on the part of the audience. The term "negative example" refers to the predilection for including within an argument something which is heterogeneous to it, so as to stimulate responses that provoke dialectical questions. In certain plays, for example, Brecht takes as a starting point the argument that the world must be changed. To explore the ways that change can occur, he sets as examples people supporting changes in moral and ethical attitudes that do not challenge the broader political reality. The failure of these paradigms intends to make the audience understand change beyond the limits of moral reformism. This method is used by Brecht in plays such as *The Good Person of Szechwan* and *The Saint Joan of the Stockyards,* in which the characters act good-heartedly only to realize that the reality of capitalism demands different actions. In the first play, Brecht tells the story of a young prostitute, Shen Te, who is offered a tobacco shop as a "gift" from the Gods on the condition that she will lead a "good" life. Shen Te, who has a natural instinct for goodness, ends up being exploited by the deprived people she wants to help. To protect her business and her self-interests, she occasionally performs a simulated identity of an imaginary cousin of hers named Shui Ta. The latter, unlike her, is cynical and pragmatic and instigates fear in the townspeople. Whenever she is in need, she assumes this identity, and eventually, she realizes that only her alter ego can survive in the capitalist reality. The play presents an experiment which explores whether it is possible to lead a good life in the capitalist reality. At one point, Shen Te observes that when she acts benevolently, she gets exploited, but when she acts wrongly, she becomes powerful. Brecht formulates the idea that changes in the world can only take place given that the wider social structures are altered.

Significantly, the play also elaborates on the ways the oppressed, that is, the poor and the deprived, can also be acclimatized in a social reality of exploitation. Instead of fighting to change the dire social circumstances, they can become habituated in exploiting what is available, for example, others that are below them, or even to reconcile themselves with the role of the victim, who is keen on being inactive and depending on others' "good intentions." Along the lines of this configuration is the thesis that passive reconciliation with the role of the underdog and the destitutes' receipt of benevolence result in reproducing, rather than questioning, the structures of social oppression. Similarly, in the *The Saint Joan*, Brecht tells the story of Johanna, who is a member of the Black Straw Hats, a Christian group dedicated to the moral enhancement of the poor. Importantly, the play includes references to the Bible, and, as G. Ronald Murphy accurately explains, the biblical influences on Brecht's work operate as a form of *Verfremdungseffekt*, which aims at making the audience see the Bible "in an entirely different situation from its original context" (cited in Jovanovic 2012, 70). Johanna understands that the dire social conditions are to be blamed for the poor's depravity, but she does not support political actions determined to change these circumstances. By contrast, she admonishes the underprivileged to pursue spiritual goals and provides them with charitable contributions. Toward the end, she becomes conscious of the fact that religious and moralist idealism reproduces social injustice by withdrawing the poor's attention from their social and material predicament. The moralist approach to historically specific problems turns to a roundabout justification of the status quo.

The parallels with *Dogville* and *Manderlay* are more than apparent, since in the first film Grace and Tom uncritically adopt an ethical/universalist rhetoric that leads to the town's violent destruction. Likewise, in *Manderlay* Grace initiates the emancipation of the slaves, but in the end she turns out to indict them for failing to conform to the existing state of things. Her respect for "the rights of the other" gives rise to their disempowerment. According to Grace's liberalist ethic, black people can be free as long as they conform to social structures which are not, however, produced by them. The similarities that *Dogville* and *Manderlay* share with these two plays by Brecht may make one perceive them as "models" that are reworked to open out a set of different questions. Brecht employs the term "model" to refer to the imitation of patterns from widely known works with the view to presenting them in a different context (1964, 211).

Von Trier has admitted *Dogville*'s parallels to many Brechtian plays and has explained that one of the film's starting points was Pirate Jenny's song in *The Threepenny Opera*. As he says: "I listened to that a lot and was seduced by the revenge motif in the song 'And they asked me which heads should fall, and the harbour felt quiet as I answered, all'" (cited in in Björkman 2003, 233). In *Manderlay*, except for the obvious references to Brecht's plays, von Trier has also pointed out Jean-Paulhan's introduction to Pauline Réage's novel *Story of O*. As he says:

> Then, it's about a situation in the Caribbean where slaves were freed by law, but went back to their former master asking to be slaves again. He refused—because of the law—and they killed him. This story, I believe, has nothing to do with

masochism, but with the fact that they'd nothing to eat, no way to survive and had been better off under the system of slavery. It's ironic. (cited in Merin 2006)

Von Trier's reference to this anecdote signals an important point which accords with some of the Brechtian ideas mentioned above, that is, that the whole concept of freedom is not an abstract universal one. Unless the right to self-determination goes hand in hand with the right to change material and social conditions that replicate repressive states of affairs, the notion of freedom becomes a misnomer that gives individuals the right to integrate themselves in different, but still repressive, conditions and situations. Grace's father in *Manderlay* articulates this rather eloquently, albeit cynically, when he expresses his skepticism regarding his daughter's initiative to abolish slavery in Manderlay.

FATHER: And what do you think those Negroes in there are? How many generations do you think these families made their homes behind that fence? I bet you most of them have taken up employment in their former jobs with the family contracts and all. Of course, now they'll get a few dollars for their efforts, but they'll soon drink that up, and maybe they'll borrow a bit more from their employers, who have no doubt, opened a little store full of colorful wares just for them. And of course they'll never be able to pay back the money and they'll be trapped yet again.

While voicing these thoughts from a position of power, his points are worthy of attention for the very reason that as a gangster he is quite aware of processes of tyrannical assimilation. That said, it is not astounding that in both films, the gangster father seems to be even more conciliatory compared to Grace, who allegedly embodies ideas of forgiveness and generosity. Prior to Dogville's catastrophe, he asks her whether shooting the dog would be a good symbolic gesture only to be surprised by Grace's response that "it would only make the town more frightened. But hardly a better place." Later on she proposes something more problematic:

GRACE: There is a family with kids. Do the kids first and make the mother watch. Tell her you will stop if she can hold back her tears. I owe her that. I'm afraid she cries a little too easily.
BIG MAN: We've better get you out of here. I'm afraid you've learned far too much already.

In both films, the end of the experiment finds one in confusion and the audience is forced to take a position, since von Trier throws us material and asks us whether we consent to the films' resolution or not. The dialectical collisions show situations and attitudes from the perspective of their changeability and not as static, but in ways that frustrate the attainment of one-dimensional conclusions.

On the other hand, it is remarkable that even von Trier, as mentioned above, understands the films to have a pedagogical element, something which is worthy of further comment. This idea of pedagogy should not be understood as the reproduction of a unilateral "message," but as a means of training the audience to think in dialectical oppositions. In other words, pedagogy refers to a process of teaching the audience the dialectical method of thinking and this pertains to Brecht's *Lehrstücke* (usually translated as learning plays in English). The *Lehrstücke* constitute experiments in theatrical form and intend to experiment with exercises in political, ethical, and social behavior. In these plays, there are no distinctions between actors and audience, since they are pedagogical exercises for those who perform them. Brecht intended to raise points of tension that render the very idea of *Einverständnis* [consent] problematic. The most popular examples are plays such as *He Who Says Yes, He Who Says No, and The Measures Taken*. In the first two plays, Brecht questions the individual's sacrifice for a collective cause; and while *He Who Says Yes* seems to approve the whole idea of the individual self-sacrifice, *He Who Says No* contradicts it. *In The Measures Taken*, a young Communist acquiesces to his own extermination because his actions endanger the Party's mission.

Brecht explains that these plays have an experimental scope, since they need to be seen as dialectical exercises aiming to encourage practical thinking. They produce *Gestus* and *Haltungen* so as to explore the individual's adaptability to a variety of social situations or to expose how the conflict between individual and social interests shapes one's postures and behavioral patterns. "Denn es gibt ein gewisses praktisches Verhalten des Menschen, das ebenfalls Situationen schaffen kann, die dann neue Haltungen nötig machen oder ermöglichen" (Because people's practical behavior can also create situations that necessitate or enable new attitudes) (*Schriften* 2, 128). What these plays question is the very idea of consent, and by performing them, the participants learn to think dialectically and to reject one-dimensional solutions to complex problems. A key term here is "theatricalization," which is equivalent to the very idea of experimentation. Emphasis is not placed on the imitation of actions, but on their theatricalization, that is, their reenactment. In reenacting specific actions and questioning decisions that have been previously taken, the performers learn to think dialectically and discover the thin boundaries between consent and dissent. For instance, in the conclusion of *The Measures Taken* the control chorus approves of the political killing. However, the performers can either agree or disagree with this absolute conclusion. Notably, Brecht made clear that the *Lehrstücke* do not intend to abolish empathy, but to manipulate it so as to foster responses to complex questions. As he says: "when i [*sic*] could no longer make any headway in the theatre with empathy, try as i [sic] might, i devised the *Lehrstück* for empathy. it [*sic*] seemed to me that if people stopped merely empathizing intellectually, then that was enough, and something fruitful could be extracted from the old kind of empathy" (1993, 6). Thus, the *Lehrstücke* oscillate between empathetic identification and detachment, so as to make the audience feel and reflect on the feelings at the same time. The feelings generate unresolved contradictions regarding ethical decisions, only to focus on morality itself as the problem, and reveal that ethics cannot be dissociated from social and political interests. On this basis, actions that aim at the promotion of progressive politics are constantly questioned and analyzed so as to demonstrate that unless the moral, traditional certainties of the past are changed, progress can easily lapse into regression.

Brecht wanted to create misunderstandings (*Mißverständnis*) which clarify that solutions or even more the whole idea of consent is contingent on different situations and conditions. He says in the same journal entry, "my love of clarity comes from the unclear way I think" (1993, 6). This complex quotation synopsizes in a succinct way the intricate connection between experimentation and pedagogy. Evidently, there are signs of connection between the *Lehrstücke*'s experimental pedagogy and *Dogville* and *Manderlay*. Particularly germane to the films' themes is Brecht's skepticism concerning consent. Obviously, given the medium differences, *Dogville* and *Manderlay* do not assume the *Lehrstücke*'s radical abolition between stage and auditorium, but both films experiment with attitudes that activate questions regarding decision-making. They proceed to confront the audience with situations that show how an act of solidarity can lead to reactionary politics. In *Dogville*, Grace's entry into the town aims at making its residents change their individualist ethic. Nonetheless, both parties are more intent on introducing changes that preserve certain norms instead of changing them. Thus, Dogville accepts Grace only to take advantage of her and preserve the community's individualist ethic. Similarly, Grace acquiesces to the gangster rule with the intention of "changing the world," and one can see how an act of change can turn into a means of enforcing the social norms and customs that it theoretically opposes. In the same way, Grace's "benevolence" in *Manderlay* is committed to changing a reality of slavery, but her attitudes shift from compassionate identification with the oppressed to violent repugnance. Meanwhile, the former slaves' attitudes are also problematic. Despite their "liberation," their previous social status keeps on conditioning their current behavior and this also derives from Grace's expectations that they shall conform to a new reality, not produced by them, but imposed by her and the gangsters.

As such, both films question the idea of social consent, which is ostentatiously structured upon a "social contract." But the most problematic form of consent is advanced by the films' ending. In *Dogville*, Grace consents to her father's view of power as something "not necessarily wrong." The question that arises is whether the audience consents to this solution or not. Empirical research from student screenings shows that reactions can vary and most of the viewers are perplexed by the film's moral ambiguity (Mór 2006, 129). Linda Badley, for instance, brings evidence from plenty of IMDb users, who demand "payback," and, like Grace, they consent to the gangster rule (2010, 110). The feelings of relief that these spectators experience become problematic. Von Trier assaults the audience's desire for solution and revenge, as if he wants to expose one's *indre svinehund* (inner bastard)—a Danish expression which, as Nikolaj Lübecker explains, "became popular during the 1980s when it was introduced into debates about xenophobia" (2011, 160). In *Manderlay*, the initial identification with Grace and her project is once again disheartened, chiefly after seeing that her presence in the town mechanically reproduces the preceding relationships of power. The audience has to take a stance and undoubtedly one cannot remain neutral. Both films manipulate empathy, in order to question the very tropes of identification employed by mainstream cinema and expose the social aspect of emotions, which according to Brecht are not universally human, but "ein widerspruchsvolles Gemisch" (a contradictory mixture) (*Schriften* 7, 209).

Theatricality: Attitudes in space

An important formal and stylistic element in both films is that the restriction of the action to a limited diegetic space problematizes identity and offers an analytical depiction of the character's postures, attitudes, and gestures. Space thus becomes heuristic to understanding the primacy of social processes in the formation of human relationships and to comprehending the thin boundaries between oppressors and oppressed. This employment of space corresponds with Mieke Bal's argument that in certain cases space can become "an object of representation itself" and not just a backdrop. "Space thus becomes an 'acting place' rather than the place of action" (1997, 136). Bal's central point is that when space is thematized, the story line is also influenced by it and the presentation of space becomes part of the story itself. The same is true for an empty space, since spatial emptiness becomes a challenge "that must be filled" (1997, 136). Correspondingly, the challenge posed by this emptiness is the encouraging of a more productive investigation of relationships that goes beyond the parameters of the dramatic cosmos. In *Dogville* and *Manderlay*, spatial emptiness is filled with analytical gestures and postures that reveal the primacy of the social in the depicted actions, but they also blur the frontiers between inside and outside, within the story and beyond it, asking the audience to "fill" specific gaps in the story line.

Critical to both films' purposes is the camera work, which enters into a productive dialogue with the static space and eventually discloses it as a dynamic locus of social and political interaction. In effect, the spatial emptiness complicates identity, privileging collective attitudes over the individuals. A good starting point to explore these issues is to discuss the ways the camera and the diegetic space provoke *Gestus* and *Haltungen,* which dissect dramatic actions and reveal a set of social contradictions. Antony Dod Mantle, who, along with von Trier, acted as cameramen in *Dogville* and in *Manderlay*, explained the former's interest in fostering a dynamic dialogue between the camera and the space. As he says:

> I think when Lars came with this idea of this naked room/set for *Dogville* to tell a pretty big story in such a potentially plain way—he always has something up his sleeve—apart from the actor direct kind of almost wiseman relationship between the main camera, which Lars operated a great deal of, most of it in *Dogville* with the actors [*sic*]. Apart from that section, they are the whole shots from above, the beautiful images of above that they are all shot in consumer cameras. He has the idea about "let's do a shot when you start on the knob of a radio being switched on or being turned off and then I'd like to come out and crane out—just crane out—come up to a shot where you can see the whole town please"... Anybody who's seen *Dogville* or *Manderlay* knows that those shots are basically impossible unless you have a warehouse or a hangar... Simply there was a rack of cameras, twelve thirteen cameras, looking down on the actors below, doing all sorts of incredibly, complicated, sophisticated techniques, green screen, painting, all sorts of multipurpose into the computers, then matrixing all these together and creating shots that not only are glorious aesthetically, some of them really beautiful, but they more than marry off with the shots on the ground. (cited in *From Dogma to Dogville: Don't Try This at Home*, 2006)

Thereby, one can see how the interplay between gestic camera and space produces important connections that transmit a sense of totality and agility. The camera joins shots from above with the ones below so as to frame connections that point toward the social totality. In effect, the final outcome communicates a sense of theatricality that serves subtler purposes rather than the sole transmission of narrative content. Discussing theatricality with reference to the film medium, Samuel Weber defines it as "a problematic process of placing, framing, situating, rather than as a process of representation" (2004, 315). This definition applies eloquently to *Dogville* and *Manderlay*. The first film frames collective interactions founded upon the capitalist ethic of exchange,[1] while *Manderlay* analyzes the interactions between the liberated slaves and their "liberators" only to obfuscate the distinction between liberation and coercion.

In *Dogville*, the restriction of the action in demarcated boundaries becomes an allegory for the community's isolation, since, as the voice-over informs us, Dogville is a town that does not have many exchange relations with the world outside its boundaries. There is a feeling that the town's citizens are embedded in an ideological sense of inevitability and unchangeability. While the place is inflicted by poverty, the narrator explains that the people living there saw no reason to change anything in their lives and this is also communicated formally. Particularly telling in this regard is a frame in the film's prologue which captures Tom while leaving his house. The camera follows him and zooms out, showing all the characters' activities in the background. The unity of space gives us a panoptic view, but the characters' movements within it look stylized and they appear as mechanical reproductions of tasks (figure 4.1). The camera pans to frame the action, while characters are reported by the voice-over, making them look like a collection of semes.

Dogville's formal asceticism assists us in seeing the characters as part of a collective reality. Yet what von Trier omits is the idea that the self-realization

Figure 4.1: *Dogville* (2003).

of the individual as part of a collective is the route to radical transformation. The residents of Dogville see themselves as part of a community, but what unites them is their acceptance of the social circumstances of their town, which has not really followed modernization. Their collective spirit is not an act of class consciousness but a way of reproducing the existing reality of their rural economy. They share a collective understanding of social life as a process of self-preservation. Consequently, the collective subject is shown as being implicated in an uncritical mimicry of nature and not as a force of transformation. The community's isolation transmits a sense of unfreedom and fixity which can be attributed to the fact that Dogville is more or less a "primitive" and poor, but self-reliant, society and not one that has been properly adapted to the reality of modern capitalism. It is this lack of interaction that forces the town's intellectual to argue in favor of "openness and acceptance." Tom speaks from the moral point of view which intends to identify meaning in the life of the community, beyond the goals of self-preservation. When Tom meets Grace and asks the people to show an attitude of acceptance, he actually manages to introduce Dogville to an exchange-value relationship with someone beyond the town's limits.

The voice-over intentionally foregrounds an economic vocabulary that makes one rethink the agreement between the two parties. Eventually, the town lets Grace do things that the people "don't want to be done, but would make their lives better." A conflict arises here, given that the community succeeds in adopting the Christian values of "openness and acceptance," but these values are solely achieved by means of an economic interaction. Thus, Tom's intention to let Grace enter into the community does not challenge the attitude of self-preservation that characterizes Dogville. The film does not expose this point until the fifth chapter of the film, in which a policeman lets the town know that Grace is wanted for criminal activities. Until that moment we are given the impression that Grace's arrival in Dogville has reinforced the community spirit. Prior to the policeman's arrival, a scene challenges this idea through jerky camera movements and framings that invite the audience to adopt a more inquisitive attitude toward the material. Dogville's residents and Grace are shown celebrating the Fourth of July. At this point, one senses that the community ties are stronger than before. When people finish singing the American national anthem, the camera zooms out to capture all characters while dining and then it focuses on Jack McCay (Ben Gazzara). The latter addresses Grace on behalf of the town and expresses the people's gratitude for making Dogville a better place to live. Jack's position in the frame is on the left-hand side, while Grace and Tom are placed on the right one opposite him (figure 4.2). When Jack starts his speech, the camera zooms in toward him and then briefly captures the people placed on the right side of the frame. Suddenly, a close-up of Grace's face is interjected, but at this point her position is on the left side of the frame (figure 4.3). The image that follows captures Jack while giving his speech, who is on the left side again (figure 4.4). Here the characters' position within the frame is changed. Both appear on the left, while they are meant to face each other and not to share the same position. The camera cuts once again to Grace and ultimately ends on Jack, who is now placed on the right side of the frame (figure 4.5). A rapid camera movement captures the people at the table, and at this point the characters are shown in different positions from the ones they had at the beginning of the scene (figure 4.6).

Here von Trier violates the 180-degree rule and the function of this violation is not a matter of formalist trickery. This movement indicates the camera's inquisitive function, which plays a dual role, namely it represents an object and subverts it at the same time. The audience's sense of orientation and stability is challenged and the camera movement functions as a means of urging them not to reconfirm the material facing them. Von Trier here baffles the viewers with the intention of showing the dynamic aspect of image-reading. In processing the material from different angles that disorientate the viewer, von Trier aims

Figures 4.2, 4.3, 4.4, 4.5, and 4.6: *Dogville* (2003).

at focusing on the way the characters perform the "ritual" of the functional community so that we can question it. The camera movement captures the actors embodying the characters and the characters performing a social "ritual" in an inauthentic space per se. In effect, this formal deviation stresses the simulation of the event. The formulation is telling, for it implies that the reconciled and happy community of Dogville is a copy that does not have an original.

This point is made visible by the scene that follows, in which a policeman informs the town that Grace is wanted for having participated in criminal activities and a reward is offered to anyone knowing her whereabouts. From now on, the social dynamics change against Grace, because another exchange opportunity has been given to Dogville by the outside world. This scene negates the previous image of Dogville as a reconciled and tolerant community. The characters' reactions make clear the economic foundation upon which Grace's admission is established and the town's adaptability to a reality of exchange-value relationships. The community decides to make Grace work for longer hours, because, as Tom puts it, "her presence in Dogville has become more costly." Tom's "illustration" has unconsciously introduced Dogville to the capitalist reality of making profit through exchangeability. Moreover, by offering services that are not necessarily needed, Grace creates needs analogous to the ones created by advertising in a capitalist society. Grace's affective labor is replaced by the exploitation of her use-value, that is, of her labor and eventually of her body. In taking advantage of the short-term benefits of Grace's value, the community unconsciously reproduces its forthcoming destruction.

In the aforementioned passages, it is evident that the gestic camera reveals the characters' contradictory *Haltungen* so as to de-individuate their actions and reveal a set of intrinsic contradictions. Similarly, in *Manderlay* the camera frames connections that bring to the fore postures and attitudes that disclose a surplus of tensions that interrogate Grace's liberalist project in *Manderlay*. A conspicuous example is a passage from the fourth chapter of the film, in which Grace delivers lessons in democracy to the population. The scene starts abruptly showing three gangsters coercing the black community into a room. One black woman is shown raising her hands (figure 4.7) as if she is threatened at gunpoint. On the right side of the frame, Mr Kirspe (Udo Kier) forces a family with kids to follow the rest of the people. In the next frame, the audience is surprised to realize that this enforced gathering is not intended to compel the people to perform labor, but to receive a "lesson in democracy." Grace teaches the confused community that "democracy means government by the people," and though

Figure 4.7: *Manderlay* (2005).

von Trier does not offer a psychoanalytic understanding of her intentions, one cannot avoid noticing the irony, which is communicated by the authoritarian presence of the thugs. The opposition is pervasive and it suggests that Grace's liberalist intervention is a form of coercion not very different from the forced labor imposed by the previous landowners.

During the lesson, the camera invites the kind of inquiry which underpins the former point. When Grace starts her speech on democracy, the camera pans away from her and focuses on the former slaves, who listen passively (figure 4.8). Violating repeatedly the 180-degree rule, the camera zooms in and out, creating a sense of instability. Grace's rhetoric is heard in the background, but the image-track captures the submissive black community, and when it finally returns to Grace, one cannot fail to observe the antithesis between the active speaker and the subservient community. This antithesis is strengthened when Grace delivers a speech on collective labor while behind her two gangsters are strolling slowly and whispering to each other. Throughout the lesson the audience is asked to reconsider the concept of freedom, since the scene makes clear that freedom without cultural capital replicates the former reality of oppression. The first thing to be put on a ballot is a trivial matter of a rake ownership. Grace takes the whole thing quite seriously only to conclude that "that's what ballots are like. There are winners and there are losers." Immediately after the end of her speech, the camera zooms out and registers Mr Kirspe while lifting and eventually lowering his carbine (figure 4.9).

Figure 4.8: *Manderlay* (2005).

Figure 4.9: *Manderlay* (2005).

In these instances, the camera movement and the actors' gestures endow the material with a dialectical significance that goes beyond the mere dramatization of events. The dramatic significance is toned down in favor of the gestic one that produces dialectical contradictions which bring dialogue and body in extreme oppositions. These contradictions point to the ideological, material, and historical relations that produce a set of corporeal attitudes. Thus, it is precisely by means of the processes of liberation of the slaves that the audience is asked to consider how past forms of slavery might persist in different setups. This gestic handling of the material provides a useful framework to understand the Brechtian method in these scenes. As Marc Silberman insinuates, for Brecht "truth cannot be uncovered, revealed or exposed behind the surface appearance, but rather that the process of concealment is the structure of truth" (1987, 11). Indeed, this comment describes powerfully von Trier's method in both films, since the camera and the actors make the most of the seemingly static space to present a set of experimental arrangements that point to the totalitarian aspect of democratic liberal thinking and, as a result, to reveal the ways it conceals its own absolutism. The implication then is that this *modus operandi* corresponds with the Brechtian intent to teach an experimental method of thinking via the *Lehrstücke*, which, as Rainer Nägele accurately develops, "are didactic not in the sense of transmitting political or ideological knowledge, but in the sense of an 'apprenticeship', or as Brecht called it *Einübungen in Haltungen*: experimental exercises in postures" (2006, 164).

It is via similar experimental postural exercises that von Trier politicizes our perception, and indicative from this point of view is the rape scene in the sixth chapter of *Dogville*, which hints that violence is an inseparable element of a political system founded on exchange. In this particular scene, von Trier manipulates the restricted space to arrange a variety of corporeal postures and attitudes that unveil the collective dimension of an individual deed. The scene starts when Chuck (Stellan Skarsgård) enters his house and finds Grace helping his children with their homework. Chuck forces the children out of the room and informs Grace that the police is looking for her, implying that unless she submits to his sexual desires he will betray her. The camera follows Grace while she confronts Chuck's sexual advances. When the latter imposes his body on top of her, the camera shifts away and captures a policeman asking information about Grace. Simultaneously, images of Dogville's everyday routine are interjected (figure 4.10). The jerky camera shifts from one person to another and juxtaposes different point-of-view shots that create a sense of disorientation. These shots are interrupted by images of Chuck raping Grace. One senses that the characters can see what takes place within Chuck's house and ignore it, something that heightens the scene's affective impact (figure 4.11). Panoramic shots follow this uneven registration of different materials and put the very act of rape in the background.

The camera manipulates the unity of space in such a way that the impression we get is that the individual cannot be dissociated from the collective. Elaine Canning convincingly argues that "the non-existence of frames and boundaries means that the whole community is implicated in the rape of Grace" (2007, 162). Therefore, von Trier displays the collective complicity in an act of individual abuse, and here this complicity is joined together with the very idea of exchange. The police cars in the background emphasize the

Figures 4.10 and 4.11: *Dogville* (2003).

price Grace has to pay for her safety. Here, the film demonstrates clearly the connection between relationships founded upon exchange value and violence. The narrator's comments that conclude the chapter highlight this point: "Yet again, Grace had made a miraculous escape from her pursuers with the aid of the people of Dogville. Everyone had covered up for her, including Chuck."

This sound and image counterpoint allows us to perceive the scene in its dialectical complexity and not as an isolated dramatic event. Moreover, there is another aspect of the rape scene that complicates matters more. When the camera cuts from Grace's rape to the actors, who are shot unawares, there are moments when they are reproduced as spectators of her abuse, as if they cannot avoid looking. For instance, the moment the camera captures Ma Ginger (Lauren Bacall), Liz (Chloë Sevigny), and Martha (Siobhan Fallon Hogan) while Grace is being raped, the minimalist setting gives the illusion that they can see what takes place inside the house. The characters seem busy not looking, but the actors, as sentient human beings, cannot help but look. This effect is a violation of the characters' position within the story, according to which they are ignorant of Grace's rape. Certainly, the actors do not have their vision trained on the rape scene as the audience does, but clearly von Trier plays with their attempt to pretend that they do not see something that takes place in front of them.

Subsequently, the characters reproduce our own status as audience and here von Trier questions once again the very act of being a spectator. Of particular interest is the way the camera captures the rape scene in the context of the political condition of the town's collective guilt, and the way it shifts from Dogville's collective subject to the collective in the auditorium. In making the characters reproduce our spectatorial position, von Trier makes a parallel between their complicity and our film-viewing process so as to challenge the safe distance between screen and auditorium. The characters challenge our spectatorial position, but, unlike Brecht, von Trier offends the collective in the auditorium, instead of declaring them to be a positive force of change. This shock is heightened by the fact that on the diegetic level, the audience identifies with Grace's misfortune. Yet on the metalevel, when the camera captures the actors (or the characters?) looking at Grace's rape, we share their point of view and not the victim's.

Evidently, von Trier's aim is to denounce the audience, and this gesture operates as a means of preventing us from being placed in a position of superior knowledge that is not accountable for the portrayed reality on the screen.

Discussing analogous Brechtian self-reflexive practices in the films of Michael Haneke, Thomas Elsaesser maintains that:

> The effect is not to make us aware of being voyeurs and in the cinema, but to undermine even the voyeuristic ground on which we normally arrange ourselves as cinema-goers. If until that point in the film we thought ourselves safe and "outside", we now realize how generally unsafe we are and how we may be caught "inside" whenever we are in the cinema: if classical narrative cinema's spectator felt safe at any distance, however close he or she got, the spectator of Haneke's films might be said to be unsafe at any distance, however far that person thinks he or she is. (2010, 62)

Elsaesser's comments apply to *Dogville*'s aforementioned scene, which blurs the boundaries between inside and outside and indicates the audience's subordination to a collective reality of violence. From this perspective, neither the collective on the screen nor the one in the auditorium is produced positively by von Trier. This theme of collective complicity has its repercussions on both films' desire to expose wider social structures that contradict the ethical handling of complex political issues, given that the filmmaker does not treat the audience as a revolutionary subject in process, but displays the spectators' complicity too.

Performative contradictions

Describing von Trier's practice in *Dogville*, Julia Helmke argues that von Trier is "ein Detektiv des Kinos mit der Absicht aufzudecken und die Wahrheit zu suchen" (a detective of the cinema with the intention of uncovering and searching for the truth) (2006, 56). While Helmke posits the whole concept of truth in terms of abstract universal human ideas, I am more inclined to understand von Trier's method in both films as a process of exposing not a simple and unilateral understanding of "truth" but the performative contradictions of an attitude committed to the pursuit of humanist ideals of progress that backfires into domination and violence. The term "performative contradiction" has been analyzed by Terry Eagleton, who offers an analysis of the ways that social practices collide with "the ideas by which we live them" (1991, 24). Simply, the term "performative contradiction" describes the collision between social actions and the theoretical utterances that accompany them.

In the course of *Dogville* and *Manderlay*, von Trier employs the camera in a performative way, emphasizing the act of showing an action over the action itself. The camera scrutinizes the characters and splits their bodies so as to explore the discrepancies between their actions and their pronouncements. In doing so, von Trier questions the short-term reformist attitude as embodied by Tom and Grace in *Dogville*; the representation of Grace in *Manderlay* follows a similar reasoning, while the former slaves' attitudes are also scrutinized to disclose how the oppressed are also complicit in their oppression. Von Trier's practice corresponds to Elena del Río's concept of the "affective performative," which describes a process in which the mimetic mirroring of identity is replaced by performative moments that fragment the body and produce frames that are not fetishized, but "become an actively dislocated force" (2008, 33). This performative process reveals the transformative potential of identity and, at the same time, disrupts, questions, and affects the narrative.

There is one particular scene in the fifth chapter of *Dogville* where von Trier mobilizes performativity to reveal a set of contradictions. Tom explains to Grace the town's decision to make her work longer hours after the second police visit to Dogville. The camera alternates between him and Grace. When Tom announces to her the news, the camera stays persistently on him and we have a view of the right angle of his face. A jump cut follows, while the character continues speaking. The visual track is interrupted but not the acoustic one, and at this point we see his face from the same angle, but his alignment with Grace has changed. While he keeps on speaking to Grace, the camera moves back and forth abruptly and we expect that it has assumed his point of view to produce an eyeline match. Surprisingly, the camera returns to Tom again and he is now placed at the center of the frame (figures 4.12–4.14).

Figures 4.12, 4.13, and 4.14: *Dogville* (2003).

The unusual framings complicate the communication of storytelling material. What the camera makes conspicuous is the character's body, which is manipulated in such a way to bring forth contradictions that are hidden underneath Tom's pronouncements. The camera's role here is not simply to represent objects but to analyze the character so as to bring our attention to the transformability of his identity. On the narrative level, this is put forward by the fact that the character is placed in-between his fondness for Grace, while he simultaneously reports to her the town's decisions. Throughout the scene, it is quite difficult to distinguish the boundaries between Tom as the member of the collective—whose decisions he reports—and Tom as the person who wants to help Grace. It is this performative contradiction that is stressed by the camera, which destabilizes the image so as to question it. The question that arises is how Tom's intention to help Grace accepts the very logic of exchange value, which will eventually lead to the latter's exploitation. When he tells Grace that the people expect "some counterbalance" (a term from physics euphemistically used by economics—and here the economic exchange is stressed) for their decision to protect her from the police, she responds astonished: "that sounds like words that the gangsters would use."

Tom's portrayal crosses the frontier between humanism and self-interest. This performative contradiction is also made evident in a scene in the eighth chapter. People embarrassed by Grace's public disclosure of her abuses challenge Tom to take sides and choose either them or Grace. Frustrated by the town's response, Tom returns to Grace's house. Initially, we get to see both characters lying down and sharing an affectionate moment. When Tom explains to Grace that he has been asked to choose between her and Dogville, the camera alternates between the left and the right angle of the frame. This alternation is followed by Tom's radical change of *Haltung*. His calm and passive body composure is replaced by a gesture of aggression and he starts making sexual advances toward Grace. The moment he imposes himself on her, the camera zooms out and the material is captured by a high-angle shot. This high-angle shot remains at a distance from the characters and shows them at a great remove (figure 4.15). Ultimately, the camera slowly zooms and highlights Tom's exaggerated posture and attitude (figure 4.16).

Tom's shift from passivity to sexual aggression does not advance a psychological change. The scene releases an amount of energy that can be observed in Tom's postural behavior and in the sudden camera movement that decreases the magnification of the image and then zooms in so as to adopt an analytical

Figures 4.15 and 4.16: *Dogville* (2003).

stance toward the material. Here, von Trier's representation of the body follows the Brechtian practice, according to which the body becomes the medium that enhances our perception of the social laws that regulate an individual's relations to other bodies. The social law that regulates Tom's relation to Grace's body is the law of exchange value. By rejecting everyone else, he acquires the right to enjoy her body. Here, a natural instinct, namely sexual desire, is estranged, and calls attention to the connection between sexuality and power. Thus, sexuality is not treated as natural but as part of a relationship founded upon exchange value, which is heightened by Tom's use of language that alludes to an economic terminology. Von Trier confronts us with a question that could be summed up like this: "how Grace's entry into Dogville which is based upon an act of reciprocal exchange assumes the form of a coercive exchange?"

Tom's example is crucial to our understanding of the film's critique of an abstract "liberal and humanist" attitude. In the beginning of the film, Tom challenges the residents of Dogville to be more receptive and suggests that the whole country would benefit from mutual collaboration. The town achieves social cohesion, but through acts, such as sexual exploitation, that promote an individualist mental outlook. Essentially, the individualism that characterized Dogville before Grace's entrance is firmly entrenched by Tom's "illustration." Liberal humanism of this sort derives from an idealist standpoint that individuals can change morally, without altering the broader social mechanisms. Fredric Jameson phrases this very accurately: "For the liberal view is generally characterized by the belief that the 'system' is not really total in that sense, that we can ameliorate it, reorganize it, and regulate it in such a way that it becomes tolerable and we thereby have 'the best of the best worlds' " (1991: 207). In light of Jameson's comments, one can see that Tom's initial plea for an attitude of "openness" is centered on a "moral righteousness" rhetoric that intends to restore to the community a higher form of "moral purpose." By the time Tom introduces Grace to Dogville, he starts a "reciprocal financial" exchange between the town and the young fugitive. From its very inception, Tom's "illustration" has to emphasize Grace's repayment so as to guarantee her the right to stay despite the ethical rhetoric that accompanies it. Consequently, people's ethics change when they realize that Grace benefits more than them from this exchange.

Clearly, *Dogville* manifests the very falsity of the capitalist idea of "reciprocal exchange" and demonstrates that the reduction of social relationships to financial interactions is bound to backfire into violence. Embedded in von Trier's negative view of capitalism is a mistrust of moralist values predicated upon abstract ideas of freedom and universal rights. Tom's example demonstrates that oppositional forces based upon such a rhetoric end up propagating the reality that they negate. Emblematic of this point is a scene in the ninth chapter, in which Tom delivers Grace to the gangsters and asks them in a roundabout way for a financial reward. The performative contradiction evidenced in Tom's and Dogville's attitude is that a gesture of acceptance assumes the form of domination and abuse.

Importantly, sexuality provides the impetus for analyzing power relationships and this is also elaborated in *Manderlay* in a very categorical way. Echoing Fassbinder, von Trier maintained that one cannot separate the sexual from the political, since the exercise of power is interconnected with sexuality (cited in Nicodemus 2005). This point can be cemented by considering a scene in the fifth chapter of the film, when Grace experiences a sexual fantasy. Grace is shown sleeping and the off-screen narrator describes her dream; a series of close-ups are collated while a number of jump-cuts interrupt the visual track. The voice-over in rather sarcastic way reads: "It manifested itself as a dream. There were women in exotic costumes and men in turbans. Even in her sleep she hated with a passion any idea in allowing that her father might be right. But it was a harem." The diegetic music in the background evokes an exotic atmosphere, which intensifies the irony. Meanwhile, close-ups of Grace's face are followed by distant tableaux of black figures, including Timothy's. Remarkably, the camera endures while registering Grace's facial expressions. But the layered images of the black

Figures 4.17 and 4.18: *Manderlay* (2005).

people are brief and out of focus and are only shown in flashes (figures 4.17 and 4.18). Furthermore, the antithesis between white skin in focus and out-of-focus black one turns into a metacommentary on cinema as a white institution par excellence, and here this gesture blurs once again the frontiers between inside and outside.

The core conjecture is that only Grace is represented as an individual, while the black people are reduced to exoticized figures. The camera work here manifestly visualizes the film's central theme, which is how the liberalist "respect for the right to difference" can culminate in a process of exoticization of the "Others," with the view to controlling them. For Grace, the African American identity is reduced to a fetishized color difference. This was also suggested in a scene in the third chapter of the film, when she decides to offer Jim (Emmanuel Idowu) a gift, but mistakenly gives it to his brother Jack (Javone Prince), only to be mocked by Timothy: "As a matter of fact I've never been able to tell them apart either. They're both colored, and they both got curly hair." Hence, Grace's liberalist rhetoric turns into a process of making the "Other" harmless. Roland Barthes expresses brilliantly this practice of exoticization in an essay written in 1957.

> How can one assimilate the Negro, the Russian? There is here a figure for emergencies: exoticism. The Other becomes a pure object, a spectacle, a clown. Relegated to the confines of humanity, he no longer threatens the security of

the home. This figure is chiefly petit-bourgeois. For, even if he is unable to experience the Other in himself, the bourgeois can at least imagine the place where he fits in: this is what is shown as liberalism, which is a sort of intellectual equilibrium based on recognized places. (1972, 152)

In other words, the process of exoticization becomes a process of violent adjustment of the "Other" to a new supposedly "reformed" reality, which serves the purpose of depoliticizing difference, that is, of preventing the oppressed from becoming active political beings. In effect, this supposedly democratic process of integration leaves untouched maleficent hierarchical structures that perpetuate oppression, albeit in ameliorated ways.

The film works to answer its questions in ways that the clichéd divisions between victims and perpetrators do not account for, since it openly acknowledges the role of the oppressed in the continuation of their submission. From the very first chapter of the film, the spectator is faced with a series of problematic *Haltungen* on the part of the black population. An exemplary illustration is offered in a scene when the plantation Mam threatens Grace and the gangsters with a gun. When they seize her rifle, she faints, and the first person willing to hold her and help her back to her room is Wilhelm, the eldest slave in Manderlay. In the scene immediately after that, Wilhelm shows analogous signs of submission; even when Mam insults him and asks him to leave the room, he acquiesces obediently. Later on, when Grace is ready to leave Manderlay with her father, Wilhelm is the one who asks her to stay a bit longer and give the population the chance to show their "gratefulness," instinctively laying the groundwork for her entry into the community, which will perpetuate the black population's dependency on a different form of white rule.

The deduction is that the former slaves hesitate to leave behind the security provided by their enslaved past. Nowhere is this made clearer than when we realize that Wilhelm was the one who cowrote Mam's book. At this point, the audience gets to know that Timothy does not belong to the category of "the proud Nigger," as Grace also misleadingly assumed. It turns out that Timothy is a "Pleasin Nigger," who can transform himself to the image anticipated by his beholder. A scene in the fourth chapter forewarns us of the performativity of Timothy's identity, who is shown battling with the dust storm, only to satisfy Grace's voyeuristic gaze. Again, Timothy is out of focus and shown from a great distance, and the camera shares Grace's point of view while gazing at "the spectacle" with excitement (figure 4.19). The voice-over comments: "Whether it would make the slightest difference in the grand scale of things was hard to tell,

Figure 4.19: *Manderlay* (2005).

but it was a battle, no matter how senseless it might be, heroic and dangerous." In Grace's eyes Timothy turns into an object of pleasure, not far from what Donald Bogle defines as a "coon" in his renowned study of the representation of blacks in American cinema (2006, 7). But Timothy's performativity is slightly more complicated, because he serves the role of the "coon" by seemingly appearing as a "Brutal Black Buck" (2006, 10). In doing so, he still assumes the exotic postures and attitudes desired by Grace.

Implicit in this scene is the idea that long-term oppression is not one-way process. It is rather a dialectical one, for the oppressed can be content with what they are offered, instead of fighting to change their circumstances. This is a political gesture, because it does not desire to create empathy with the victim. It is a polemical formulation which intends to make the oppressed angry, in order to transform this anger into political action. In this respect, *Manderlay* is not a "protest film"; that is, it is not concerned with ameliorating the present situation, but a radical one, which aims at transforming it and revealing that one of the reasons why the racial problem has not been resolved is the black population's preference to adapt themselves in a white reality, instead of fighting to change it. The film also reveals the totalitarian aspects of standardized forms of social reconciliation, since the implication is that liberal initiatives grounded in abstract ethical/universal ideas can be quite totalitarian. Alain Badiou has perfectly analyzed this, arguing that according to the "ethical ideology" the particularity of difference is valued as long as the "Other" can conform to a course of action that could be summarized as follows: "Become like me and I will respect your difference" (2001, 25).

Through this lens, one may well reexamine Grace's representation in *Dogville*. A closer assessment of a set of contradictions that arise from her depiction may help one perceive the film's intricate texture and go beyond the understanding of it as a story of female exploitation. It is vital here to consider some of von Trier's comments that draw attention to the fact that Grace is not a "Goldheart figure." The term "Goldheart" derives from a Danish picture book titled *Guld Hjerte*. The book's story referred to a young girl "good enough," who played the role of the martyr (Schepelern 2000a, 15). Von Trier employs this term to describe the role of women in his *Goldheart* trilogy, *Breaking the Waves*, *The Idiots*, and *Dancer in the Dark*, where the main characters demonstrate self-renunciation as a means of saving someone else. In contrast to these paradigms, von Trier explains that Grace does not belong to this category.

> Yes Grace acts good-heartedly, but she isn't—and will not be—a "Goldheart figure". She has to possess a capacity for something else. I tried two or three things to get it to work, but I don't know if it does. This is where the concept of arrogance comes in, a refusal to discuss things and analyse them. (cited in Björkman 2003, 252)

In both films, Grace as a character stresses the tension that arises when one is dedicated to enforcing values upon people not prepared to accept them. *Dogville*'s critical reception has not really identified this idea and this is probably the reason why von Trier presses on this so forcefully in *Manderlay*.

However, in *Dogville* there are also moments that question Grace's seemingly flat character and her portrayal as the embodiment of unconditional generosity and forgiveness. Apart from her metamorphosis in the last chapter of the film, nowhere is this point more acutely evident than in a scene in the third chapter, in which she forces Jack, a blind man not reconciled with his disability, to admit that he is blind. Besides the obvious allegory, what renders the scene quite distinctive is the camera's examination of the character and its emphasis on gestures that attest to Grace's transformative potential. Oblique close-ups of Grace's face are followed by frantic camera movements that capture Jack and the very diegetic space, creating a complex interaction between the bodies and space (figures 4.20 and 4.21). The scene merges a series of images that have a narrative significance with others that focus on the very idea of performativity as a process of movement and readjustment. The sequence reaches a climax when Grace opens the curtains in Jack's room and the light accentuates the performative space. Interestingly, the intrusion of light changes Grace's composure, a change that is irreducible to psychological explanation.

In this scene, von Trier's manipulation of the body in space becomes a process in which character, identity, and space are set apart and analyzed. The actress/character's relation to the diegetic space becomes multifaceted. The space

Figures 4.20 and 4.21: *Dogville* (2003).

encompasses the actress performing the character, the character as a narrative agent, and the character as a performative persona, namely as a person who is caught in the process of working to embody and display certain social qualities. Formally and thematically, the scene addresses Grace's performative struggle and the very performative contradiction, which is that an act of kindness results in an aggressive enforcement of values. Grace is implicated in a reality that she opposes, so as to enforce certain values on people not prepared to accept them, and it is in this vein that her moral attitude entails a violent side. Her performativity involves both the process of integrating herself in a set of relationships that contradict her "ideals" and the means she employs to resist her complete assimilation into Dogville.

Commenting on Grace's behavior in *Manderlay*, von Trier stated something that applies to her attitude in *Dogville* too. As he says: "The idea of spreading your values to other places is that's what in the past used to be called a mission and is problematic" (cited in *The Road to Manderlay*: 2005). This standpoint is rendered visible by the film's ending, in which Grace decides that the town's actions "were not good enough." In the midst of a lengthy camera movement, the lighting changes, and we get to see a high-angle shot of Dogville. The camera slowly zooms in and, in a choreographic movement, pans from right to left to capture the people of Dogville in a state of bewilderment (figure 4.22). Critical here is the antithesis between the camera's mobility and the static position of the actors. Then, the camera returns to Grace, who performs a circular movement that heightens

Figure 4.22: *Dogville* (2003).

stylization. When Grace comes to her final conclusion, she walks backwards in a steady and stylized movement that unleashes an energy which prognosticates the forthcoming catastrophe. Here the camera privileges the performing of connections between the bodies; it is by means of this performing that the image dissolves our certainties vis-à-vis the boundaries between oppressors and oppressed.

It is useful now to go back to del Rio's discussion of the affective performative, which I mentioned earlier, so as to explain the effects of this stylization. Del Rio explains that the "eruption" of performative moments that privilege the bodies of the actors is a means of freezing dramatic action and bringing to the fore "unforeseen connections between bodies and concepts." As she says:

> The affective-performative unfolds as an interval demarcated by first the cessation and then the resumption of narrative. Prior to the affective-performative event, ideology seems to be securely in place, yet certain narrative causes or psychological motivations build up a pressure that leads to the moment of performative eruption. In the aftermath, we witness a certain wreckage of ideological stability, the debris of a passing storm, as former corporealities and their relations appear profoundly altered or dislocated. (del Rio 2008, 16)

In light of del Rio's comments, one can see the performative excess of the aforementioned scene as a moment that disrupts "ideological stability," and here "ideological stability" refers to the ethical certainties that the audience has formed so far. Grace's stylized movement toward her father's car becomes a gestural exposition of an attitude and a rhetorical statement that uncovers the thin boundaries between liberal humanism and violence.

This rhetorical statement is intensified by the ironic voice-over which asserts that:

> And all of a sudden she knew the answer to her question all too well. If she had acted like them she could not have defended a single one of her actions and

could not have condemned them harshly enough. It was as if her sorrow and pain finally assumed their rightful place. No. What they had done was not good enough. And if one had the power to put it to right it was one's duty to do so—for the sake of other towns, for the sake of humanity. And not least for the sake of the human being that was Grace herself.

Seen through the prism of Brecht's concept of the social *Gestus*, one recognizes that the voice-over here becomes gestic; that is, it discloses a concrete attitude. According to Brecht, "a language is gestic when it is grounded in a gest and conveys particular attitudes by the speaker towards other men." The sentence "pluck the eye that offends thee out" is less effective from the gestic point of view that "if thine offend thee, plucks [*sic*] it out" (1964, 104). The social *Gestus* in the former scene is also to be found in the contrapuntal use of sound and image. Moreover, the extra-diegetic music—Vivaldi's Cum dederit (Nisi Dominus)— does not describe emotional states, but it also assumes an attitude and intensifies the tableau's gestural shock effect. Grace's thoughts are reported by the voice-over, which de-individuates her and places emphasis on the performative contradiction of effacing a whole town "for the sake of humanity." The voice-over becomes ironic and exposes how appeals to morality and "universal values" may serve certain social interests. Self-abnegation and unconditional giving are exhibited to be simulacra, which conceal deeper political conflicts and processes.

Von Trier's critique of liberal humanism puts forward the conjecture that the moralist reform of a system is an illusion given that ethics are inextricably linked with a specific social context. This point is particularly elucidated in *Manderlay*, and this is why these two films must be discussed in concert with each other. Indeed, *Manderlay* lacks *Dogville*'s complexity, and one can argue that it reduces the first film's questions to bare bones. Either way, the film's ending provides a paradigm of dialectical thinking. We see Grace whipping Timothy viciously, for stating the obvious: "Aren't' you forgetting something? You made us!" Later on, when Grace's father congratulates her for "having a good grip on things," one can clearly see that liberal humanism and social oppression are shown as two sides of the same coin. The fact that the former slaves start chasing Grace for not acquiescing to become their new Mam complicates matters further. Thus, the complex interplay between violent imposition of ethics and the former slaves' collective complicity to their oppression is left unfinished. In this regard, both films are pedagogic, not in the sense that they offer a single-minded message; they rather teach a dialectical method of thinking determined to dissolve liberal ideas based upon a generalized concept of social progress.

Narrative openness as negative dialectics

Political cinema is based on the condition that society and the individuals it consists of are changeable and is not anchored in changes in ethical attitudes that merely conceal the roots of oppression. Such an argument figures importantly in Brecht's theory and practice, and as the philosopher says in *The Messingkauf Dialogues*, a dialectical representation "would treat the moral problem as a historical one too" (1965, 37). Von Trier's depiction of the individual and his or her handling of ethics follow Brecht's approach, since the moral questions are not dissociated from political ones. Both films exhibit the persistence of social antagonisms without pointing to a definite resolution. In *Dogville*, one can identify neither with Dogville's depoliticized working class nor with Tom's and Grace's moralism, which reproduces the causes of social injustice. Similarly, *Manderlay* does not submit to binary moralist contrasts and neither Grace's liberalist ethic nor the former slaves stand for positive forces of change.

Then, how are we to understand this narrative openness that characterizes both films? Are they simply reactionary objects that propagate one-dimensional ideas and do they prescribe to Brian Goss' aphorism that "von Trier's fictional worlds suck the oxygen out for struggles for social betterment" (2009, 131)? In order to see the two films out of the cul-de-sac of nihilism, one needs to acknowledge that they do not produce an all-encompassing worldview that implies a concrete solution to the social problems. However, it is of paramount importance to mention that the lack of positive narrative resolution is not necessarily tantamount to nihilism or reactionary aesthetics, though pessimism seen under a historical context can be understood politically. Michael Haneke, a filmmaker who is also committed to politicizing the audience's perception, phrases this accurately in the following quotation: "I always respond that the true pessimists are those who consider people so stupid that it all comes down to fleecing them with stupefying material, because they do not believe in discussing things seriously" (cited in *News and Stories*). Haneke cogently describes that the production of pseudo-harmonizing effects is a defeatist gesture rather than a positive one, as it is routinely assumed. On this account, experimentation in *Dogville* and *Manderlay* operates as a means of production, but here the term "production" refers to the generation of contradictions and not to their synthetic resolution. This signals an important point: The post-Brechtian merging of materialist dialectics with uncertainty may give rise to negative dialectics.[2]

"Negative dialectics" is a term associated with Theodor Adorno, who argued in favor of a dialectical process that does not produce tangible results and immutable theoretical axioms. Put simply, negative dialectics refers to an accumulation of dialectical contradictions that cannot be synthesized into a harmonious end-result. Suspicious of the Enlightenment ideas of progress, Adorno values a dialectical thinking concerned with producing disintegration and disharmony and thinking "in contradictions for the sake of contradiction once experienced in the thing, and against that contradiction" (2004, 145). The fundamental tenet in his phrasing of negative dialectics is that there is not a direct equation between reason and reality; he, instead, proposes a dialectical practice that does not intend to sublate contradictions, but to expose the nonidentical between concepts and objects. For Adorno, it is via a process of critical negation that dialectical thinking can avoid intellectual conformity and its assimilation by the status quo. The task, therefore, of negative dialectics is to expose the reified character of social relationships and to avoid reducing complex concepts to binary contrasts, for example, myth versus rationality, progress versus regression, and so on. Negative dialectics intends to demystify the standardized liberal thinking of idealist philosophy and to juxtapose antithetical concepts that self-negate each other. For instance, idealist concepts of progress have been negated by the course of history, making it hard to distinguish the boundaries between progress and barbarism.

Adorno defines negative dialectics as an "anti-system" (2004, xx), whose refusal of conformity aspires to negate the fetishization of critical thinking and its assimilation by the status quo in the form of an institutionalized product. Commitment to critical negativity can reveal the "untruth" of social reality, so as to expose its structures to critical understanding. Adorno's aim was the production of ceaseless dialectical collisions and as Susan-Buck Morss idiosyncratically suggests, "this lends to negative dialectics the quality of the quicksilver: just when you think you have grasped the point by turning into its opposite it slips through your fingers and escapes" (1977, 186).

Precisely, this feeling of puzzlement, which aspires to open out social reality to dialectical understanding, is encountered by the audience after the end of *Dogville* and *Manderlay*. To illuminate matters further, I would like to explore the dialectical collisions that work upon the films' key metaphors. In *Dogville*, Tom's preliminary argument that Dogville is not a receptive community is negated by Grace's admission in the town and by her eventual integration. Yet the temporary harmony brought about by Grace's admission is negated by the exchange ethic upon which her residence is founded and by the abuses she suffers. Additionally, Tom's willingness to help Grace is negated by his subordination to the "reciprocal exchange" ethic, which eventually makes him betray her. Finally, Grace's attitude of unconditional generosity and forgiveness is negated by her siding with the gangsters, and by the fact that her decision to destroy a whole town is justified upon the same ethical grounds. Thus, the opposite side of the preliminary negative force, namely Dogville's lack of acceptance and community values, is negated by another negative force, which is the town's brutal catastrophe.

In *Manderlay*, the institution of slavery is abolished by Grace's altruistic intervention, but Grace's optimism apropos the empowerment of the community is negated by the former slaves' compliance with their previous submissive status. Grace's liberation of the slaves is also negated by her forceful attempt to impose a set of values and morals to the black community. Her aspiration to transform them into active citizens makes them conform to a model that she vehemently enforces. In effect, the process of liberation is negated by a process of aggressive enforcement that interrogates the frontiers between freedom and manipulation. One can clearly see that the dialectical collisions in both films do not unify to a synthetic resolution. Von Trier offers them to the audience to stimulate argumentative experimentation, and this treatment of the material avoids the pitfalls of easy conclusions. Each antithesis that comes as a negation of a preliminary thesis does not become a positive force, but an act of negativity that refutes an answer to the questions.

Like Brecht's plays, both films' open-endedness shifts the questions from the screen to the auditorium but without sharing the closed form of the Brechtian *Fabel*. One of the fundamental tenets of Brecht's theory and practice is that catharsis should be replaced by contemplation, something that has influenced political cinema too. One may recall Peter Wollen's table of countercinematic traits, in which he argues that narrative closure that characterizes classical cinema is replaced by "narrative aperture" in "counter-cinema" (1982, 91). Brecht considered that the Aristotelian valorization of the emotional purging of the audience flattened out the portrayed contradictions and failed to implicate the audience in a productive way. In this fashion, narrative openness served the role of awakening the audience, so as to perceive its historical role. Furthermore, this formal element aimed at changing the social function of the medium, which restricted the audience to the status of consumers. As mentioned in Chapter 1, in Brecht's utopian view, the reinstating of the audience's productive position within the theater/cinema could be a means of rethinking their productive role in the social field.

Nonetheless, Brecht's interest in leaving the contradictions unresolved is restricted by the closed form of the *Fabel*, which implies that socialism can be a means of combating social injustice. One has to recall the last scene in *Kuhle Wampe*, which makes quite evident that socialism could resolve the peoples' misery. Similarly, Joan's assertion that "where force rules only force can help" in *Saint Joan of the Stockyards* becomes an agitational call for change (1997, 308). According to Brecht, the *Fabel* is the logic of history, and, for the socialist left of his time, history—the negation of the old world by means of dialectical collisions of antithetical social interests—was the route to social and political progress. In contrast to Brecht's progressive view of history, von Trier's deployment of narrative openness does not put forward any specific political proposition that might tackle the causes of social oppression. In many respects, *Dogville*'s and *Manderlay*'s ending is pessimistic (but not nihilistic), and this pessimism can be understood historically. The establishment of late capitalism after the collapse of a socialist alternative forces us to reconsider politics and representation, and radical politics can be joined together with historical pessimism. Thus, a critique of the existing social reality can be effective given that one combines it with a critique of the perception of history as progress. Buck-Morss formulates this quite eloquently:

> Traditionally it was the socialist left that believed in historical progress, while the right, the social conservatives were the nostalgic critics of history's course. But in this century, revolutionary politics and historical pessimism have been brought together because intellectual integrity would not allow otherwise. One cannot have lived in the twentieth century, which is grinding and bumping to a close as we speak and still maintain an unshaken belief, either in capitalism as the answer to the prayers of the poor, or in history as the realization of reason.... Meanwhile as the grey background of these political events, the economic gap between rich and poor not only persists; it has become an abyss, a situation for which the new global organization of capitalism—unchallenged as the winner in history—no longer even tries to apologize. (2002, 212)

Buck Morss' argument can help us see both films' pessimism historically and clarify their post-Brechtian dialectics. Contrary to the forward-looking politics of Brecht's dialectics, *Dogville* and *Manderlay* exhibit the falsehood of the very notion of historical progress, which informs the rhetoric of right-wing forces that celebrate capitalism's establishment.

One could object that both films offer a very abstract and static perception of social relationships and a fixed view of "human nature," implying that social change is unfeasible. However, von Trier's treatment of identity is dynamic and not static, since changes in social circumstances and shifts in power relations modify the characters' attitudes. When it comes to violence, *Dogville* takes a dialectical view of it to show the impossibility of mutual collaboration and prosperity within a system structured upon the capitalist ethic of making profit by means of exploitation. As such, the characters' uncritical reproduction of this ethic and the violence that accompanies it assume the form of dialectical negations that indicate the unlikely prospect of change within capitalism. In *Manderlay*, violence is the outcome of the vicious circle of racial oppression that has been ameliorated, but certainly not eradicated. In these terms, von Trier presents us with uncomfortable truths that refer to pernicious social structures outside the narrative. This is reinforced by both films' end-credits that offer a succession of still images taken from Jacob Holdt's book *American Pictures*. In *Dogville*, we see images of the Great Depression, of poverty, racism, and violence accompanied by David Bowie's song *Young Americans*. Similarly, *Manderlay*'s end-credits are accompanied by the same song and press forcefully on the persistence of structures that perpetuate racial divisions. A plethora of images ranging from the American Civil War to the Rodney King abuse and the Iraq war succeed one another in a frenetic way. The images become rhetorical manifestations, and here von Trier connects the filmic with the extra-filmic reality. The obvious inference is that the world needs to be changed, but the director is not in the position to provide the audience with a thesis that can lead to social transformation. His commitment to critical negativity is not a defeatist gesture, but it is exactly this refusal to provide the audience with harmonizing effects that stresses the need for social change.

Notes

1   Robert Sinnerbrink also discusses the idea of exchange in the film, but while I see the act of exchange as a social law that motivates the characters' actions, Sinnerbrink discusses it in different terms, that is, as the "libidinal economy of desire" that infiltrates the system. Robert Sinnerbrink, "Grace and Violence: Questioning Politics and Desire in Lars von Trier's Dogville," in *SCAN/Journal of Media Arts Culture*, 4:2 (2007) available online at http://www.scan.net.au/scan/journal/display.php?journal_Id=94.

2   David Barnett makes a similar point in his forthcoming article "Performing Dialectics in an Age of Uncertainty, or: Why Post-Brechtian Does Not Mean Postdramatic," in *Postdramatic Theatre and the Political International Perspectives on Contemporary Performance* (London: Bloomsbury, 2013).

Epilogue: Dialogue with the "Dissensual" Past

In the course of a prolonged camera movement, Justine guides her little nephew (Cameron Spurr) to a shelter made out of wood sticks. Then she grasps her petrified sister's (Charlotte Gainsbourg) hand and accompanies her inside the shelter. A typical von-Triersque scene follows, in which the camera does not simply capture dramatic action but registers each character from a variety of angles or half-out of frame, rarely placing the three of them together in the same frame. Moving frantically from one face to another, the camera disembodies the characters capturing their hands and their postures and then cutting to close-ups of their faces. The buildup of visual tension in tandem with the extra-diegetic employment of Wagner's *Tristan and Isolde* creates a feeling of hokeyness. Ultimately, the three characters are framed together and in the background we see the planet Melancholia approaching and finally destroying the earth (figure E.1). This is a passage from the finale of *Melancholia,* in which once again we encounter the characteristic von-Trieresque method, which is committed to showing the process of showing an action rather than reproducing clear-cut dramatic effects. The frantic camera movements destabilize subjective points of view and the produced material joins together drama, irony, parody, and a performative excess on the part of the camera and the actors. Peculiarly, the end of this sequence produces a sense of relief rarely generated in the endings of his previous films. The film is divided into two chapters, and in the first one von Trier shows in stretched-out sequences Justine's wedding. The guests and her family are representative of a world of wealth, hypocrisy, and social conventions. The prolonged sequences of the wedding ceremony inundate the audience with social *Gestus* which bring to the fore the emptiness and meaninglessness of this bourgeois reality. The question posed rather simply is, can this world be changed? Failing to present an alternative to this reality, the film's ending underpins the epistemological crisis and implies that we must start from the beginning.

Figure E.1: *Melancholia* (2011).

It is beyond dispute that the film's employment of digital effects acts as a form of negation and not aestheticization, and this is firmly confirmed by its concluding visual, which implies that "we must do away with the old." That said, *Melancholia*'s stylization and its merging of excessive visuals with a more standardized von-Triersque post-Dogme camera work has little to do with the aestheticized and reproductive use of digital technology in contemporary Hollywood. In other words, the film's employment of technology as a form of negation of "the old" (the old world and the current state of cinema) does not differ much from *The Idiots*' aesthetic which proposed that technology should commit itself to the production of films that do not simply narrate stories but promote a radical criticism of conventional forms of cinematic narration and of conformist social practices and modes of behavior too. This provides the means to recapitulate the post-Brechtian aspect of von Trier's cinema. The quintessence of Brecht's theory is to deconstruct everyday actions into their social-determining factors and offer the audience time to think and reflect on social relations that need not to be preserved, but demolished. The process of making the familiar strange is primarily a method of negation as confirmed by Brecht himself: "Verfremdung als ein Verstehen (verstehen—nicht verstehen—verstehen), Negation der Negation" (Making the familiar strange to produce comprehension (to understand, to not understand, to understand), negation of negation) (*Schriften* 3, 180). As such, defamiliarization aims at negating the old, a process that precedes the heralding of the new and this is one of the important aspects of Brecht's theory which is generally overlooked by film studies scholars. But as the aforementioned quotation implies, there is an optimistic insinuation in Brecht's thinking which suggests that the concrete new is possible based upon his Marxist view of the unity of theory and practice.

I began this book in an attempt to accentuate the ways in which form in von Trier's films generates *Verfremdungseffekte* that perform dialectical negations which do not lead to categorical conclusions, but operate as unfinished materials that the audience needs to rework and rethink. These negations are in accordance with Brecht's intention to understand social phenomena and interactions beyond the realms of the natural, that is, the reductive view of the social present as permanent and unchangeable. In all his films, von Trier stages dialectical clashes and emphasizes the social component in the characters' gestures and attitudes, but the depicted relations do not provide conclusive resolutions. The reason for this commitment to critical negativity rests on the fact that von Trier is not constrained by what Heiner Müller defines as "the ideological gaze." In a quite polemical statement, Müller synopsizes the post-Brechtian dialectical open-endedness arguing that "every ideological gaze [...] is a false gaze and prevents seeing what is really there" (cited in Barnett 2010, 18). The key to the comprehension of this statement is that political art should not provide a secure hermeneutical interpretative system, not only because history has disputed the optimism for a rational, progressive world made of enlightened individuals but also because the propagation of definite resolutions can end up institutionalizing even the most radical politics by reducing the audience to the status that they are accorded by mainstream systems of narration, that is, to consumers of "messages." After all, as stated in the previous chapter, critical negativity is not principally synonymous with nihilism, but it can be seen as a way of imagining something that is not available. In these terms, von Trier's deployment of *Verfremdungseffekte* does not follow the Orthodox Brechtian interpretative system, but is more in line with a point that Brecht phrased in the early 1940s while his ideas on dialectical theater were at an embryonic stage: "the mysteries of the world are not solved, they are demonstrated" (1993, 120). Accordingly, von Trier's cinema is compliant with the polemical nature of the *Verfremdungseffekt*, which intends not to produce unity and harmony in the auditorium, but to confront the audience with questions that can revive conflict.

It is of paramount importance to emphasize that von Trier's intention to reanimate film practice is very much influenced by the past historical/cinematic debates. Von Trier can be paralleled to Walter Benjamin's historian, who quotes the fragments of the past to make sense of the past and the present. Many of his formal experiments are not innovative, and as he says, "I don't think I am becoming increasingly extremist within film. I just take some old principles and try to do something funny with them. Like a carpenter, who explores wood's many possibilities" (cited in Schepelern 2005c, 120). Elsewhere he stated, "Mange af de ting, jeg bruger, er jo filmiske klichéer. Det er byggesten, som jeg har, klichéer, som jeg godt kan lide" (Many of the materials I am using are cinematic clichés. These clichés that I am fond of are my starting point) (cited in Schepelern 2005a). My discussion of the films' form has already pointed out that some of the films' formal features are not necessarily innovative. For example, how can one characterize the Dogme 95 project as original, or the strategies of representation employed in the *Europa* trilogy, or even the Fassbinderian manipulation of melodramatic clichés in *Breaking the Waves* and *Dancer in the Dark*? Perhaps, there is something historically important in this dialogue with the cinematic/historical past and this is something that can account for my own anachronistic methodology, which returns to a figure like Brecht so as to understand the politics of von Trier's cinema.

Von Trier's oeuvre is drenched with references to the modernist cinema of the past, and his politicization of the medium is combined with his insistent belief in the European art cinema narration. Commenting on *Melancholia*, Steven Shaviro intimates that the film assumes an antimodernist stance implying that even modernist forms are now bereft of their "subversive edge" (2012, 29). We return again to the fundamental mistake committed by film scholars in associating modernism and Brechtianism with a set of stylistic devices instead of considering it as a methodology and a form of negation. To this it should be added that modernism in the arts was not a unified whole as it is wrongly assumed, but it included a plethora of different trends. For instance, even fascist artistic experiments are products of modernism in the wider sense and they also assume a critique of modernity, not to foreground the new, but to express nostalgia for premodernist social hierarchies. On the other hand, radical modernist filmmakers of the likes of Pasolini, Antonioni, and Fassbinder included an auto-critique of modernity in their own films, suggesting that capitalism homogenizes social environments, human interactions, and artistic experiments. Subsequently, the criticism of modernity from within is not something new, and as David Harvey accurately intimates one can even identify this in Charlie Chaplin's *Modern Times* (1936) (1990, 32). To return to von Trier, one cannot avoid noticing the persistent references to the major art cinema figures of the past. Even in the notorious interview at the Cannes film festival in May 2011, von Trier admitted that some of the major sources of influence for *Melancholia* were modernist filmmakers, such as Antonioni, Visconti, and Bergman.

Von Trier's work, thus, is a reanimation of a practice with its roots in a number of modernist predecessors such as Brecht. This return to modernism is not a postmodern nostalgic gesture, but a means of resisting the assimilation of his work on the part of the cinematic institution. The cinematic and pedagogical institutions have absorbed even the most radical filmmakers of the past of the likes of Godard, Fassbinder, and Antonioni, as a result of treating their works as museum pieces and not as objects that can help us politicize our perception of the present. Antithetically, von Trier's dialogue with the past aspires to reevaluate and rethink the resistant aspect of the modernist art cinema in the current historical circumstances. Put simply, his films retain the modernist will to negate the old, and here the old stands for the institutionalized. In the Manifesto that accompanied his first feature film he wrote, "We will no longer be satisfied with 'well-meaning films' with a 'humanist message' " (Manifesto 1, Appendix). This statement clearly castigates the institutionalization of the European art cinema. Then again, this critique of art cinema comes from within, since von Trier's films dispense with the institutionalized elements of the past and at the same time make use of the elements that produce an aesthetics of resistance. This can help us understand the reason why his films do not subscribe to a postmodernist celebration of commodification and depoliticization. However, von Trier is an artist who has witnessed the failures of the utopian aspirations of modernity and this is why he is more concerned with disclosing social disharmonies instead of providing one-sided resolutions. What does then this dialogue with the past indicate?

A pertinent starting point would be that modernist art cinema's formal experimentation can still perform conflict and reveal contradictions, which do not produce uniform interpretations based upon the "humanization" of complex political issues. As a first step in clarifying this point, I want to consider the writings of Jacques Rancière. Despite Rancière's reservation toward *Dogville*, his writings can illuminate the historical aspect of von Trier's dialogue with the past and the historicity of my Brechtian methodology. Rancière has published various essays on film and it is important to point out his insistence on figures of the past, such as Brecht, Rossellini, Godard, and Straub/ Huillet. What he identifies as relevant in the aforementioned figures is the sense of conflict, which he considers to be necessary for the politicization of art. Their works communicate "dissensus" that is absent from many contemporary films. According to Rancière, "dissensus" describes a political process which intends to confront our established framework of perception. As he says:

> What "dissensus" means is an organization of the sensible where there is neither a reality concealed behind appearances nor a single regime of presentation and interpretation of the given imposing its obviousness on all. It means that every situation can be cracked open from the inside, reconfigured in a different regime of perception and signification. To reconfigure the landscape of what can be seen and what can be thought is to alter the field of the possible and the distribution of capacities and incapacities. Dissensus brings back into play both the obviousness of what can be perceived, thought and done, and the distribution of those who are capable of perceiving, thinking and altering the co-ordinates of the shared world. (2009, 48–49)

To retain its countercultural force, cinema should avoid generating "consensus" in the auditorium. Producing a unity of ethics, aesthetics, and politics in the auditorium is tantamount to depoliticizing the medium and reproducing the social reality as natural. For this reason, contemporary cinema has much to learn from the European art cinema and from the modernist debates of the past.

Rancière's point that there is more to be sought and found in the "dissensual" politics of Brecht, Godard, Rossellini, and Straub/Huillet can be seen as a negation of the reign of the commodity and as a desire to reactivate conflict and repoliticize the medium (Conley 2005, 105). Mostly, this gesture implies that films do not become political by reproducing a political subject matter, but by helping to disrupt our perception of reality as self-evident and unchangeable. Seen through the prism of Rancière's argument, von Trier's dialogue with the past as well as his insistence on the art cinema narration demonstrate a willingness to avoid the commodification of the medium and to produce films that challenge our social certainties. In a historical period that alternatives find no firm foothold, von Trier's films build upon the "dissensual" politics of the art cinema of the past so as to challenge the politics of perception.

His ability to experiment with film form and to challenge the institution of cinema is largely attributed to his involvement with Zentropa, a film production company he cofounded with Peter Aalbæk Jensen in 1992. Initially set up to produce von Trier's films, Zentropa has now turned out to be the largest film production company in Scandinavia. Zentropa produces a plethora of films including both risk-taking projects and other objects that respond to a wider audience. Currently von Trier and Jensen own 25 percent of the company; 25 percent is shared by its employees, while the remaining 50 percent is owned by Nordisk films. Zentopa's *modus operandi* allows von Trier to engage in projects without worrying about the box office success. It is not accidental that both von Trier and Jensen consider *Dogville* as one of their most important achievements, simply because very few companies would invest their money in such a project. One has also to acknowledge the role of the Danish film policy. Denmark is a country with a significant film tradition and provides state funding for filmmaking, priding itself on being a nation that funds arts. Since 2003, the Danish Film Institute introduced a new policy titled New Danish Screen, which encourages "interesting failures" and risk-taking projects by new talents, and the funding is allocated without any "recovery requirements" (Redvall 2012, 214). Meanwhile, contemporary filmmakers like Christopher Boe and Simon Staho continue renewing the Danish cinematic tradition by making films that do not follow uniform patterns of narration. Commenting on the Danish film funding policy, von Trier has stated, "I can't imagine being able to make the films I've made in any other country than Denmark. Maybe I could have made them in the Soviet Union before things changed" (cited in Björkman 2003, 102). Von Trier's comments help us understand the amount of freedom he has in the filmmaking process and the reasons why he can still make films that would have been difficult to produce under a more standard financing system, something that he and Jørgen Leth acknowledge in the interviews they gave me.

This industrial context allows von Trier to experiment with new ideas, rather than following the canons of the industry or even repeating formulas that have been previously proved commercially successful. For instance, the international box office success of *Breaking the Waves* was followed by *The Idiots*, a film whose formal and thematic treatment of a sensitive subject matter made it inaccessible to a wide audience. Similarly, the popularity of *Dancer in the Dark*, which sold 4.4 million tickets globally and earned him the *Palme d'or* in the Cannes film festival, was followed by the release of *Dogville*. The film's cinematic austerity and experimentation was bound to appeal to a smaller audience, something that did not prevent von Trier from following the same formula in *Manderlay*. Finally, the release of such a provocative film as *Antichrist* was bound to stir controversy and respond to a smaller audience compared to his past works. *Melancholia* subscribed to a more mainstream aesthetic only to be followed by the coming *Nymphomaniac,* which seems to do away with the polished aesthetic of the previous film. As he says, "You can become so good at producing things that they become nauseatingly boring to look at. That might have happened had I continued to make the same film again and again, as some people do" (cited in Bondebjerg 2000, 213).

Lars von Trier's films continue dividing audiences and critics and perform conflicts revealing the persistence of historical, social, and sexual antagonisms, challenging film form and subject matter without offering reductive messages. It remains to be seen whether detailed formal/political analyses of his films will minimize discussions of the director's eccentric persona. I hope, nonetheless, that this book will have introduced the reader to the political implications of form in the films under discussion. Von Trier's approach toward filmmaking is rooted in a practice that renders the familiar strange so as to create conflict in the auditorium, in the press, and in the media. It is by means of such a division that he activates questions regarding the world outside the cinema. In effect, his films do not produce relief to the audience by means of moralist assertions, but negations that are not complemented by positive instructions on how to overcome the impasse. It is time to draw our attention to the politics of form in the films of Lars von Trier.

Appendix
Interview with Lars von Trier

The following interview took place on Friday, November 12, 2010, in Lars von Trier's office in Zentropa Productions.

AK: One of my favorite experiments is showing your films to people that have no background in art cinema. What interests me is that they always provoke discussions and strong responses as opposed to other art films that cannot address the nonexpert. I use the term "narrative avant-garde" to describe your films. What do you think?

Lars von Trier: Yes, yes I agree. I am just right now editing *Melancholia* and it seems I am back, for various reasons, to very sentimental issues. It is very strange because even when I am writing a script that has no sentimentality whatsoever, when I am working with the actors extreme emotions seem to take over. It is a kind of perversion. It always comes back to these extreme themes—persons suffering etc.—which is very nonart cinema. I do not know. If it is fun to write something it is fun on a narrative level. But when you direct it, it is fun to direct it so that it works on an emotional level. It is different things you are after in a different level of a work. I asked myself today how this film (*Melancholia*) turned out to be so emotional and it should not be at all.

AK: Speaking of emotions, since *Breaking the Waves* some of your films are characterized by an excess of affect and emotionality. It is interesting because this excess renders emotions and feelings strange.

LvT: I can only say that, when I do something I tend to do it very much. That is technical-wise too. I think I started with *Breaking the Waves*. I wanted to do a film that my parents would hate, in order to investigate emotions a bit. It is like bad taste that I like working with. You should not underestimate the pleasure of doing it. It's like painting something and putting blue into green. It is a strange pleasure when things become very emotional. It is also a forbidden area too, because we tend to adhere to logic and rationality. In my childhood we laughed a little at films that were very sentimental. The right way to see a film was to be detached. I am quite emotional…

AK: Just a footnote in this question. Despite this excess of emotionality, I think that you do not force feelings to someone. One cannot digest this excess easily. So, I think that there is an element of detachment.

LvT: But here you are talking about technique. Emotion is like using very strong colors in a painting and after you are done with the painting you are using some stuff to hide and disguise it. That is how I see it.

AK: Yet all your films are self-reflexive; they do not just reproduce a story; they reflect the process of their making too.

LvT: Yes that is true. Earlier in my career it was very important to show how things were done. For instance, in *Europa*, I wanted to show that I am superimposing images and not to hide it. Not so much with the last film, which is all about computers. Though you could do that with a computer.

AK: Sometimes your manipulation of genres brings to the surface some of their most reactionary aspects. For instance, *Antichrist* created so much commotion, because it manipulates a genre which has reproduced many misogynist stereotypes.

LvT: The portrayal of the sexes in *Antichrist* has to do with my big love for Strindberg. There is something about the battle of sexes that is quite interesting. Strindberg was a kind of a hero also because he allowed himself to be completely unreasonable.

AK: Yet speaking of Strindberg, it is interesting that he was not politically correct. The same applies to you. Your films are not politically correct. Political correctness normally tries to hide something.

LvT: There are different ways of doing a film. I am trying to avoid the obvious. Also, you have no respect for your audience when you do a film that is politically correct. Political correctness kills everything. I think that people who see a film should have an opinion about it and form their own views and even protest against the film. Political correctness is inartistic. Especially American political correctness is really tiresome.

AK: So you see your audience as collaborators in the construction of meaning?

LvT:	Yes certainly. The audience has to participate when watching my films.
AK:	I want to go back to the *Europa* trilogy. Recently I organized a screening of *Europa,* and it is interesting to see how the film works under the current historical circumstances in Europe.
LvT:	Well, you know that I used to be a communist. I am still getting fascinated when I see a documentary about Mao. Especially the Cultural Revolution was a great idea. I must admit some of these people, like Lenin and Mao, are icons that I can understand. Even though, they were all quite horrible, because they killed millions of people. Lenin was horrible too. But they have this celebrity status that I feel I know them. The cynical aspect of a film director can be evil also. It is a cynical pursuit of a goal. And I can become a bit cynical with my actors. Of course, I do not gas them or put them into camps!
AK:	You just mentioned communism and it is interesting that in the past progress was associated with left-wing forces and nowadays the word "progress" has been appropriated by right-wing ones.
LvT:	It is difficult for me to see that there is any historical progress. I am too old fashioned.
AK:	All the characters in the *Europa* trilogy become voyeurs of history and they are punished for that.
LvT:	Of course, being a spectator can be tantamount to being a criminal! If you are a spectator of a crime!
AK:	Since *Breaking the Waves,* you have this shooting method according to which the actors are not aware whether they are on frame or not.
LvT:	That's how it should be in principle, but I kept telling them off. Especially in *Breaking the Waves* I kept telling them: "You just waited for the camera!"
AK:	Yes but there are moments that one senses that the actors act out of character due to this shooting style. Especially in *The Idiots.*
LvT:	Oh yes. I am very interested in this. I am interested in capturing the actors when they are in and out of character. The borderline between the private individual and the character is very

intriguing. Especially, when it overlaps and you cannot tell whether a reaction can be attributed to the actor or the character. That is where I try to go very often.

AK: Thus, in a way the characters manifest their own fictionality.

LvT: Yes you could say that.

AK: Also most of your films have a kind of semidocumentary form, as if they document the process of their own making.

LvT: But this is like cheating as well. I had this camera operator in *Breaking the Waves* that I had to lie to so as to do these strange movements. I told him, for example, pan to the left the actors are going to the left, and the actors would move to the right. The aim was to use the camera to find things instead of framing things. But that is not very easy for a lot of camera operators. For me, it is not interesting when I am watching a scene and know where the camera movement starts and where it is going to end.

AK: But you have acted as a camera operator in *The Idiots*, in *Dancer in the Dark,* and in *Dogville*. Does it allow you more freedom?

LvT: Oh yes I have been a camera operator. Unfortunately, not in my last film, because I was not capable of directing and being the camera operator at the same time. I like it very much because it lets your interest move the camera… That is the best, I like it very much. But that is also because we were using a handheld camera. A handheld camera tells you more, while a camera on the tripod tells you less. A handheld camera is like handwriting.

AK: So it is less an interest of reproduction.

LvT: I become a spectator of the scene and that means that I am going at different places. Anyway, it is not an attempt to capture truth. There is a little scene—very improvised—in *Dancer in the Dark*. Selma's son has just got his bike and they walk around by a bridge. In that scene everybody was pretty much out of character. The actors improvised and they talked about strange things that made no sense. Somebody says something like "women are like rust." I do not know where that came from. This is one of my favorite scenes. Mainly because you see Catherine Deneuve and Björk becoming also private and not being in character, while both are used to a more controlled way of performing.

AK:	I am very interested in the role of language in your films. Sometimes, I have the feeling that language stages its own performance. I have in mind the dialogue between Grace and her father in *Dogville*.
LvT:	Ok I will talk to you about this particular scene. I wanted to show Grace's potential for something else and this could only emerge through this long dialogue. It was really difficult for me. Normally, when you have your characters so well laid out, they cannot say anything that contradicts their behavior. I was so interested in making her do something that she would not do—that would go against the character. That is why the conversation became so long. I struggled to do this. The film's ending became so long because of this. But Nicole and James Caan were great.
AK:	Yet out of this conversation Grace ends up justifying the town's catastrophe. This is achieved through rationalized arguments and this is where language's rationalism becomes the synonym for terror. The same happens with the male character in *Antichrist*.
LvT:	I know what you are getting at and I can see it working as an argument, but I have not thought about it.
AK:	I want to go back to the *Dogme Manifesto*. The Manifesto implies that technology should go back "to the right hands." This is something that we can see in political modernist writings too. Brecht, in his cinematic writings, argued that technology should be taken from the "merchants" so as to be used in a radical way.
LvT:	Interesting, I have not seen Brecht writing anything about film. You know better than me where these things come from. I know in principle Brecht's basic theory of the *Verfremdungseffekt*. I can understand this effect. On the other hand, truth is difficult to define and in particular, when we are dealing with the media. It is not just how a character says something, but it has to do with all aspects of cinema. It is more the feeling you have as a director. There are moments that I can understand that I got a second of "truth," though it is a banal word. For me, it is very obvious when I capture a moment of truth.
AK:	Yes Brecht wrote on film too and he kept on doubting any productive outcome stemming from the simple reproduction of

dramatic situations. Previously you have also said that you are not interested in "pure reproduction."

LvT: That is right. I am not interested in reproducing a film. But a lot of people are interested in this process. Even though a filmmaker reproduces material or even steals from others.

AK: The *Dogme Manifesto* argued in favor of an anti-illusionist film practice together with a realist style. For many years realism was seen as pure reproduction. In *The Idiots,* you managed to make a film which is realist and self-reflexive at the same time.

LvT: Don't ask me too much about the Manifesto. I remember the rules but not the first page. I used to be a keen reader of Breton's Surrealist Manifesto. And "Manifesto" is a great word.

AK: But can realism be political? Can you make a realist film that is not reproduction?

LvT: Without being very clever about it, I think that *The Idiots* is a very political film. But I am not sure whether I can explain how and why.

AK: Some of your films have a very dramaturgical simplicity and this simplicity renders them very complex.

LvT: Well, in this film that we are doing now—*Melancholia*—we have this very simple thing that this planet is approaching the earth and they are going to collide, which is very simple, but it leaves you a lot of space and I think it is like a very simple melody in a symphony that you can do anything with it. Imagine a simple theme in a Beethoven symphony, which starts in a very melodic way and then explodes. As long as you have that theme, you can do anything with it. Relatively quickly I thought that it is a good idea to start with a simple story. Simple stories want to make you go into the film. It is as if you want to enter a wild and mystical forest and you can only go with a friend that can show you around. And here "the friend" stands for this very simple narrative level.

AK: After *Breaking the Waves*, though this applies to *Epidemic* too, your use of music is much more austere. In *The Idiots* you have no extra-diegetic music at all. Some of your best scenes in all your films have no music at all.

LvT: To me it is just extremely irritating when you see a film and then the director tries to force your ways to feel a film by means of music. You just listen to the music and you realize that the way you feel, your idea of the film are just forced to you. I am like oh fuck! I want to see it in my own way. But this is going to be very different in this film. We are using Wagner in *Melancholia*. It is all very romantic.

AK: What strikes me in your films is that the boundaries between the oppressors and the oppressed are not easily distinguishable.

LvT: Oh yes. But I am old fashioned. I do not believe in good and evil. I think that there are tendencies inside an individual; it is like a more complex understanding of human nature.

AK: I have the feeling that the portrayed relationships in your films can be understood historically. You even mentioned in an interview that the most banal films are the ones that have a very definite idea of human nature.

LvT: I am definitely trying not to make one-dimensional films and I intend to show human relationships in their complexity.

AK: People used to consuming very violent films find it difficult to deal with your employment of violence, which is normally kept to a minimum. Is violence a formal tool in your films?

LvT: Well I do not take violence easily. But when you are a melancholic person as I am, it is very interesting to see yourself as a victim. By doing that, you can easily see how you can make it even worse for yourself. I feel very much from the point of view of the victim and that is what interests me when it comes to violence.

AK: In *Dogville* and *Manderlay* you set up film experiments that fuse elements from literature, theater, and philosophy. After so many years of cinematic production people are still resistant to such a formal experimentation in narrative cinema. Is it because film is still considered to be a reproductive medium?

LvT: Well the main reason for this has to do with the fact that earlier on and right now—maybe not in the future—films are very expensive to make. People tend to reproduce more and only move a little bit, because it is so expensive. People tend to stand on the shoulders of the ones before... Film also depends on a large crew. It is not like sitting in front of your computer and writing a novel. It is not costly for a writer to experiment a lot, but it is not the same when you are making a film. I am in a privileged situation here that I can still finance my films. I am kind of working with this in mind, that is, that I do not have problem funding my films. And this obliges me to be a bit freer than most directors. It is difficult for me to see a film like *Dogville* being made under a more standard financing system.

AK: To my understanding you are a political filmmaker.

LvT: Interesting, people tend to think that political cinema is something like Ken Loach, which I do not think is right.

Interview with Jørgen Leth

This Skype interview with the filmmaker took place on Wednesday, July 18, 2012. Certain answers were slightly modified by the filmmaker after e-mail contact in November 2012.

AK: You keep on saying "that my basic idea is that I know nothing, but I would like to know something."

Jørgen Leth: That's the starting point. I do not know anything. I want to learn something. I am learning throughout the process. I do not have a meaning that I want to sell to others. I learn what I see. The process of creating is in itself sometimes a mystical process. Strange things happen during the writing or the filmmaking process which lead me to new directions.

AK: You mentioned writing and there are numerous references in the act of writing in your films. Take as an example *The Erotic Man* (*Det Erotiske Menneske*, 2010) or in your film *I'm Alive—Søren Ulrik Thomsen* (*Jeg er levende—Søren Ulrik Thomsen, digter*, 1999), where you focus on the materials of writing, for example, typewriters and pens.

JL: I always saw a relationship between filming and writing. For me filming is a similar process like poetry. It is a wonder to write poetry, because you do not know where it takes you. That's a process which is both mystical and spontaneous. I follow a similar practice when I am filming. I am trying to reach that kind of clarity, that kind of simplicity that you get when you put pen to paper. From my earlier films, for example, *The Perfect Human* (*Der Perfekte Menneske*, 1968), to the most recent ones, I am trying to bring things back to basics, to bring a sense of spontaneity like the one you get when you write.

AK: But this naïve approach to reality is the key to complexity.

JL: I pretend to be naïve as you know from the questions I pose in films like in *Life in Denmark* (*Livet I Danmark*, 1972). These are simple questions and quite naïve. It is a simplistic

way to deal with life. This is a play. I choose the concepts
that I am trying to play with. It makes more sense to ask
simple, naïve questions. When I film people, I ask them very
simple questions, I ask them where they work, what they do,
etc. I want you to understand that my generation of poets,
artists, reacted against the modernism of the 40s and 50s.
Godard with Vivre Sa Vie (1962) was close to that feeling of a
generational turning point. He was working with language as
building bricks and so were we. Other sources of inspiration
were Duchamp's, William Bourroughs, Warhol, John Cage,
and Jules Supervielle, who once said he wanted to invite the
smallest, the gayest words of language to a glorious party. I am
doing something similar in my poetry. I use no metaphors at
all. I am keeping it simple. The same I am doing in my films.
I ask my actors to "just be there and face the camera." I prefer
one maximum two persons in a frame. It is an aesthetic choice
which is quite clear in *Life in Denmark*. I asked various people
to come in a black studio dressed in their own clothes and to
bring their own props and to say simple sentences. I expect
simple answers, for example, "I like dogs." That's all I need to
know. Just a few words, like Warhol's line in *66 Scenes from
America* (*66 Scener fra Amerika*, 1982): "My name is Andy
Warhol and I just finished eating a hamburger." In *Life in
Denmark*, I was also inspired by the anthropologist Bronisław
Malinowski, whose approach relied very much on simple
observation. My work corresponds to this idea. I want to put
pictures in a box. I do not want drama.

AK: Brecht thought that there is a connection between political art
and naiveté. It strikes me that in the seminar we had with you,
many people thought of your naïve approach to filmmaking
as political. Brecht also suggested that the camera should be
searching for things rather than copying things.

JL: Yes, Brecht's idea of the *Verfremdungseffekt* was another essential
part of the horizon, also for me, and through Godard. But I
never thought I made political statements in my films or in my
writing. Unless you say, as some do, that every uttered word or
image is a political statement in itself. I don't want to get into
that. Brecht of course is right in saying that the camera should

search instead of copy. The camera should be studying things, trying to show secrets.

AK: You mentioned somewhere the idea of collapsable fictions.

JL: That's—I think—a great idea which I developed in my film *Interference* (*Udenrigskorrespondenten*, 1983), the original title was *Foreign Correspondent*. I had a sketch of a story about a foreign correspondent in a dangerous place, whose life is falling apart. In a way it is a classical story, you've seen it in *Foreign Correspondent* (1940), in *Professione: Reporter* (1975), and in other films. But inside that what I am doing is, I am bringing two actors from Denmark and place them in Haiti. I went to Haiti in 1982 and I witnessed many situations that I wanted to include in a fictional story.

AK: This is also indicative of your tendency to be "in-between" on the border between reality and fiction.

JL: Yes that's certainly an important aspect of my work. Even in my documentary films, there is always an element of fiction. For instance, in *Erotic Man* fiction plays an important role. But in *Interference*, it is very clear, since fiction takes place in a setting and in situations which are very "real." I put the actors in real situations and I am trying to see what happens, I want the story to float and unfold. Thus, the film unfolded scenes from real life and let them become part of the fiction. There's a scene when the actor is received by a real policeman. We had seen him dance in an airport lounge and then asked him to do the same for us in the film. It is one example of what I call the gift of chance (also the title of a book I wrote about my method and especially my confidence in what chance can give you). This scene is one of my favourite ones, because it is exactly on the borderline between reality and fiction. One more example of this practice is when the character enters the police station downtown. He is quite drunk, desperately looking for his love. He asks the policemen to find the woman he is in love with. This is a "real" scene: The policemen ask him to speak in French and they react in their own way—as policemen. And mind you, these are the feared brutal police of the Duvalier *Dictature*. Their response is not acted. The actor that dealt with them had the courage to go in and do what I asked him to do.

AK: In some films your use of the long-take is recurring and in a way it affects the boundaries between reality and fiction.

JL: I like to observe life in a certain amount of time. John Cage and Andy Warhol were important figures for me. I am still faithful to the 1960s art principles. One of them was the authenticity of time. I am setting up a scene. I observe the situation and when the shot starts I want to see what happens—to see what happens when you have set up the rules of the situation. That's basic for me. This is the concept. I like time passing in film, because even when nothing seems to happen, there is always something taking place. The film breathes. In one of my early writings about film, I say that a film is a series of images and what matters is not dramatic continuity. I am fascinated by the idea of exploring the depth of each scene and the duration of time, rather than cutting to the next image. In a way, I am against overediting in cinema.

AK: In many respects, your films are based on deictic representational strategy. They show the showing, something similar to Carl Dreyer's work and to Brecht's idea of quoting the action.

JL: I am big admirer of Dreyer's work. My practice is synopsized as follows: I show things and then I tell you what you have seen. *Life in Denmark* is very much in line with this. I show the information and then I pause and disrupt the continuity. I use the text as something that confirms or contradicts the immediate reading of an image, for instance, the iconic image of a woman. I like showing a woman and having the voice-over reading: "This is a woman." I like playing with the obvious in the same way that a musician plays his instrument.

AK: In *Moments of Play* (*Det Legende Menneske*, 1986) you experiment with this in a very productive way, when you show an image and you quote the gestures, the feelings.

JL: I am glad that you mentioned *Moments of Play*. In this film I am very aware of how to use words. I am trying to be inside the persons, by getting inside the action and then explaining it from the outside. I explain what people are doing even if it is already obvious. It is a play with the very act of explaining. I like playing games with different words and with film language itself. This is what maybe makes it poetry. At the same time, I am very conscious of the ways I am using sounds, words, and music. I definitely do not want sounds to be in harmony with the images. I want to add something different; sometimes simply by using sound to double the image, sometimes to question it, to contradict it.

AK: In the film you have codirected with Lars von Trier, *The Five Obstructions*, there is certainly a connection between restraints and productive inventiveness.

JL: I cannot work without having a set of rules. For example, both *66 Scenes from America* and *New Scenes from America* (*Nye Scener fra Amerika*, 2002) were made according to strict rules. The camera could not move. Zooming was not allowed. The camera does not follow action. Action derives from the static frame. Action is movements inside a frame. In the same film, I play with people's consciousness and with their habits. The rules of the game are the route to creativity. Similarly, in *Sunday in Hell* (*En Forarsdag i Helvede*, 1976) I wanted strict framing toward a very dramatic material. This allowed the intrusion of "uninvited things" in the narrative universe. As a film teacher, I always taught my students to work with certain rules. It is more fun to use few means and tell yourself—"you can't do this or that." This was picked up by the Dogme Brothers. Lars von Trier and Thomas Vinterberg have referenced the influence that my teaching had on the very idea of Dogme.

AK: Denmark has a strong cinematic tradition dating back to the beginning of the 20th century. In many ways, Danish cinema is still very productive. This, to an extent, can be attributed to the state funding of cinema. On the other hand, you recently had some problems, since you did not manage to get funding for a sequel to *Life in Denmark*.

JL: The Danish film system is very good. There are consultants and each consultant deals with a specific genre of films. For instance, one consultant reads funding proposals for documentaries, another one for children films, etc. The procedure is very transparent, since you can see who makes the decision. This has been working well for many years. We are a small country and we rely on the state funding of the arts. I have been extremely privileged because my films are not commercial and they would not have been materialized was it not for the Danish funding system. Moreover, in Denmark it was possible to produce art films, since the state recognized that we had to produce some films that do not have primary commercial entertainment value, but something more, that is, artistic value. Recently, though, I had a problem with getting funding for the sequel to *Life in Denmark*. Perhaps, because my vision of Denmark is different compared to the people living here, I spend much time outside the country and the point of the film was to see my own country from an outsider's perspective. But the consultant did not like the idea. She did not think that this is an important project.

AK: A last question about von Trier's connection to your own work. It strikes me that his films also employ the same deictic strategies as yours and at times—especially in the early ones—he's also using sound as a means of quoting the image.

JL: Yes this is the case in *The Element of Crime*…

AK: And in *Europa* (1991)… Then even his later less stylized films follow your own *modus operandi*. The camera has the desire to discover things.

JL: He says that my work has been influential on his own films. What I like about his films is exactly that they value the act of exploring, the very process of making a film. A lot of filmmakers pretend to know everything about the world. Lars explores the world by making films and that's exactly what I am doing. He's using the camera to examine and that's how cinema should be. Both of us do not like fixed answers to fixed questions. This is something that you can even see in some classic filmmakers, Hitchcock for example.

Manifestoes

Manifesto 1

Everything seems to be all right: film-makers are in an unsullied relationship with their products, possibly a relationship with a hint of routine, but nonetheless, a good and solid relationship, where everyday problems fill the time more than adequately, so that they alone form the content! In other words, an ideal marriage that not even the neighbours could be upset by: no noisy quarrels in the middle of the night ... no half-naked compromising episodes in the stairwells, but a union between both parties: the film-maker and his "film-wife", to everyone's satisfaction ... at peace with themselves ... but anyway.... We can all tell when the Great Inertia has arrived!

How has film's previously stormy marriage shrivelled up into a marriage of convenience? What happened to these old men? What has corrupted these old masters of sexuality? The answer is simple. Misguided coquetry, a great fear of being uncovered (what does it matter if your libido fades when your wife has already turned her back on you?) ... have made them betray the thing that once gave the relationship its sense of vitality: *Fascination*!

The film-makers are the only ones to blame for this dull routine. Despotically, they have never given their beloved the chance to grow and develop in their love ... out of pride they have refused to see the miracle in her eyes ... and have thereby crushed her ... and themselves.

These hardened old men must die! We will no longer be satisfied with "well-meaning films with a humanist message", we want more—of the real thing, fascination, experience—childish and pure, like all real art. We want to get back home to the time, when love between film-maker and film was young, when you could see the joy of creation in every frame of the film!

We are no longer satisfied with surrogates. We want to see religion on the screen. We want to see "film-lovers" sparkling with life: improbable, stupid, stubborn, ecstatic, repulsive, monstrous and not things that have been tamed or castrated by a moralistic, bitter, old film-maker, a dull puritan who praises the intellect-crushing virtues of niceness.

We want to see heterosexual films, made for, about and by men. We want visibility!

Lars von Trier May 3, 1984.

Manifesto 2

Everything seems fine. Young men are living in stable relationships with a new generation of films. The birth-control methods which are assumed to have contained the epidemic have only served to make birth control more effective: no unexpected creations, no illegitimate children—the genes are intact. These young men's relationships resemble the endless stream of Grand Balls in a bygone age. There are also those who live together in rooms with no furniture. But their love is growth without soul, replication, without any bite. Their "wildness" lacks discipline and their "discipline" lacks wildness.

LONG LIVE THE BAGATELLE!

The bagatelle is humble and all-encompassing. It reveals creativity without making a secret of eternity. Its frame is limited but magnanimous, and therefore leaves space for life. *Epidemic* manifests itself in a well-grounded and serious relationship with these young men, as a bagatelle—because among bagatelles, the masterpieces are easy to count.

May 17, 1987
Lars von Trier.

Manifesto 3—I Confess!

Everything seems fine: the film director Lars von Trier is an artist and a scientist and a human being. Yet all the same I say that I am a human being, AND an artist, AND a film director.

I am crying as I write this, because I have been so arrogant in my attitude: who am I to think that I can master things and show people the right path? Who am I to think that I can scornfully dismiss other people's life and work? My shame keeps getting worse, because my apology—that I was seduced by the pride of science—falls to the ground a lie! Certainly it's true that I have tried to intoxicate myself in a cloud of sophistries about the goals of art and the artist's duties, that I have worked out ingenious theories about the anatomy and nature of film, yet—and I am admitting this quite openly—I have never succeeded in suppressing my inner passions with this feeble veil of mist: MY FLESHY DESIRES!!

Our relationship to film can be described in so many ways, and is explained in many myriad ways: We have to make films with a pedagogical purpose, we can desire to use film as a ship that can carry us off on a voyage of discovery to unknown lands, or we can claim that we want film to influence our audience and get it to laugh or cry—and pay. All this can sound perfectly OK, but I still don't think much of it.

There is only one excuse for suffering and making other people suffer the hell that the genesis of a film involves: the gratification of the fleshy desires that arise in a fraction of a second, when the cinema's loudspeakers and projector, in tandem, and inexplicably, allow the illusion of movement and light to find their way like an electron leaving its path and thereby generating the light needed to create ONE SINGLE THING: a miraculous blast of LIFE! THIS is the only reward a film-maker gets, the only thing he hopes and longs for. This physical experience when the magic of film takes place and works its way through the body, to a trembling ejaculation...

NOTHING ELSE! There, now it's written down, which feels good. So forget all the excuses: "childish fascination" and "all-encompassing humility", because this is my confession, in black and white: LARS VON TRIER; THE TRUE MASTURBATOR OF THE SILVER SCREEN.

And yet in *Europa*, the third part of the trilogy, there isn't the least trace of derivative manoeuvring. At last, purity and clarity are achieved! Here there is nothing to hide reality under a suffocating layer of "art" ... no trick is too mean, no technique too tawdry, no effect too tasteless.

JUST GIVE ME ONE SINGLE TEAR OR ONE SINGLE DROP OF SWEAT AND I WOULD WILLINGLY EXCHANGE IT FOR ALL THE "ART" IN THE WORLD.

At last. May God alone judge me for my alchemical attempts to create life from celluloid. But one thing is certain: life outside the cinema can never find its equal, because it is HIS creation and therefore divine.

Lars von Trier
December 29, 1990.

The dimension manifesto

However omnipresent time—the so-called fourth dimension—may be, we describe and maybe even "experience" it as if it were invisible and quite impossible to depict. To us, its presence is only known from what we generally regard as its ceaseless march—a march we in our cultural hemisphere typically describe with the help of various verbal inflections. The effect of this march of time is at once aging and rejuvenating on organic as well as inorganic, natural and man-made materials, and in this process time is what we might call a waste product.

Our idea is to make a feature film, with the march of time as its all-prevailing undercurrent. A film that not only presents, in "documentary" form, the march of time as inherent to the action it decorates, but also as a suspense-creating element—"the pursuer of all living things".

In order to visualize the march of time in the actors and their surroundings as concretely as possible—that is to say, without the aid of the medium's characteristic use of illusory effects—we have decided upon a production time of about 30 years with premiere in 2024. In other words, we intend to concentrate a span of about 30 years into a feature film of about 100 minutes (the present normal length) and produce a good 3 minutes of effective running time per annum.

As to how people—their situation, surroundings and products—will change, and what they will change into by the year 2024, as the result of political, economic, technological, climatic, linguistic and other developments, no one, as we all know, can tell us. Nor do we know which of us will still be alive in 10, 20 or 30 years time.

Thus, we wish as far as possible to guarantee the completion of the film by drawing up and appending wills to the final contracts. These will transfer to others the responsibility for any of the jobs on the film team that might become vacant in the intervening interval as the result of death or serious disablement.

Time has always constituted an unavoidable—and often regular—element of every dramatic work. In this film we wish to employ time in a non-fictional manner by making use, though in concentrated form, of its actual passage, whereupon it will become more manifest—as an active and absolutely veracious factor—than in any film hitherto.

Naturally, in the case of a draft plan for a feature film as outlined here—where, with the help of a typical film team (actors, technicians, instructor, scriptwriter and producer), we move about 30 years into the future, precisely in order, dramaturgically speaking, to make the very most of the time factor—to start the production with a ready-made script already specifying which scenes, with dialogue, are to be shot in 2007, would directly conflict with our aim. Thus, on the script level, our idea is to formulate the necessary and sufficient starting point for the characters involved—a zero point for the action—and let time, with the influence it has on everything and everybody, be a dummy; which doesn't mean to say that it is any less important as a partner in the further development of the drama.

A film production that lasts 30 years can also give immediate rise to speculations of a technical nature. Will films as a medium still exist in 2024, or will the electronic—or other hitherto unknown media—have conquered the entire field by then? Before starting production, therefore, we wish to do some technical research centring, for example, around the normative strategies adopted by the film and similar industries, in the hope of being able to make a financially wise and well-timed choice of shooting technique.

Thirty years is a long time—half a human lifetime, and an unheard-of duration for a film production. In retrospect, however, 30 years is not an incredibly long period, really amounting only to a couple of brief flashbacks, despite everything that happens to the human and global substance. In several productions the film media has turned historical material and human memory to its own advantage, precisely, like history, by turning to look at what has already happened. In such cases the medium has adopted the same curious attitude as the audience, we might say. In this project our memory is forward-looking, as it were—and naturally the major part of this film's potential audience has not yet come into being. At the premiere in 2024 the film, like all other historical films, will generally be regarded as retrospective, but in this case the intervening thirty years will be truthfully depicted, because the shooting of this historical film will take place parallel with the period of the time covering the change of century.

DIMENSION is a grand idea. It is easy to visualize this film drama enacted on the stage of the future United Europe, and the interest in DIMENSION will most certainly spread far beyond the circles in which films are normally financed and consumed, solely on account of its tremendous perspectives as a work of art.

DIMENSION is a film that transgresses boundaries, geographical as well as cultural and conceptual ...

There is a future in this new creation.

Copenhagen, October 5, 1990
Lars von Trier and Niels Vørsel

The Dogme 95 manifesto and the vow of chastity

Dogme 95 is a collective of film directors founded in Copenhagen in the spring of 1995.

Dogme has the expressed goal of countering certain tendencies in the cinema today.

Dogme 95 is a rescue action!

In 1960 enough was enough! The movie was dead and called for resurrection. The goal was correct but the means not! The Wave was up for grabs, like the directors themselves. The Wave was never stronger than the men behind it. The anti-bourgeois cinema itself became bourgeois, because the foundations upon which its theories were based was the bourgeois perception of art. The auteur concept was bourgeois romanticism from the very start and thereby ... false!

To Dogme 95 cinema is not individual!

Today a technological storm is raging, the result of which will be the ultimate democratization of the cinema. For the first time anyone can make movies. But the more accessible the media becomes, the more important the avant-garde. It is no accident that the phrase "avant-garde" has military connotations. Discipline is the answer ... we must put our films into uniform, because the individual film will be decadent by definition!

Dogme 95 counters the individual film by the principle of presenting an indisputable set of rules known as THE VOW OF CHASTITY.

In 1960 enough was enough! The movie had been cosmeticized to death, they said: yet since then the use of cosmetics has exploded.

The "supreme" task of the decadent filmmaker is to fool the audiences. Is that what we are so proud of? Is that what the "100 years" have brought us? Illusions via which emotions can be communicated? By the individual artist's free choice of trickery?

Predictability (dramaturgy) has become the golden calf around which we dance. Having the characters' inner lives justify the plot is too complicated and not high art. As never before, the superficial action and the superficial movie are receiving all the praise.

The result is barren. An illusion of pathos and an illusion of love.

To Dogme 95 the film is not an illusion!

Today a technological storm is raging of which the result is the elevation of cosmetics to God. By using new technology anyone at any time can wash the last grains of truth away in the deadly embrace of sensation. The illusions are everything the movie can hide behind.

Dogme 95 counters the film of illusion by the presentation of an indisputable set of rules known as the VOW OF CHASTITY.

"I swear to submit to the following set of rules drawn up and confirmed by Dogme 95":

1. Shooting must be done on location. Props and sets must not be brought in (if a particular prop is necessary for the story, a location must be chosen where the prop is to be found).
2. The sound must never be produced apart from the images, or vice versa. (Music must not be used unless it occurs where the scene is being shot.)
3. The camera must be hand-held. Any movement or mobility attainable in the hand is permitted. (The film must not take place where the camera is standing; shooting must take place where the film takes place.)
4. The film must be in colour. Special lighting is not acceptable. (If there is too little light for exposure the scene must be cut or a single lamp may be attached to the camera.)
5. Optical work and filters are forbidden.
6. The film must not contain superficial action. (Murders, weapons, etc., must not occur.)
7. Temporal and geographical alienation are forbidden (That is to say that the film takes place here and now).
8. Genre movies are not acceptable.
9. The film format must be Academy 35 mm.
10. The director must not be credited.

Furthermore, I swear as a director to refrain from personal taste! I am no longer an artist. I swear to refrain from creating a "work" as I regard the instant more important than the whole. My supreme goal is to force the truth out of my characters and settings. I swear to do so by all means available and at the cost of any good taste and any aesthetic considerations.

Thus I make my VOW OF CHASTITY.

Copenhagen, Monday, March 13, 1995
On Behalf of Dogme 95
Lars von Trier, Thomas Vinterberg.

Selma's manifesto

Selma comes from the east. She loves musicals. Her life is hard, but she can survive because she has a secret. When things get too much to bear she can pretend she's in a musical ... just for a minute or two. All the joy that life can't give her is there. Joy isn't living ... joy is there to make it bearable for us to live. The joy that she is able to conjure up from within is her spark of happiness.

Selma loves The Sound of Music and the other big song-and-dance films. Now she's got the chance to play the lead in an amateur version of The Sound of Music.... At the same time, she is about to fulfil her life's greatest goal. It looks like dream and reality are going to melt together for Selma.

So, popular music and famous musicals are what fills the spaces in her brain. But she isn't just a dreamer! She is someone who loves all of life! She can feel intensely about the miracles that every corner of her (fairly grim) life offers. And she can see all the details ... every single one. Strange things that only see can see or hear. She's a genuine watcher ... with a photographic memory. And it's this double-sided nature that makes her an artist: her love and enthusiasm for the artificial world of music, song and dance, and her keen fascination for the real world ... her humanity. Her art consists of the musical interludes that she takes refuge in when she needs to ... fragments of Selma's own musical ... like no other musical ... it's a collision of splinters of melodies, folk songs, noises, instruments, texts and dances that she has experienced in the cinema and in real life, using the components that she—because of her gift—can find there.

This isn't pure escapism! ... It's much more ... it's art! It stems from a genuine inner need to play with life and incorporate it into her own private world.

A situation might be incredibly painful, but it can always provide the starting point for even a tiny manifestation of Selma's art. It can be incorporated into the little world that she can control.

About the film

In order to tell Selma's story the film must be able to give concrete form to her world. All the scenes that don't contain her musical fantasies must be realistic as possible as far as acting, décor and so on are concerned, because the scenes from Selma's daily life are the model for what she adds to her musical numbers ... and these have to be true to life. What she sees at the cinema is flawless ... painless ... in other words, entirely at odds with real life ... where it's the flaws and the pain that make it shine. The intimation of humanity ... of nature ... of life!

So the events that form part of the story will partly be expressed by the finest, most beautiful music, recorded according to unambiguous methods—and mixed with all the muddles and mistakes that reality can contribute. These two orchestras will play together.

This is also the principle for Selma's musical. Punk is the word I would use to underline the whole thing: as I see it, punk is a collision between tradition and nature. It isn't destructive ... it isn't solemn, because it's trying to get back to basics ... by confronting the system with a modern, more honest view of life ... and forcing life into something that has become stale and enclosed ... using violent means. This is probably the only violence that Selma participates in?

The music

The musical elements that include instruments and melodies come from the musicals that she loves. They might be fragments that are incorporated into different contexts ... or instrumental sounds that are used in unusual ways. Selma loves the cheapest musicals effects: riffs and other clichés ... and she uses them in ways that have nothing to do with good taste ... but these elements are mixed with the sounds of life, and through this she becomes far from banal. She loves the simple sounds of living expression ... hands, feet, voices, and so on... (the sighs caused by hard work?) ... the noise from machines and other mechanical things ... the sounds of nature ... and above all the little sounds caused by chance ... the creak of a floor when a floorboard develops a defect. Her music extols dream on the one hand, life on the other. She uses her own daily life to create music. Mostly to use this positively ... but occasionally to sing out her pain.... It's important that the artificial is allowed to remain and sound artificial ... we have to be aware of where things come from ... the clichés from musicals ... and even more important: the sounds from the real world ... they should never be "refined" ... the closer to reality the better ... we prefer a rhythm created by hand using a rattling window than a sampled version of the same thing... if sampling is to be used here, then it must take its place on the artificial side. The music should sway from one side to the other ... let there be occasions when only natural noises reign (stomp).

In any case, there will be an explosion of feelings and above all a celebration of the joy that fantasy can bring. The sounds of reality do not only come from machines and daily routine ... they also come from creative people like Selma who can use anything and everything in every scene as an instrument! This is an area where Selma is superior. She can weave gold from mud. She can hear music in noise ... and when she shows it to us ... we can also hear ... that the noise contains life and it is as beautiful as any traditional, celebrated masterpiece from the stage. Both sides are there ... alike and not unlike.

The dancing

The principle is the same; Selma exploits and loves grand effects: poses, homogeneity ... glamour ... but she combines all this with real people ... with real movements and faults. With the chaos of life. With acting. Efficiency and inefficiency. Her use of effects is a challenge to good taste ... and her consideration of life's vicissitudes is immense. Every arena is utilized. She can see possibilities in any unexpected thing. The dancers can see whatever they like in their dance and their music. She has worked in a factory for a long time and takes pleasure in the slightest human gesture. She knows what a body can do ... when it does its best to attain perfection in dance, like in the big films, and she knows how the joy and pain of everyday life can be expressed in movement. Selma dances like a child ... for herself ... in ecstasy ... it might look terrible ... but suddenly, in a fraction of a second, the whole room is in harmony ... and she is its queen. The dance has no façade ... it faces every direction ... it has no boundaries ... a fingertip touching a surface is dance! (If we should need explanations or preparations for a shift from reality ... we can show it in the non-musical episodes.)

The songs

The songs from the musicals provide the bass ... and they've got rhythm! They're primitive ... they're Selma's naïve way of telling a story through a song ... but sometimes her fascination with sounds, rhythms, words and rhymes fights through ... then she starts to play with it and forgets everything. The songs are Selma's dialogue with herself ... even if sometimes they are put in other characters' mouths, who express her words, her doubts, fears, joys, and so on. They are naïve songs, with all her well-used words, from popular music ... but often things don't work for her ... and certain deeper truths seep out.... When that happens Selma is quick to turn it all into a game again ... playing with words ... or fragments of words ... like a child! ... sheer astonishment at letting sounds come out her mouth!

And remember she enjoys mimicry ... she can sound like a machine or a violin. A mistake can suddenly also be used as an effect ... a micropronounced word can gain its own meaning when thirty people pronounce it the same way!

The décor

Super-realism! Neither more nor less. No one should be able to say that this is a film that wasn't made on location ... and that these places have never been documented by a camera before. Everything in these places and that is used in dance or music ... must be there because of the story or the location of the characters. We are working against the principle of musicals entirely here ... there are NOT suddenly ten identical things to use in a dance. The same applies to costume ... there shouldn't be a troupe of dancers wearing the same clothes. The costumes are also an expression of realism, and they say something about the person wearing them.

And, as usual, it's the sudden gaps in logic that make things credible and alive! That make everything human! And this all has its origin in Selma .... She is the person seeking and speaking!

"Defocus"

We are searching for something fictional not factual. Fiction is limited by our imagination and facts by our imagination and facts by our insight, and the part of the world that we are seeking cannot be encompassed by a "story" or embraced from an "angle". The subject matter we seek is found in the same reality that inspires fiction-makers, the reality that journalists believe they are describing. But they cannot find this unusual subject matter because their techniques blind them. Nor do they want to find it, because the techniques have become the goal itself.

If one discovers or seeks a story, to say nothing of a point that communicates, then one suppresses it. By emphasising a simple pattern, genuine or artificial; by presenting the world a puzzle picture with solutions chosen in advance.

The story, the point, the disclosure and the sensation have taken this subject-matter from us—this; the rest of the world which is not nearly so easy to pass on, but which we cannot live without!

The story is the villain. The theme presented at the expense of all decency. But also the case in which a point is presumably submitted for the audience to evaluate, assisted by viewpoints and facts counterbalanced by their antitheses. The worship of pattern, the one and only, at the expense of subject-matter from which it comes. How do we rediscover it, and how do we impart or describe it? The ultimate challenge of the future—to see without looking: to defocus! In a world where the media kneel before the altar of sharpness, draining life out of sharpness, draining life out of life in the process, the DEFOCUSIST will be the communicators of our era—nothing more, nothing less!"

Lars von Trier
March 22, 2000.

The Dogumentary manifesto[1]

Dogumentarism relives the pure, the objective and the credible. It brings us back to the core, back to the essence of our existence.

The documentary and television reality which has become more and more manipulated and filtered by camera people, editors and directors must now be buried.

This takes place with the following documentarist content guarantee:

The goal and content of all Dogme documentary projects must be supported and recommended in writing by at least seven people, companies or organisations who are relevant and vital.

In its content and context which plays a primary role in Dogumentarism, format and expression are secondary to this process.

Dogumentarism will restore the public's faith as a whole as well as the individual's. It will show the world raw in focus and in "defocus".

Dogumentarism is a choice. You can choose to believe in what you see on film and television or you can choose **Dogumentarism.**

The documentarist code for Dogumentarism

1. All the locations in the film must be revealed (This is to be done by text being inserted in the image. This constitutes an exception of rule number 5. All the text must be legible).
2. The beginning of the film must outline the goals and ideas of the director (This must be shown to the film's actors and technicians before filming begins).
3. The end of the film must consist of two minutes of free speaking time by the film's "victim". This "victim" alone shall advice regarding the content and must approve this part of the finished film. If there is no opposition by any of the collaborators, there will be no "victim" or "victims". To explain this, there will be text inserted at the end of the film.
4. All clips must be marked with 6–12 frames black (Unless it is a clip in real time, that is a direct clip in multi-camera filming situation).
5. Manipulation of the sound and/or images must not take place. Filtering, creative lighting and/or optical effects are strictly forbidden.
6. The sound must never be produced exclusive of the original filming or vice-versa. That is, extra soundtracks like music or dialogue must not be mixed in later.
7. Reconstruction of the concept of the directing of the actors is not acceptable. Adding elements, as with scenography, are forbidden.
8. All use of hidden cameras is forbidden.
9. Archived images of footage that has been taken for other programs must never be used.

Lars von Trier Zentropa Real
October 2001.

Note

1 The words in bold as in the original document.

Bibliography

Lars von Trier Filmography

Early Films (With the exception of the last five ones most of them are unavailable. Recordings are available at the University of Copenhagen.)

Turen til Squashland (*The Trip to Squash Land*) (Denmark, 1967).
Nat, scat (Denmark, 1968).
En røvsyg oplevelse (*A Kick-ass Experience*)(Denmark, 1969).
Et skakspil (*A Game of Chess*) (Denmark, 1969).
Hvorfor Flygte Fra Det Du Ved Du Ikke Kan Flygte Fra? Fordi Du Er En Kujon (*Why Run Away from What You Cannot Escape From? Because You Are a Coward*) (Denmark, 1970).
En blomst (*A Flower*) (Denmark, 1971).
Orchidégartneren (Denmark, 1977).
Menthe—la Bienheureuse (Denmark, 1979).
Nocturne (Denmark, 1980)
Der sidste detalje (*The Last Detail*) (Denmark, 1981).
Befrielsesbilleder (*Images of Relief*) (Denmark, 1982).

Feature Films

The Element of Crime (Denmark, 1984).
Epidemic (1987), (Denmark, 1987).
Europa (Denmark, Sweden, France, Germany, Switzerland, 1991).
Breaking the Waves (Denmark, Sweden, France, Netherlands, Norway, Iceland, 1996).
The Idiots (Denmark, Sweden, France, Netherlands, Italy, 1998).
Dancer in the Dark (Denmark, Germany, Netherlands, Italy, USA, France, UK, Sweden, Finland, Iceland, Norway, 2000).
Dogville (Denmark, Sweden, Norway, Finland, France, UK, Germany, Netherlands, Italy, 2003)
De Fem Benspænd (*The Five Obstructions*), codirected with Jørgen Leth (Denmark, Switzerland, France, Belgium, 2003).
Manderlay (Denmark, Sweden, Netherlands, France, Germany, UK, 2005).
Occupations (France, 2007).

Direktøre For Det Hele (*The Boss of It All*) (Denmark, Sweden, Iceland, Italy, France, Norway, Finland, Germany, 2006).
Antichrist (2009), (Denmark, Germany, France Sweden, Italy, Poland, 2009).
Dimension (unfinished/Denmark, France, 1991-1997/released in DVD in 2010).
Melancholia (Denmark, Sweden, France, Germany, 2011).
Nymphomaniac (Denmark, Germany, France, Belgium, 2013) (forthcoming).

As a Scriptwriter

Dear Wendy, directed by Thomas Vinterberg (Denmark, France, Germany, UK, 2005).
De unge år Nietzsche sagaen del 1 (*The Early Years: Erik Nietzsche Part 1*) (Denmark, Italy, Sweden, Austria, France, 2007).

TV Films

Medea (Denmark, 1988).

TV Projects

Lærerværelset (*The Teacher's Room*) (Denmark, 1994).
Riget (The Kingdom) (Denmark, 1994).
Riget II (The Kingdom II) (Denmark, 1997).
D-Dag (*D-Day*), co-directed with Kristian Levring, Thomas Vinterberg, Søren Kragh-Jacobsen (Denmark 2000).

Other Films Cited

Documentaries

Signals Through the Flames, directed by Sheldon Rochlin (USA, 1983).
Ennenstadt Europa, uncredited director (Denmark, 1984).
The Making of Europa uncredited director (France, 1991) in *Europa* DVD extras.
Trier's Element, directed by Nikolaj Buchardt, in *The Element of Crime* DVD extras (Denmark, 1991), in *Europa* DVD extras.

Tranceformer: A Portrait of Lars von Trier, directed by Stig Björkman (Sweden, Denmark, 1997).

De Ydmygede (The Humiliated), directed by Jesper Jargil (Denmark, 1998).

De Udstillede (The Exhibited), directed by Jesper Jargil (Denmark, 2000).

De Lutrede (The Purified), directed by Jesper Jargil (Denmark, 2003).

A Short Film About a Big Company, directed by Carsten Bramsen (Denmark, 2003), http://www.zentropa.dk/zen-video/zentropafilm/, accessed 7 April 2011.

The Road to Manderlay, directed by Carsten Bramsen (Denmark, 2005), in *Manderlay* DVD extras.

From Dogma to Dogville: Don't Try This at Home, directed by Matthias Maaß (Germany, 2006).

News and Stories: Ich geh nicht in den Keller lachen! Michael Haneke über seine Haltung beim Filmmachen: Michael Haneke Interview with Alexander Kluge, dcp 22 June 2008, 00:00-00:30 (Germany).

Works Cited

Adorno, Theodor. 1984. "The Essay as Form". Translated by Bob Hullot-Kentor and Frederic Will, *New German Critique* 32 (2): 151–171.

——. 1998. "The Meaning of Working Through the Past", in *Adorno Critical Models: Interventions and Catchwords,* 89–103. New York: Columbia University Press.

——. 2004. *Negative Dialectics.* Translated by E. B. Ashton. London, New York: Routledge.

Agamben, Giorgio. 1978. "Notes on Gesture", in *Infancy and History: the Destruction of Experience.* Translated by Liz Heron, 133–140. London, New York: Verso.

Alter, Jean. 1990. "Reference and Performance", in *A Sociosemiotic Theory of Theatre,* 31–90. Philadelphia, PA: University of Pennsylvania Press.

Alter, Nora M. 1996. "The Political Imperceptible in the Essay Film: Farocki's Images of the World and the Inscription of War", *New German Critique* 68 (2): 165–192.

Altman, Rick. 1987. *The American Film Musical.* Bloomington, IN: Indiana University Press.

Artaud, Antonin. 1989. *Artaud on Theatre.* Edited and translated by Claude Schumacher and Brian Singleton. London: Methuen.

Badiou, Alain. 2001. *Ethics: An Essay on the Understanding of Evil.* Translated by Peter Hallward. London, New York: Verso.

Badley, Linda. 2010. *Lars von Trier.* Urbana, Chicago, Springfield: University of Illinois Press.

Bainbridge, Caroline. 2007. *The Cinema of Lars Von Trier: Authenticity and Artifice.* London, New York: Wallflower Press.

Bakhtin, Mikhail. 1984. *Problems of Dostoyevsky's Poetics*. Translated by Caryl Emerson London, Minneapolis: University of Minnesota Press.

Bal, Mike. 1997. *Narratology: Introduction to the Theory of Narrative*. Toronto, Buffalo, London: University of Toronto Press.

Barnett, David. 2010. " 'I Have to Change Myself Instead of Interpreting Myself ': Heiner Müller as Post-Brechtian Director", *Contemporary Theatre Review* 20 (1): 6–20.

——. 2011a. "Undogmatic Marxism: Brecht Rehearses at the Berliner Ensemble", in *Edinburgh German Yearbook Volume 5: Brecht and the GDR: Politics, Culture, Posterity*. Edited by Laura Bradley and Karen Leeder, 25–44. New York, Rochester: Camden House.

——. 2011b. "Toward a Definition of Post-Brechtian Performance: The Example of in the Jungle of the Cities at the Berliner Ensemble, 1971", *Modern Drama* 54 (3): 333–357.

——. 2013. "Performing Dialectics in an Age of Uncertainty, or: Why Post-Brechtian Does Not Mean Postdramatic", in *Postdramatic Theatre and the Political International Perspectives on Contemporary Performance*. Edited by Jerome Carroll, Steve Giles, Karen Jürs-Munby. London: Bloomsbury.

Barthes, Roland. 1972. *Mythologies*. Translated by Annette Lavers. New York: The Noonday Press.

——. 1977. "Diderot, Brecht, Eisenstein", in *Image, Music, Text*. Edited and translated by Stephen Heath, 69–78. London: Fontana Press.

——. 2000. "Literature and Signification", in *Critical Essays*, 261–279. Evanston, IL: Northwestern University Press.

Baudrillard, Jean. 1994. *Simulacra and Simulation*. Translated by Sheila Faria Glaser. Ann Arbor, MI: University of Michigan Press.

Bazin, André. 1971. *What Is Cinema?* Vol. I&II. Edited and translated by Hugh Gray. Berkeley, Los Angeles, London: University of California Press.

Benjamin, Walter. 1998. *Understanding Brecht*. Translated by Anna Bostock. London: Verso.

——. 1999. "Theses on the Philosophy of History", in *Illuminations*. Edited by Hannah Arendt, translated by Harry Zorn, 245–255. London: Pimlico.

Berlau, Ruth, Brecht, Bertolt, Hubalek Claus, Palitzsch Peter and Rülicke Käthe. 1952. *Theaterarbeit: 6 Aufführungen des Berliner Ensembles*. Dresden: Dresdner Verlag.

Björkman, Stig. 2003. *Trier on von Trier*. Translated by Neil Smith. London: Faber and Faber.

Bogle, Donald. 2006. Toms, *Cooons, Mulattoes, Mummies and Bucks: An Interpretative History of African Americans in Films*. New York: Continuum.

Bondebjerg, Ib. 2000. "Lars von Trier", in *The Danish Directors: Dialogues on a Contemporary National Cinema*. Edited by Ib Bondebjerg and Mette Hjort, 208–223. Bristol, Portland: Intellect.

Bordwell, David. 1985. *Narration in the Fiction Film*. Madison, WI: University of Wisconsin Press.

———. 2006. "Another Pebble in Your Shoe", http://www.davidbordwell.net/
blog/2006/12/13/another-pebble-in-your-shoe/, accessed 2 November 2011.

Brady, Martin. 2008. "Brecht in Brechtian Cinema", in *"Verwisch Die Spuren!"*. *Bertolt Brecht's Work and Legacy: A Reassessment*. Edited by Robert Gillet and Godela Weiss- Sussex, 295–306. Amsterdam, New York: Rodopi.

Brecht, Bertolt. 1963–4. *Schriften zum Theater* volumes 1–7. Frankfurt: Suhrkamp Verlag.

———. 1964. *Brecht on Theatre: the Development of an Aesthetic*. Edited and translated by John Willett. New York, London: Methuen.

———. 1965. *Messingkauf Dialogues*. Translated by John Willett. London: Methuen.

———. 1983. *Texte Für Filme* I&II. Frankfurt: Suhrkamp Verlag.

———. 1993. *Journals 1934–1955*. Edited by John Willett, translated by Hugh Rorrison. London: Methuen.

———. 1997. *Saint Joan of the Stockyards*. in *Brecht Collected Plays: Three*. Edited by John Willett, translated by Ralph Manheim, 202–231. London: Methuen.

———. 2001. *Bertolt Brecht: On Film and Radio*. Edited and translated by Marc Silberman. London: Methuen.

———. 2003. *Brecht on Art and Politics*. Edited by Tom Kuhn and Steve Giles, translated by Laura Bradley. London: Methuen.

Brewster, Ben. 1977. "The Fundamental Reproach (Brecht)", *Ciné-Tracts* 1 (2): 44–53.

Buck-Morss, Susan. 1977. *The Origin of Negative Dialectics: Theodor W. Adorno, Walter Benjamin and the Frankfurt Institute*. London, New York: The Free Press.

———. 1981. "Walter Benjamin: Revolutionary Writer (I)", *New Left Review* 128 (1): 50–75.

———. 1992. "Aesthetics and Anaesthetics: Walter Benjamin's Artwork Essay Reconsidered", *October* 62 (3): 3–41.

———. 2002. "Revolutionary Time: The Vanguard and the Avant-Garde", in *Perception and Experience in Modernity*. Edited by H. Geyer Ryan, P. Koopman, and K. Ynterna, 210–225. Amsterdam, New York: Rodopi.

Burch, Noël. 1981. *Theory of Film Practice*. Translated by Helen R. Lane. Princeton, NJ: Princeton University Press.

Bühler- Dietrich, Annette. 2008. "Theater im Film—Film als Theater: DOGVILLES Formen der Intermedialität", in *Dogville Godville: Methodische Zugänge zu einem Film Lars von Triers*. Edited by Stefan Orth, Michael Staiger, and Joachim Valentin, 87–106. Marburg: Verlag Schüren.

Byg, Barton. 1995. *Landscapes of Resistance: The German Films of Danièle Huillet and Jean-Marie Straub*. Berkeley, Los Angeles, London: University of California Press.

Callinicos, Alex. 1995. *Theories and Narratives: Reflections on the Philosophy of History*. Cambridge: Polity Press.

Canning, Elaine. 2007. "Destiny Theatricality and Identity in Contemporary European Cinema", *Journal of Contemporary Film* 4 (3):159–171.

Chatman, Seymour. 1980. *Story and Discourse: Narrative Structure in Fiction and Film*. Ithaca, London: Cornell University Press.

Chion, Michel. 1999. *The Voice in Cinema*. Translated by Claudia Gorbman. New York: Columbia University Press.

Christensen, Ove. 2000. "Spastic Aesthetics-*The Idiots*", in *P.O.V. A Danish Journal of Film Studies* 10 (2):35–46.

Conley, Tom. 2005. "Cinema and Its Discontents: Jacques Rancière and Film Theory", *Substance* 34 (3): 96–106.

Cook, Pam. 2005. *Screening the Past. Memory and Nostalgia in Cinema*. London: Routledge.

Corrigan, Timothy. 2011. *The Essay Film from Montaigne, After Marker*. Oxford, New York: Oxford University Press.

Coulthard, Lisa. 2011. "Interrogating the Obscene: Extremism and Michael Haneke", in *The New Extremism in Cinema: From France to Britain*. Edited by Tanya Horeck and Tina Kendall, 180–181. Edinburgh: Edinburgh University Press.

Debord, Guy. 1995. *The Society of the Spectacle*. Translated by Donald Nicholson-Smith. New York: Zone Books.

Del Rio, Elena. 2008. *Deleuze and the Cinemas of Performance: Powers of Affection*. Edinburgh: Edinburgh University Press.

Derrida, Jacques. 1977. "Signature, Event, Context", in *Limited Inc*. Translated by Samuel Weber, 1–24. Evanston: Northwestern University Press.

———. 1994. *Spectres of Marx: The State of the Debt, the Work of Mourning and the New International*. Translated by Peggy Kamuf. New York, London: Routledge.

Eagleton, Terry. 1991. *Ideology: An Introduction*. London, New York: Verso.

Elsaesser, Thomas. 2010. "Performative Self-Contradictions: Michael Haneke's Mind Games", in *A Companion to Michael Haneke*. Edited by Roy Grundmann, 53–74. Oxford: Willey-Blackwell.

Elsaesser, Thomas and Hagener, Malte. 1973. "The Cinema of Irony" *Monogram* 5 (1): 1–7.

———. 1987. "The Irresponsible Signifier or 'The Gamble with History': Film Theory or Cinema Theory", *New German Critique* 40 (1): 65–89.

———. 2009. "World Cinema: Realism, Evidence, Presence", in *Realism and the Audiovisual Media*. Edited by Lúcia Nagib and Cecíllia Mello, 3–19. New York: Palgrave Macmillan.

———. 2010. *Film Theory: An Introduction Through the Senses*. London, New York: Routledge.

———. 2011. "James Cameron's *Avatar*: Access for All," *New Review of Film and Television Studies* 9 (3): 247–264.

Fargier, Jean-Paul. 1971. "Parenthesis or Indirect Route", Translated by Susan Bennett, *Screen* 12 (2): 131–144.

Flemming, Antje. 2010. *Lars von Trier: Goldene Herzen, geschundene Körper*. Berlin: Bertz and Fischer.

Galt, Rosalind. 2006. *The New European Cinema: Redrawing the Map.* New York: Columbia University Press.

Gaut, Berys. 2000. "Naked Film: Dogma and Its Limits", in *Purity and Provocation: Dogma 95.* Edited by Mette Hjort and Scott MacKenzie, 89–101. London: BFI.

Gemünden, Gerd. 1999. "Brecht in Hollywood: *Hangmen also Die* and the Anti-Nazi Film", *Theatre Drama Review* 43 (4): 65–76.

Genette, Gérard. 1980. *Narrative Discourse.* Translated by Jane E. Lewin. Oxford: Basil Blackwell.

Gersch, Wolfgang. 1975. *Film Bei Brecht.* München: Carl Hanser Verlag.

Giles, Steve. 1997. *Bertolt Brecht and Critical Theory: Marxism, Modernity and the Threepenny Lawsuit.* Berne: Peter Lang.

———. 2008. "Photography and Representation in Kracauer, Brecht and Benjamin", in *"Verwisch Die Spuren!" Bertolt Brecht's Work and Legacy: A Reassessment.* Edited by Robert Gillet and Godela Weiss-Sussex, 115–125. Amsterdam, New York: Rodopi.

Goss, Brian, Michael. 2009. *Global Auteurs: Politics in the Films of Almodóvar, von Trier and Winterbottom.* New York: Peter Lang.

Greenberg, Udi E. 2008. "The Holocaust Repressed. Memory and the Subconscious in Lars Von Trier's *Europa*", *Film and History* 38 (1): 45–50.

Griffiths, Keith. 2003. "The Manipulated Image", *Convergence: The International Journal of Research into New Media Technologies* 9 (4): 12–26.

Gruzinski, Serge. 1997. "*Europa*: Journey to the End of History", in *Documenta-X the Book.* Edited by Catherine David and Jean-Francois Chevrier, 508–513. Ostfildern: Verlag Gerd Hatje.

Hampton, Howard. 1995. "Wetlands: The Kingdom of Lars von Trier", *Film Comment* 13 (6): 40–46.

Hansen, Miriam Bratu. 2012. Cinema and Experience: Siegfried Kracauer, Walter Benjamin and Theodor W. Adorno. Berkeley, LA, London: University of California Press.

Hart, Christopher. 2009. "What Does It Take for a Film to Get Banned These Days", *Daily Mail*, http://www.dailymail.co.uk/debate/article-1200742/CHRISTOPHER-HART-What-DOES-film-banned-days.html, accessed 11 October 2012.

Harvey, David. 1990. *The Condition of Postmodernity: An Inquiry into the Origins of Cultural Change.* Cambridge, Oxford: Blackwell.

Harvey, Sylvia. 1982. "Whose Brecht? Memories for the Eighties", *Screen* 23 (1): 45–59.

Haycock, Joel. 1990. "The Sign of the Sociologist: Show and Anti-Show in Godard's *Masculin Féminin*", *Cinema Journal* 29 (4): 51–74.

Heath, Stephen. 1974. "Lessons from Brecht", *Screen* 15 (2): 103–128.

Hemke, Julia. 2008. "Die zitternde Oberwelt in der schmutzigen Pfütze", *Dogville Godville*, 47–60.

Hjort, Mette. 2005. *Small Nation Global Cinema: The New Danish Cinema.* London, Minneapolis: University of Minnesota Press.

Hjort, Mette, Bondebjerg, Ib. 2000. "Jørgen Leth", in *The Danish Directors: Dialogues on a Contemporary National Cinema*, 58–74.

———. 2003. "Style and Creativity in the Five Obstructions", in *Decalog 1: On the Five Obstructions*, 15–37. London: Wallflower Press.

———. 2011. "On Lars von Trier: Enfant Terrible of Danish Art Film", *Kinema: A Journal of Film and Audiovisual Media* 34 (2), http://www.kinema.uwaterloo.ca/current_issue.php, accessed 20 August 2011.

Jameson, Fredric. 1991. *Postmodernism or the Cultural Logic of Late Capitalism*. Durham: Duke University Press.

———. 1998. *Brecht and Method*. London, New York: Verso.

Jerslev, Anne. 2002. "Dogma 95, Lars Von Trier's *The Idiots* and the 'Idiot Project'", in *Realism and 'Reality' in Film and Media*. Edited by Anne Jerslev, 41–66. Copenhagen: Museum Tusculanum Press.

Jovanovic, Nenad. 2012. "Estranging the Postmodern: The Brechtian Resonances in Lars von Trier": *The Brecht Yearbook* 37: 62–81.

Kaes, Anton. 1989. *From Hitler to Heimat: the Return of History as Film*. Cambridge, Massachusetts, London: Harvard University Press.

Kelly, Richard. 2000. *The Name of This Book Is Dogme 95*. London: Faber and Faber.

King, Geoff. 2000. *Spectacular Narratives: Hollywood in the Age of the Blockbuster* London, New York: Tauris.

Knudsen, Peter Øvig. "The Man Who Would Give Up Control", in *Lars von Trier Interviews*. Edited by Jan Lumholdt, 117–124. Jackson: University of Mississippi Press.

Koutsourakis, Angelos. 2011. "Brecht Today: Interview with Alexander Kluge", *Film-Philosophy* 15 (1): 220–228.

Kracauer, Siegfried. 1990. "Caligari", in *The Cabinet of Dr. Caligari: Texts, Contexts, Histories*. Edited and translated by Mike Budd, 242–255. New Brunswick, London: Rutgers University Press.

———. 1995. "Photography", in *The Mass Ornament: Weimar Essays*. Translated by Thomas Y. Levin, 47–64. Cambridge, Massachusetts, London: Harvard University Press.

Lambek, Michael. 1996. "The Past Imperfect: Remembering as Moral Practice", in *Tense Past: Cultural Essays in Trauma and Memory*. Edited by Paul Antze and Michael Lambek, 235–254. London, New York: Routledge.

Larsen, Jan Kornum. 2003. "A Conversation Between Jan Kornum Larsen and Lars von Trier", *Lars von Trier Interviews*, 32–46.

Lehmann, Hans-Thies. 2006. *Postdramatic Theatre*. Translated by Karen Jürs-Munby. London, New York: Routledge.

Lellis, George. 1982. *Bertolt Brecht, Cahiers du Cinéma and Contemporary Film Theory*. Ann Arbor, MI: University of Michigan Research Press.

Leth, Jørgen. 2002. "Working Credo" *Film* Special Issue/Leth: 3.

———. 2006. "Gifts of Cinema: Poetics of Chance", DVD booklet Jørgen Leth: *The Anthropological Films* (Edition Filmmuseum).

Lubecker, Nikolaj, "Lars von Trier's *Dogville*: A Feel-Bad Film", in *The New Extremism in Cinema: From France to Britain*, 157–168.

Lundtofte, Anne Mette. 2004. "Jørgen Leth" in BOMBSITE, http://bombsite.com/ issues/88/articles/2656, accessed 14 October 2012.

Lyotard, Jean- François. 1991. "Time Today", in *The Inhuman: Reflections on Time*. Translated by Geoffrey Bennington and Rachel Bowlby, 58–77. Cambridge: Polity Press.

MacCabe, Colin. 1974. "Realism and the Cinema: Notes on Some Brechtian Theses", *Screen* 15 (2):7–27.

Malkin, Jeanette R. 1999. "Memory, History, Postmodern Drama", in *Memory-Theater and Postmodern Drama*, 17–36. Ann Arbor, MI: The University of Michigan Press.

Manovich, Lev. 2001. *The Language of the New Media*. Cambridge, Massachusetts, London: MIT Press.

Margulies, Ivone. 1996. "Introduction: Chantal Akerman's Films: the Politics of the Singular", in *Nothing Happens: Chantal Akerman's Hyperrealist Everyday*, 1–20. Durham, London: Duke University Press.

Martig, Charles. 2008. *Kino der Irritation: Lars von Triers theologische und ästhetische Herausforderung*. Marburg: Verlag Schüren.

Marx, Karl. 1990. *Capital: A Critique of Political Economy* Volume I. Translated by Ben Fowkes. London: Penguin Books.

———, Engels Friedrich. 1970. *The German Ideology*. Edited by C. J. Arthur, translated by W. Lough. London: Lawrence and Wishart.

Merin, Jennifer. 2006. "Interview: Lars von Trier", *New York Press*, http://www.nypress. com/article-12778-interview-lars-von-trier.html, accessed 2 April 2011.

Metz, Christian. 1991. "The Impersonal Enunciation, or the Site of Film (In the Margin of Recent Works on Enunciation in Cinema)". Translated by Béatrice Durand-Sendrail and Kristen Brookes, *New Literary History* 22 (3): 747–772.

Meyerhold, Vsevolod. 2005. "The Director as Superstar". Translated by Margorie L. Hoover, in *Theater and Film: A Comparative Anthology*. Edited by Robert Knopf, 21–23. New Haven and London: Yale University Press.

Monte Mór, Walkyria. 2006. "Reading *Dogville* in Brazil: Image, Language and Critical Literacy", *Language and Intercultural Communication* 6 (2): 124–135.

Mueller, Roswitha. 1987. "Montage in Brecht", *Theatre Journal* 39 (4): 473–486.

Mulvey, Laura. 2004. "Passing Time: Reflections on Cinema from a New Technological Age", *Screen* 45 (2): 141–155.

Nägele. 2006. "Body Politics: Benjamin's Dialectical Materialism, Between Brecht and the Frankfurt School", in *The Cambridge Companion to Walter Benjamin*. Edited by David S. Ferris, 152–177. Cambridge: Cambridge University Press.

Narboni, Jean. 1986. "Towards Impertinence". Translated by Norman King, in *Cahiers du Cinéma Volume 2, 1960–1968. New Wave, New Cinema, Re-evaluating Hollywood*. Edited by Jim Hillier, 300–301. Cambridge, MA: Harvard University Press.

Naremore, James. 1995. "American Film Noir: The History of an Idea", *Film Quarterly* 49 (2): 12–28.

Nicodemus, Katja. 2005. "I am an American Woman", in *Signandsight.com*, http://www.signandsight.com/features/465.html, accessed 4 April 2011.

Novrup Redvall, Eva. 2012. "Encouraging Artistic Risk-taking Through Film Policy: The Case of the Danish Screen", in *Film and Risk*. Edited by Mette Hjort, 209–225. Detroit, MI: Wayne State University Press.

Oppenheimer, Jean. 1996. "Von Trier and Müller's Ascetic Aesthetic: On *Breaking the Waves*", *American Cinematographer* 77 (1): 18–22.

Oxholm, Jan, Nielsen Jakob Isak. 2000. "The Ultimate Dogma film. An Interview with Jens Albinus and Anne-Louise Hassing on Dogma 2- *The Idiots*", *P.O.V.: A Danish Journal of Film Studies* 10 (2):11–35.

Peucker, Brigitte. 1995. "Incorporation: Images and the Real", in *Incorporating Images: Film and the Rival Arts*, 104–167. Princeton, NJ: Princeton University Press.

———. 2007. *Material Image: Art and the Real in Film*. Stanford, CA: Stanford University Press.

Probst, Lothar. 2003. "Founding Myths in Europe and the Role of the Holocaust", *New German Critique* 90 (1): 45–58.

Rancière, Jacques. 2004. *The Politics of Aesthetics*. Translated by Gabriel Rockhill. London, New York: Continuum.

———. 2006. "The Ethical Turn of Aesthetics and Politics". Translated by J.P. Deranty, *Critical Horizons* 7 (1): 1–20.

———. 2009. *The Emancipated Spectator*. Translated by Gregory Elliott. London: Verso.

Ravetto, Kriss. 2001. *The Unmaking of Fascist Aesthetics*. Minneapolis, MN: University of Minnesota Press.

Renov, Michael. 1989. "History and/as Autobiography: The Essayistic in Film and Video", *Framework: A Journal of Images and Culture* 2 (3): 6–13.

Rhodes, John David. 2012. "Style as Work", *Framework: The Journal of Cinema and Media* 53 (1): 47–64.

Rodowick, David Norman. 1998. *The Crisis of Political Modernism*. Urbana, IL: University of Illinois Press.

Schatz, Thomas. 1993. "The New Hollywood", in *Film Theory Goes to the Movies*. Edited by Jim Collins, Hillary Radner, and Ava Preacher Collins, 8–36. New York: Routledge.

Schawander, Lars, "We Need More Intoxicants in Danish Cinema", in *Lars von Trier Interviews*, 13–23.

Schepelern, Peter. 2000a. *Lars von Triers Film Tvang Og Befrielse*. København: Rosinante.

———. 2000b. "'Kill Your Darlings': Lars von Trier and the Origin of Dogma 95", in *Purity and Provocation: Dogma 95*, 58–69.

———. 2005a. "Drillepinden", *EKKO*, http://www.ekkofilm.dk/artikler/drillepinden/, accessed 10 October 2012.

———. 2005b. "The King of Dogme", *Film*/Special Issue Dogme, 8–12.

———. 2005c. "The Making of an Auteur: Notes on the Auteur Theory and Lars von Trier", in *Visual Authorship: Creativity and Intentionality in Media*. Edited by Torben Grodal, Bente Larsen, and Iben Thorving Laursen, 103–127. Copenhagen: Museum Tusculanum Press.

———. 2010a. "Triers Ufuldendte", *EKKO*, 48–49.

———. 2010b. "The Element of Crime and Punishment: Aki Kaurismäki, Lars von Trier, and the Traditions of World Cinema", *Journal of Scandinavian Cinema* 1 (1): 87–103.

Schneider, Rebecca. 1997. *The Explicit Body in Performance*. London: Routledge.

Schoeps, Karl-Heinz. 1989. "From Distancing Alienation to Intuitive Naiveté: Bertolt Brecht's Establishment of a New Aesthetic Category", *Monatshefte* 81 (2): 186–198.

Shaviro, Steven. 2012. "MELANCHOLIA or the Romantic Anti-Sublime", *Sequence* 1 (1), http://reframe.sussex.ac.uk/sequence1/1-1-melancholia-or-the-romantic-antisublime/, accessed 2 January 2013.

Silberman, Marc. 1987. "The Politics of Representation: Brecht and the Media", *Theatre Journal* 39 (4): 448–460.

———. 1993. "A Postmodernized Brecht?", *Theatre Journal* 45 (1): 1–19.

———. 1995. *German Cinema: Texts in Context*. Detroit, MI: Wayne State University Press.

———. 2006. "Brecht's Gestus or Staging Contradictions", *The Brecht Yearbook* 31: 318–335.

———. 2009. "Brecht, Realism and the Media", *Realism and the Audiovisual Media*, 448–460.

Simons, Jan. 2007. *Playing the Waves: Lars Von Trier's Game Cinema*. Amsterdam: Amsterdam University Press.

Sinnerbrink, Robert. 2007. "Grace and Violence: Questioning Politics and Desire in Lars von Trier's *Dogville*", *SCAN/Journal of Media Arts Culture* 4 (2), http://www.scan.net.au/scan/journal/display.php?journal_id=94, accessed 10 August 2009.

Sontag, Susan. 2004. "From Approaching Artaud", in *Antonin Artaud: A Critical Reader*. Edited by Edward Scheer, 83–95. New York: Routledge.

Stevenson, Jack. 2002. *Lars von Trier*. London: BFI.

Stewart, Elizabeth 2005. "Hypnosis, Identification and Crime in Lars Von Trier European Trilogy", *Film Journal* 12 (1), http://www.thefilmjournal.com/issue12/larsvontrier.html, accessed 29 November 2008.

Thompson, Kristin. 1986. "The Concept of Cinematic Excess", in *Narrative, Apparatus, Ideology: A Film Theory Reader*. Edited by Philip Rosen, 130–142. New York: Columbia University Press.

Thorsen, Nils, "Longing for the End of All", http://www.melancholiathemovie.com/, accessed 11 January 2013.

——. 2011. "Lars von Trier Fortryder "Dogville", Efter det Norske Massemord', in *Politiken*, http://politiken.dk/kultur/film/ECE1349365/lars-von-trier-fortryder-dogville-efter-det-norske-massemord/, accessed 30 August 2011.

Tookey, Chris. 2009. "The Man Who Made This Horrible Misogynistic Film Needs to See a Shrink", *Daily Mail*, http://www.dailymail.co.uk/tvshowbiz/reviews/article-1201803/ANTICHRIST-The-man-horrible-misogynistic-film-needs-shrink.html, accessed 10 October 2012.

Trotter, David. 2007. *Cinema and Modernism*. Oxford: Blackwell Publishing.

Vertov, Dziga. 1984. *Kino-Eye: The Writings of Dziga Vertov*. Edited by Annette Michelson, translated by Kevin O'Brien. Berkeley, Los Angeles, London: University of California Press.

Visy, Gilles. 2008. "Europa, Lars von Trier: Un Certain Cauchemar Expressioniste", *Cadrage: La Revue du Cinema International*, http://www.cadrage.net/films/europa/europa.html, accessed 3 August 2008.

Von Trier, Lars. 1996. *Breaking the Waves*. London: Faber and Faber.

Weber, Samuel. 2004. *Theatricality as Medium*. New York: Fordham University Press.

Walsh, Martin. 1981. *The Brechtian Aspect of Radical Cinema*. Edited by Keith Griffiths. London: BFI.

White, John J. 2004. *Bertolt Brecht's Dramatic Theory*. New York: Camden House.

White, Hayden. 1996. "The Modernist Event", in *The Persistence of History: Cinema, Television, and the Modern Event*. Edited by Vivian Sobchack, 17–38. New York, London: Routledge.

——. 2007. "Manifesto Time", in *Manifestos for History*. Edited by Keith Jenkins, Sue Morgan, and Alun Munslow, 222–231. London, New York: Routledge.

Wollen, Peter. 1982. "Godard and Counter-Cinema: Vent d'Est", in *Readings and Writings: Semiotic Counter Strategies*, 79–91. London: Verso.

Wright, Elizabeth. 1989. *Postmodern Brecht: A Representation*. London, New York: Routledge.

Index

Lightning Source UK Ltd.
Milton Keynes UK
UKHW02f2251230818
327720UK00012B/597/P